THE CHANGING FACES

...a Vermes was born in Hungary i...
...y. He received a Catholic educ...
...tly after the Second World War, ...
...ish roots. He studied in Budapest and Louvain, where he read
...ntal history and languages and obtained a doctorate in theology in
... with a dissertation on the Dead Sea Scrolls. After further research
...ris he made his home in England in 1957. He taught at the
...sities of Newcastle and Oxford, where he became the first Pro-
...or of Jewish Studies. In 1991 he was granted the title of Professor
...ritus. He is a Fellow of the British Academy, the holder of an Oxford
...tt., and of honorary doctorates from Edinburgh, Durham and
...field.

...best-known books of Geza Vermes are *Jesus the Jew* (1973), *Jesus
...the World of Judaism* (1983), *The Religion of Jesus the Jew* (1993)
...*The Complete Dead Sea Scrolls in English* (1997). He played a
...ding part in the rewriting of Emil Schürer's classic work, *The History
...the Jewish People in the Age of Jesus Christ* (1973–87). In *Providential
...dents: An Autobiography* (1998) he offers a vivid account of a
...long involvement with the Bible, the Scrolls and the Jesus of history.

# GEZA VERMES

# The Changing Faces of Jesus

PENGUIN BOOKS

PENGUIN BOOKS

Published by the Penguin Group
Penguin Books Ltd, 27 Wrights Lane, London w8 5tz, England
Penguin Putnam Inc., 375 Hudson Street, New York, New York 10014, USA
Penguin Books Australia Ltd, Ringwood, Victoria, Australia
Penguin Books Canada Ltd, 10 Alcorn Avenue, Toronto, Ontario, Canada m4v 3b2
Penguin Books India (P) Ltd, 11, Community Centre, Panchsheel Park, New Delhi – 110 017, India
Penguin Books (NZ) Ltd, Private Bag 102902, NSMC, Auckland, New Zealand
Penguin Books (South Africa) (Pty) Ltd, 5 Watkins Street, Denver Ext 4, Johannesburg 2094, South Africa

Penguin Books Ltd, Registered Offices: Harmondsworth, Middlesex, England

First published by Allen Lane The Penguin Press 2000
Published in Penguin Books 2001
1

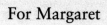

For Margaret

# Contents

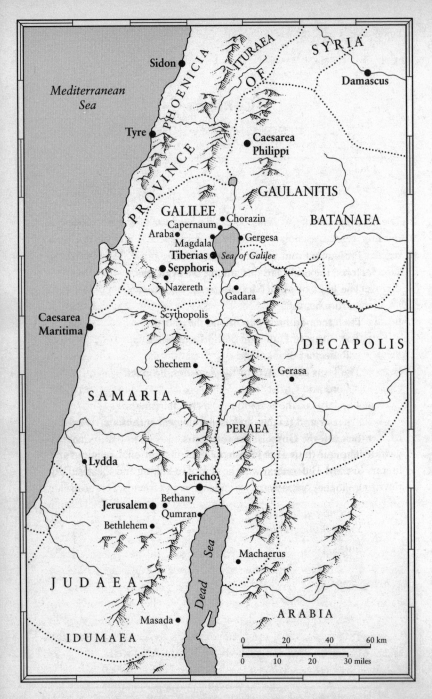

Palestine in the age of Jesus

# Prologue:
# From Christ to Jesus

*The Changing Faces of Jesus* combines the four favourite themes of my fifty years of scholarly activity. In retrospect, I find my life as a teacher, researcher and writer to be all of one piece. My publishing career began in 1949 with an article devoted to the then recently discovered Dead Sea Scrolls. This beginner's adventure developed into an academic love affair which persisted over the decades until it produced in 1997 *The Complete Dead Sea Scrolls in English*.

The study of the Qumran writings led me to an increasing involvement with ancient Jewish Bible interpretation; in 1961 after several years of work it matured in *Scripture and Tradition in Judaism*, which already signalled my awakening curiosity in the study of the New Testament.

My first close encounter with the post-biblical and rabbinic treatment of Scripture was followed, from the mid-1960s onwards, by twenty years of labour in the field of Jewish political, institutional, religious and literary history. The context was the task of re-editing and substantially rewriting – in the company of two colleagues and friends, Fergus Millar and Martin Goodman – Emil Schürer's modern classic, *The History of the Jewish People in the Age of Jesus Christ* (Vols. I–III, 1973–87).

My serious academic interest in Jesus came as an offshoot of this historical inquiry. It produced in the course of the next twenty years (1973–93) a trilogy, *Jesus the Jew, Jesus and the World of Judaism* and *The Religion of Jesus the Jew*. *The Changing Faces of Jesus* is in natural continuity with the trilogy and often relies on it, but it also takes the subject further in that it deals not just with the Synoptic Gospels (Matthew, Mark and Luke), but with the Gospel of John, the letters of Paul, and the rest of the New Testament as well.

A particular slant characterizes my approach to the study of Jesus: I envisage the New Testament not as an independent and autonomous literary composition standing apart from the Jewish world, but look at it through the prism of contemporaneous Jewish civilization, the matrix of the primitive Christian church. Of course, the idea of using Jewish writings from the Bible (c. 1000 to 200 BC) through intertestamental literature (200 BC to AD 100) to the Mishnah and the Talmud of the rabbis (AD 200 to 500) for the interpretation of the Gospels is not something new; it has been a tool employed in critical New Testament scholarship over the last three centuries, and especially during the past hundred years. However, as the vast majority of scholars dealing with the subject happened to be Christian churchmen, they explicitly or implicitly introduced a qualitative distinction between the New Testament and the non-biblical Jewish writings. For them, Jewish literature formed the background against which they made the New Testament stand out in all its presumed superiority and grandeur. Or else they saw the Gospel as the mistress and the Jewish books as servants and auxiliaries, allowed to speak only when spoken to: the agenda of the inquiry was set by the mistress herself and in her own interest.

The procedure which I advocate is much more democratic. Both parties are granted a voice, an equal voice. Put differently, as a historian I consider Jesus, the primitive church and the New Testament as part and parcel of first-century Judaism and seek to read them as such rather than through the eyes of a theologian who may often be conditioned, and subconsciously influenced, by two millennia of Christian belief and church directives.

The main aim of my historical approach is to discover the significance of words and ideas in their original language, as the original speakers meant the original listeners to understand them. The language of Jesus and his Galilean disciples was Aramaic, a Semitic language akin to Hebrew, then spoken by most Palestinian Jews. It was in Aramaic that Jesus taught and argued with friends and foes. The linguistically authentic form of his teaching, with the exception of a dozen or so Aramaic words preserved in the Gospels, soon disappeared. If there ever existed a written Aramaic Gospel, it did not survive for long; we certainly no longer have it. At the same time, as a consequence of the success of the primitive church in the Greek-speaking Gentile (i.e.

non-Jewish) world, the whole message transmitted by the apostles – the Gospels, the letters and the rest – was recorded in Greek, which is the earliest form of the New Testament that we possess. But this Greek New Testament is a 'translation' of the genuine thoughts and ideas of the Aramaic-thinking and -speaking Jesus and of his immediate disciples, a translation not just into a totally different language, but also a transplantation of the ideology of the Gospels into the completely alien cultural and religious environment of the pagan Graeco-Roman world. Therefore my task as a historian and exegete is first to find the way back to the Jewish Jesus speaking to his Jewish followers in his Jewish mode of communication and in his familiar Semitic tongue. The next step is to examine the words attributed to Jesus, and teachings about Jesus, in the Greek New Testament in order to discover changes or developments in meaning, and even potential deformation, arising from the transmission of ideas through the channel of Hellenistic civilization.

Take, for instance, the fundamentally important New Testament expression 'son of God', which will often be discussed in the forthcoming pages. In Hebrew or Aramaic 'son of God' is always employed figuratively as a metaphor for a child of God, whereas in Greek addressed to Gentile Christians, grown up in a religious culture filled with gods, sons of gods and demigods, the New Testament expression tended to be understood literally as 'Son of God', spelled as it were with a capital letter: that is to say, as someone of the same nature as God.

Today, thanks to the many manuscript discoveries in the nineteenth and twentieth centuries, the Jewish literary and religious-cultural context to which the New Testament belongs has become much more extensive and varied than ever before. It is organically preceded by the Hebrew and Aramaic Old Testament and by the Apocrypha, those Old Testament books which survived only in the Greek version of the Bible. They, as well as most of the so-called Pseudepigrapha (religious writings which remained outside both the Hebrew and the Greek Old Testament), the Dead Sea Scrolls found between 1947 and 1956, the writings of the philosopher Philo of Alexandria and the historian Flavius Josephus, antedate or are contemporaneous with the books of the New Testament. To this already rich material for literary and doctrinal comparison we have to add the vast monument of rabbinic literature, works written down mostly in the early centuries of the Christian era, but often reflecting traditional teaching current long before their redaction in script. Their use for interpreting the New Testament requires familiarity and critical skill, but if handled competently they can shed an invaluable light both on Jesus and on primitive Christianity.[1]

In one respect *The Changing Faces of Jesus* differs from my previous books. While it contains a bibliography, it hardly ever refers to any secondary literature. Naturally, I have read a great deal over the years and learned much, positively and negatively, from other scholars. I have assimilated their learning and understanding and stored everything up in my heart. In these pages, to borrow a phrase from Jesus, the mouth speaks out of the abundance of the heart.

My aim is not to instruct readers but to lead them on a voyage of discovery. They are not expected to be thoroughly familiar with the subject, and they are offered – for better or worse – all the evidence on which the argument is based. The direct quotations, which usually follow the Revised Standard Version, are accompanied by the relevant New Testament references so that those who so wish can inquire into the broader context. May they enjoy the journey.

Perhaps it is worth noting that in yet another respect this book departs from the beaten track. Students of the evolution of the image of Jesus in the various layers of the New Testament usually follow the line of chronological progression (see, for instance, such recent titles as *From Jesus to Christ* by Paula Fredriksen, 1988, and *From Jewish Prophet to Gentile God* by Maurice Casey, 1991). I have decided to

---

1. My principles are laid down in 'Jewish Literature and New Testament Interpretation: Reflection on Methodology', *Journal of Jewish Studies* 33 (1982), 361–76. One general observation may be of use. Bearing in mind Jewish unwillingness to take notice of Christianity during the early stages of their co-existence, if we find something common to the New Testament and to a later Jewish document, it is more likely that both rely on an earlier Jewish tradition than that the Jewish author has borrowed from Christianity. Quite recently I came across in a Dead Sea Scroll of the first century BC a tradition previously known only from a Jewish text of the ninth century AD. As a result, we now know that the latter repeats a tradition which was current a thousand years earlier. Cf. 'New Light on the Sacrifice of Isaac from 4Q225', *Journal of Jewish Studies* 47 (1996), 140–46.

begin with the divine Christ and then put the engine into reverse and search for the human Jesus. So in a theological diminuendo we will move from the Everest of the Gospel of St John and the high peaks of the letters of St Paul towards the much more this-worldly figure of the Jesus of Jewish Christianity in the hills and on the plain of the Acts of the Apostles and the Synoptic Gospels, in the hope of catching a glimpse of the real Jesus concealed beneath the accounts of Mark, Matthew and Luke.

While writing this book, I have greatly benefited from the sensitive comments and shrewd criticisms of my wife; in a very special way *The Changing Faces of Jesus* belongs to her. But I would like also to remember here with love my parents, Ernest Vermes, journalist (1877–1944) and Theresia Riesz, teacher (1895–1944), innocent victims of the evil and madness called antisemitism.

# I

# John: the odd-man-out
among the evangelists

Over the last quarter of a century, in addition to my academic lectures I have had many opportunities to address non-specialist groups of educated men and women, young and older, on my work on Jesus. My purpose has always been to portray 'Jesus the Jew', that is, the *historical* figure that stands behind the doctrinal elaborations of two millennia of Christian belief, worship and speculation. My non-theological sketch usually received sympathetic hearing from liberally-minded Christians, as well as from those in the auditorium who did not belong to church or chapel, while Jews listened to it with amazement and curiosity. However, it provoked, simultaneously and regularly, puzzled incomprehension among the conventional, especially evangelical or fundamentalist Christian members of the audience who believed that they were familiar with the Gospels. 'Did I hear you saying,' I was often asked, 'that there is no evidence in Scripture stating that Jesus was the Messiah or that he was God? But didn't he explicitly assert the opposite, namely that he *was* the Messiah and the Son of God? Did he not proclaim to the Jews in the Temple of Jerusalem that he and the Father were one?' And so on.

Nine times out of ten, the traditionalists' bewildered question derives from some passage in the Fourth Gospel. My customary reply, which echoes the conclusions of most critical scholars, leaves them as a rule somewhat confused, but ultimately unimpressed. They cannot swallow the view that the so-called Gospel of John is something special and reflects, not the authentic message of Jesus or even the thinking about him of his immediate followers, but the highly evolved theology of a Christian writer who lived three generations after Jesus and completed his Gospel in the opening years of the second century AD. For the average believer, the last Gospel is naturally the best and the most reliable of the four. They hold it to be the work of the apostle and eye-witness of the life of Jesus whom he cherished so much that shortly before dying on the cross he named him his heir and the guardian of his mother Mary.

It is obvious to anyone acquainted with the doctrinal tradition of the church that the theological understanding of Jesus – who he was and what he did – by historic Christianity ultimately depends on the Gospel of John and the letters of Paul. Paul, the apostle of the Gentiles, is primarily responsible for the church's teaching on Christ, the Redeemer of mankind; faith in the divinity of the Son of God and the divorce between Christianity and Judaism, on the other hand, derive first and foremost from the influence of the Fourth Gospel. John's picture of the truly divine Jesus Christ constitutes, it may be said, the climax in the evolution of Christian dogma in the New Testament, its most polished and ultimate expression. For this reason John is chosen as the best point of departure in our historical-spiritual journey. To be more explicit, we shall begin with the doctrinally most evolved stage in our search for the historical reality which lies hidden behind and beneath the earliest stages of the church's belief in the celestial Christ.

Anyone well versed in history knows that the Fourth Gospel is a unique phenomenon. It is unlike the first three Gospels, and comparison reveals that it stands out as truly *sui generis*, of its own peculiar kind. Mark, Matthew and Luke, the *Synoptic* Gospels, follow the same story line and generally can be set out in parallel columns in a so-called Gospel *synopsis*. They only differ at the beginning and the end of the life of Jesus. The story of his birth and the apparition accounts after his death are all missing from Mark, the earliest of the three, whereas both Matthew and Luke record them, though each in his own way. By contrast, John has his own special vision, aim and structure. The theological canvas painted by this evangelist, his chronology, and the style of teaching and actual message he attributes to Jesus are largely unparalleled in the Synoptics, and sometimes flatly contradict their testimony.

This view of the Gospels is that of a scholar, of a detached historian, in search of information embedded in the surviving sources. Religious authorities do not like to be faced with contradictory evidence; they strive for reconciliation and harmony. Modern Old Testament research has distinguished four layers or sources in the 'Law of Moses', but ancient Jewish tradition managed to amalgamate these into a single unified account, the books of the Pentateuch, the first five books of the Hebrew Bible, as we have them. Perturbed by the differences and dissonance in the four records of the life of Jesus, the Christian church also made two kinds of attempt at ironing out discrepancies. The first instinctively imitated ancient Judaism, which had converted the four pre-existing 'sources' into the single Mosaic Law. Likewise the early church sought to replace the four separate Gospels with one narrative incorporating *all* the details of Matthew, Mark, Luke and John, thus eliminating all the differences. This effort ultimately failed, but for a while a brilliantly conceived Gospel harmony, known as the *Diatessaron*, or the Four-in-One, attributed to the mid-second-century Christian apologist Tatian, had considerable success in the churches of Syria, where it almost managed to eclipse the individual Gospels. However, from the fifth century onwards it was consigned to near oblivion. The second line of defence has succeeded and survives to this day. It represents John as the supreme biographer of Jesus, the author of the spiritual Gospel. Familiar with the works of his predecessors, he is said to have deliberately avoided repeating most of their story, apart from the Passion account, to have restricted himself to supplementing and enriching their records with entire speeches attributed to Jesus, and in general doctrinally developing and improving their narratives.

No critical reading of the four Gospels justifies such an understanding of John. For it is obvious to any religiously unbiased reader that if the Fourth Evangelist is right, his forerunners must be mistaken or vice versa. The Synoptics and John cannot be simultaneously correct when the former assign to Jesus a public career lasting a year, while John stretches it to two or three years by mentioning two or possibly three consecutive Passover festivals during Jesus' ministry in Galilee and Judaea. Likewise, if John's dating of the crucifixion to the day *before* the Passover, i.e. 14 Nisan, is accurate, the Synoptics who depict the last supper as a Passover dinner and place the events leading to the execution of Jesus on 15 Nisan must be in error. Or to Hebraize and suitably adapt the English proverb to the Passover situation, you can't have your unleavened bread and eat it!

When and by whom was the Fourth Gospel written? The oldest

known manuscript fragments of John belong to sometime between AD 125 and 150, and equally the oldest references to John's Gospel in early Christian literature come from the mid-second century. So the work was completed before those dates. On the other hand, the highly evolved doctrine of John points to a period posterior to the redaction of the Synoptic Gospels, which is estimated to have taken place in the course of the last quarter of the first century AD. Likewise the split reflected in John between Judaism and Christianity, with followers of Jesus being expelled from the synagogue, is hardly conceivable before the turn of the first century AD. I subscribe therefore to the opinion held by mainstream New Testament scholarship that the work was published in the early second century, probably between the years 100 and 110. This chronological hypothesis best fits the evidence available to us and is preferable to the dating of the Fourth Gospel, advanced by some serious experts, to AD 150 or beyond.

The same majority opinion considers the identity of the author unascertainable. Apart from the title, 'according to John', which is ambiguous – which John? – and was only later attached to the composition, the Gospel itself from chapter 1 to chapter 20 mentions no author. In chapter 21, appended by someone distinct from the evangelist (cf. verse 24), an attempt is made to identify him with 'the beloved disciple of Jesus', who is *tacitly* assumed to be the Galilean fisherman John, the son of Zebedee.

Now, according to a garbled version of traditions current among Christians in the second century AD, the famous church father Irenaeus, bishop of Lyons, reported *c.* AD 180 that the apostle John lived to a great age in Ephesus (western Asiatic Turkey), and produced there the Fourth Gospel. However, no early evidence connects John with Ephesus. He is last mentioned in the Acts of the Apostles (8:14) as leading the evangelization of Samaria in the company of Peter. Paul also characterizes him in the company of James, the brother of the Lord, and Peter as one of the three pillars of the Jerusalem church (Gal. 2:9). No one testifies in the first century AD to John's move to the farther edge of Asia Minor. The martyr bishop Ignatius of Antioch had a splendid opportunity but failed to do so. In his letter to the members of the church of Ephesus, written in *c.* AD 110, he referred to the Ephesians as the people of *Paul*, without mentioning that just a few years earlier the great apostle and evangelist John had been residing among them!

To complicate matters further, there seems to have been a number of men named John active in that region. One of these was 'John the Elder', a disciple of the Lord according to Papias, bishop of Hierapolis (in Asia Minor), who died around AD 130. Incidentally, the author of the second and third letters of John also identifies himself simply as 'the Elder'. The first letter is not attributed to any named person in the text itself.

Finally, to envisage as the author of the Fourth Gospel an 'uneducated and common' Galilean fisherman (Acts 4:13), who was a centenarian give or take a few years, yet not only still creative but fully at home in Hellenistic philosophical and mystical speculation, requires a leap of imagination which seems to be beyond the reasonable.

In sum, one can just as well pull a name out of a hat. Candidates in addition to John the apostle could be a presbyter or elder called John; John Mark, Paul's companion (Acts 15:37), referred to by the church father, Clement of Alexandria; Lazarus, the friend whom Jesus loved ('the beloved disciple'?); or whomsoever you fancy. The total irreconcilability of the Fourth Gospel with the Synoptics, combined with the late date of its composition, would strongly militate against an author who was an eye-witness of the historical Jesus.

Recent attempts to advance the redaction of the Fourth Gospel nearer to the mid-first century AD strike me as historically unsound and theologically quasi impossible; they are inconsistent with the totality of the evidence. Judging from his work, John was either an educated Jew of mystical leanings who also had some acquaintance with Hellenistic mysticism, or, considering the evangelist's violent detestation of the Jews, a cultured Greek who first toyed with Judaism and subsequently embraced Christianity. The fact that some of the most common Hebrew words (for example *rabbi* or *rabbouni*) are regularly translated into Greek in this Gospel shows that it was primarily intended for a non-Jewish readership. Matthew and Mark, unlike John, assume that their public would understand.[1]

---

1. The question does not arise in connection with the Gentile Luke because he does not employ either Semitic term.

The portrait of Jesus and the message ascribed to him in the Fourth Gospel will be treated in the next chapter. They will be shown to be substantially in advance of the Synoptic Gospels. My main purpose here is to indicate that this discrepancy is not surprising; it is indeed to be expected, bearing in mind that we are dealing with the odd-man-out among the evangelists.

As I have noted, everything in this Gospel – its story, chronology and structure – is *sui generis*. Although John and the Synoptics purport to recount the life and teaching of the same individual, they have precious little in common. So little, in fact, that the straight correspondences are limited to a single chapter, precisely to the first twenty-five verses of John, chapter 6. They represent three consecutive episodes: the miraculous feeding of five thousand people; Jesus walking on the Lake of Galilee; and his entry into a boat heading towards the opposite shore. These accounts are roughly paralleled in Mark and Matthew, the main difference consisting in John's silence on the healing activity of Jesus in the land of Gennesaret (cf. Mark 6:32–56; Matt. 14:13–36).

Some of the prominent features of Jesus' portrait in the Synoptics are either completely absent from the Fourth Gospel, or their significance is greatly diminished. Thus one of the chief aspects of Jesus' function as a healer in the Synoptics, namely the casting-out of demons who were blamed for every kind of illness, is completely missing from John. Such a practice smacked of popular religion, if not of magic, and as such was considered unworthy of the Johannine Jesus. Even the performance of cures, perhaps the dominant feature of the portrait of Jesus in the earlier Gospels, lost its centrality in John. From among the many healing miracles listed in the Synoptics, only a single one survives in this Gospel, and that in a somewhat remanipulated form. The Synoptic story of the Roman centurion's servant healed by Jesus *in absentia* is turned by John, as I will show presently, into the curing of a Herodian official's son.

The Fourth Evangelist describes only two additional therapeutic episodes: the healing of the paralytic at the pool of Bethesda (5:2–9), and the restoration of sight to a man who was blind from birth (9:1–7). The former was made to recover simply by a verbal command, 'Rise, take up your pallet and walk!' (5:8), but for the latter Jesus had recourse to a medicinal substance, mud prepared from clay mixed with his saliva. The method is reminiscent of the healing of a deaf and dumb person (Mark 7:33), and of a blind man (Mark 8:23), by the spittle of Jesus. These are the only explicit stories, but John also alludes more generally to 'doing signs on those who were diseased' (John 6:2; cf. Mark 6:53–6 and Matt. 14:34–6).

Faint echoes of the Synoptics can be detected in a number of Johannine passages, although in a different context, or with a changed story line. The alterations always seem to be motivated by the more elevated doctrinal concepts of the Fourth Gospel. In other words, even literary considerations alone inescapably lead to the conclusion that, compared with Mark, Matthew and Luke who stand between the historical Jesus and the earliest formulations of Christianity, John reflects the fully developed form of the primitive belief, the end product of the early church's thinking about Jesus.

For example, in the Synoptic Gospels Jesus expels the money-changers and traders in sacrificial animals from the courtyard of the Jerusalem sanctuary a few days before his crucifixion. The episode is presented as the ultimate cause triggering his downfall, and as such possesses great historical probability. John, by contrast, sets the so-called cleansing of the Temple to the beginning of Jesus' activity (2:14–16) and invests it with a prophetic and theological significance. It is an act symbolically alluding to the destruction and subsequent rebuilding of the holy place, itself the prefiguration of Jesus' death and resurrection as is manifest in the words, 'Destroy this temple and in three days I will raise it up' (2:19).

Similarly, in the scenario followed by the Synoptics, the only healing act performed by Jesus from a distance benefited the servant of a Gentile army officer retired to Capernaum. The aim of the story was to bring into relief the faith of a non-Jew (Matt. 8:5–13; Luke 7:1–10). In the Fourth Gospel the father of the sick person is not a veteran Roman soldier, but a Jewish royal official, no doubt from Tiberias, where the court of Herod Antipas, tetrarch of Galilee, resided. In short, Jesus was facing a Jewish, not a Gentile, suppliant, and true to the spirit of the Johannine Gospel he immediately rebuked the man, reproaching him with the Jewish sin of greed for miracles. Nevertheless, hearing the moving plea of the distressed father Jesus relented and complied with his prayer (John 4:46–53).[2]

Take again the various Gospel narratives depicting the anointing of Jesus' feet by a woman in Bethany. According to John (12:1–8), *six days* before Passover Jesus spent the evening in the house of his friend the risen Lazarus whose sister, Mary, then proceeded with the ceremony of anointing. She was criticized by Judas, not for the immodesty of using her hair as a towel, but for wasting the precious aromatic balsam the cost of which might have helped the poor! This story is made up of elements derived from at least two original traditions. The anointing of Jesus' *hair* (not his feet) by an anonymous woman in Bethany *two* (not six) days before Passover is reported by Mark (14:3–9) and Matthew (26:6–13). However, the episode is said to have happened in the house of the otherwise unknown Simon the Leper, and not in Lazarus' home. The woman's generous and loving gesture is qualified as a waste by some of those present (Mark), or by the 'disciples'

---

2. This account furnishes a close parallel to the healing story credited in rabbinic literature to Hanina ben Dosa, a Galilean wonder-worker of the first century AD (cf. pp. 242–3).

| *John* 4:46–53 | *bBer.* 34b (*yBer.*9d) |
|---|---|
| And at Capernaum there was a royal courtier whose son was ill. When he heard that Jesus had come . . ., he went and begged him to come down and heal his son, for he was at the point of death. Jesus therefore said to him, 'Unless you see signs . . . you will not believe.' The royal courtier said to him, 'Sir, come down before my child dies.' Jesus said to him, 'Go, your son will live.' The man believed the word that Jesus spoke to him and went his way. As he was going down, his servants met him and told him that his son was living. So he asked them the hour when he began to mend, and they said to him, Yesterday at the seventh hour the fever left him. The father knew that was the hour when Jesus had said to him, Your son will live; and he himself believed and all his household. | It happened that when Rabban Gamaliel's son fell ill, he sent two pupils to R. Hanina ben Dosa that he might pray for him. When he saw them, he went to the upper room and prayed. When he came down, he said to them, 'Go, for the fever has left him . . .' They sat down, wrote and noted the hour. When they came to Rabban Gamaliel, he said to them, 'By Heaven, you have neither detracted from it, nor added to it, but this is how it happened. It was at that hour that the fever left him and he asked us for water to drink.' |

(Matthew). A parallel account is missing from Luke, who nevertheless records in a different context (Luke 7:36–50) – in the house of Simon surnamed the Pharisee (not the Leper) and much earlier in the Gospel story – that a prostitute ('a woman of the city who was a sinner') entered the room uninvited and washed Jesus' feet with her tears, wiped them with her hair, kissed them, and poured ointment on them from an alabaster flask. Reading disapproval on Simon's face, Jesus turned the story into a lesson of repentance and forgiveness. The same Luke mentions Jesus' visit in an unnamed (Galilean) village to two sisters, Martha and Mary, but with no mention of a brother called Lazarus or of any anointing of Jesus. The Fourth Evangelist produces here a garbled and conflated tradition with the significant twist that the anointing is criticized, not by the disciples who are thus put in favourable light, but by Judas, a traitor and a thief.

Again, to put into relief the difference between the Synoptics and John, consider the two episodes where in the Fourth Gospel the Baptist and Jesus are brought together. The description of the first encounter between the two at the Jordan is quite similar in John (1:29–37) and the corresponding Synoptic passages. John's phrase, 'Behold the Lamb of God', recalls in the Synoptics the heavenly voice introducing Jesus as God's 'beloved Son'. (Note that not unlike 'kid' in English, the Aramaic 'lamb' (*talya*) is used metaphorically for a child.) But there are also crucial differences. Matthew, Mark and Luke firmly assert that Jesus humbly sought to be baptized by John. The Fourth Gospel cannot tolerate such self-abasement, and accordingly this evangelist prefers to keep silent on the baptism of Jesus. He thus avoids any possible insinuation that the baptizer John might be superior to the baptized Jesus. The appropriateness of the latter's wish to undergo such a baptism of penitence had already been indirectly queried by the tradition recorded in Matt. 3:14–15. There John is supposed to have remarked in a surprised and apologetic tone: '*I* need to be baptized by you, and do *you* come to me?' A little further on (3:22–30; 4:1–2), and contrary to the respect and harmony implied to have existed between Jesus and the Baptist, the evangelist alludes to strained relations revealed by a rivalry and quarrel between their disciples. Also, to underplay the significance of kinship between the two masters, which if clearly stated might imply that they were at least of similar standing, John makes no reference to the fact, testified to by Luke (1:25–56), that their mothers, Elizabeth and Mary, were related.

This mention of the mother of Jesus helps to recall another striking difference between the Synoptics and John. In the Synoptics Jesus is portrayed as showing reserve, verging on hostility, towards his family, including Mary. Mark (3:21) bluntly reports that his relatives held him to be crazy; they wanted to seize him and remove him from the public arena. Elsewhere we are told that his mother and brothers expected, but failed to receive, preferential treatment from Jesus. They reckoned that he would interrupt his teaching when informed that they had arrived. But Jesus rebuffed them: 'Who are my mother and my brothers?' he asked. Then, pointing towards his disciples, he declared them to be metaphorically his 'mother' and his 'brothers' (Mark 3:31–5; Matt. 12:46–50; Luke 8:19–21). Apart from the Nazareth episode where Jesus, the son of Mary, is described as 'the carpenter' or 'the carpenter's son', the Synoptic story loses sight of the family of Jesus. One has to turn to the Acts of the Apostles (1:14) for the next appearance of 'Mary, the mother of Jesus and . . . his brothers' in the company of 'the women', and of the apostles, eleven in number after the defection of Judas Iscariot. Later on we learn also from the Acts of the Apostles that James, 'the brother of the Lord', became the leader of the Jerusalem church. Moreover Jude, another of Jesus' four brothers, is presumed to be the author of one of the minor letters of the New Testament. So in time at least part of the family joined the Jesus party.

To return to Mary: the passage in Acts just quoted marks a turning-point, the beginning of a favourable attitude towards her, which culminates in the Fourth Gospel. Whereas John is still negative towards the 'brothers' of Jesus who 'did not believe in him' (John 7:5), he has a positive message about the mother of Jesus.

John, in common with the Synoptics, knows the father of Jesus as Joseph (Mark 6:3; Matt. 13:55); both he and Jesus' mother are depicted as well-known citizens of Nazareth (1:45, 6:42). John, however, never uses the name Mary. The 'mother of Jesus', as the Fourth Evangelist calls her, first appears in this Gospel as a guest, together with Jesus and his disciples, at a wedding in the village of Cana, close to Nazareth. Noticing that the wine is running out, she urges Jesus, seated next to her, to do something about the embarrassing situation (2:1–3).[3] Mary ignores his evasive answer, and secure in the knowledge that Jesus will not resist her wishes, instructs the servants to follow his orders (2:4–5). After the miracle, the family group – mother, son and brothers – and the disciples leave together and go to Capernaum (2:12). John's sketch presupposes closeness and warmth between mother and son, so different from the cold and unfriendly attitude towards the interfering family discernible in the Synoptic account. The same loving atmosphere surrounds the scene of the crucifixion, too. In contrast to the accounts of Mark and Matthew where some named women, but not the mother of Jesus, were witnessing the events from a distance (Mark 15:40; Matt. 27:56), Mary according to the Fourth Evangelist stood beside the cross where the dying Jesus entrusted to each other's care his mother and his beloved disciple (19:26–7).

Another major feature distinguishing the Fourth Gospel from the Synoptics resides in their respective understanding of the miracles of Jesus. The first three evangelists consider these as 'mighty works', that is to say, acts such as curing the sick, performed for their own sake, which struck the onlookers as miraculous. Jesus is said to have generally and explicitly disapproved of 'signs' intended to demonstrate the supernatural power of the person who executed them. He refused to comply with the demand for a 'sign' or a 'sign from heaven' addressed to him by Jewish notables, Pharisees, scribes or Sadducees (Mark 8:11; Matt. 12:38; 16:1). He rebuffed them by the comment that only those who belong to an 'evil and adulterous generation' (Matt. 12:39; 16:4; Luke 11:29) needed 'signs'. In the Synoptics, the conclusion drawn from the performance of wonders is that Jesus was a prophet, a traditional element twice echoed in John (6:14; 9:17). Or else the presence of the miraculous indicates, as does the expulsion of demons 'by virtue of the finger of God' (Matt. 12:28; Luke 11:20), that the Kingdom of God or the messianic age was approaching or indeed that it had already arrived.

Go and tell John [the Baptist] what you hear and see: the blind receive their sight and the lame walk, lepers are cleansed and the deaf hear, and the dead are raised up, and the poor have good news preached to them (Matt. 11:4–5).

---

3. The shortage of wine may have been due to the arrival of the (uninvited) disciples of Jesus who, like pupils of rabbis, dutifully followed their master wherever he went.

The context of such happenings recalls the Messianic Apocalypse (4Q521) from Qumran, possibly an Essene composition, where Messiah, healing, resurrection of the dead, and Kingdom of God are mentioned in a single breath.

> ... [the hea]vens and the earth will listen to His Messiah ... He [the Lord] will glorify the pious on the throne of the eternal Kingdom, He who liberates the captives, restores sight to the blind, straightens the b[ent] ... For He will heal the wounded, and revive the dead and bring good news to the poor.

In the Synoptics, the miracles of Jesus, the charismatic prophet, mostly stem from a man of God's love and pity for the sick and the miserable, unless they are depicted as the expected prelude to the establishment of God's Kingdom, or as the signal of its actual presence, the principal goal of Jesus' mission. Yet this Kingdom of God, so central in the teaching of Jesus in the Synoptics, appears only in a single episode in John 3:3–5, and plays no real part in the theology of the Fourth Gospel. As for the Johannine miracles, they are 'signs' and are meant to prove the otherness, the heavenly origin and supernatural nature of Jesus. They manifest his glory. The signs are in the forefront of the evangelist's thinking, and it seems that in his original draft John listed them in a numbered sequence, the miraculous transformation of water into wine at the wedding feast of Cana being described as 'the beginning', and the healing of the royal official's son as 'the second' of the 'signs performed by Jesus' (2:11; 4:54). However, with sign number two the serial presentation abruptly comes to an end and the confusion begins. In fact, an earlier remark of John (2:23) suggests that an unspecified number of (unrecorded) miracles antedated the healing of the royal official's son and accounted for the faith of many Jews in Jesus. Nicodemus, too, confesses that his belief in Jesus as an envoy of God relies on 'signs' which 'no one can do unless God is with him' (3:2). Later in the Gospel story we find an incidental passing reference to 'the signs [Jesus] did on those who were diseased' (6:2).

Finally, in addition to the miraculous feeding of the crowd and the healing of a blind man (6:14, 26; 9:16–17), the raising of Lazarus was another 'sign' which particularly increased the fame of Jesus in the eyes of the crowd (12:18). Looking at the same story of Lazarus from a different perspective, imperviousness to 'so many signs' (12:37) reveals, in John's view, the enormity of the Jews' lack of faith. By contrast, 'many other signs', not written down in the Gospel but witnessed by the disciples, are there to prove that Jesus was 'the Christ, the Son of God' (20:30–31). In short, explicitly or tacitly, the Johannine 'signs' serve to manifest the supernatural character of Jesus.

In the present era of friendly Christian–Jewish dialogue, one of the most dismaying features of the Fourth Gospel is its determined claim that *the* Jews, or at least the inhabitants of Judaea – the Greek *Ioudaioi* can designate either – were profoundly and universally inimical to Jesus. Indeed to all intents and purposes the Jesus of John was almost from the start of his career the target of repeated Jewish murder plots. A twofold reason is given for such a deep animosity. According to the first, Jesus aroused the fury of his co-religionists by performing cures on the Sabbath, and thus profaned the Jewish holy day. The second reason for their outrage, according to John, was Jesus' allegedly blasphemous claim that God was his Father.

The purported antagonism receives no support from the Synoptic Gospels; neither the historian Josephus nor rabbinic literature reports killing of Jews by other Jews for religious, as opposed to political, reasons.[4] Such behaviour is completely without theological foundation in the Jewish thought of the age. Healing in the New Testament was in general performed by a verbal command; it did not entail 'work', and consequently was not a real breach of the Sabbath. Furthermore, singly or together the Jews are entitled to call themselves children of God. We may indeed discard as highly unlikely Luke's story of an attempted lynching of Jesus by fellow Jewish worshippers in the synagogue of his home town, for not even the most bigoted local patriot of Nazareth could have considered murder a commensurate and justifiable response to Jesus' performing cures in neighbouring Capernaum. Apart from this single episode in Luke 4:29, the first three evangelists do not blame the Jews as such but rather their leaders, the Pharisees, scribes or the high priests, with conspiracy to murder. Apart from one debat-

---

4. Thus the high priest Ananus was flexing his political muscles when during the interregnum between two Roman procurators he put to death James, the brother of Jesus, and others on a trumped-up religious charge. His act scandalized the fair-minded and strictly observant Jews of Jerusalem, according to Josephus (*Jewish Antiquities* XX.200–201).

able case (Mark 3:6; Matt. 12:14; Luke 6:11),[5] even they are accused only in the final stages of Jesus' public career of seeking his downfall. Contrast this with the heinous intent displayed again and again from a relatively early stage by 'the Jews' in John (5:16, 18; 7:19, 25). The Fourth Gospel represents Jesus as forced to escape to Galilee because in Judaea the Jews (*Ioudaioi*) were threatening his life (7:1). According to John, this bloodthirstiness revealed the true colour of the Jews: they behaved like their father, the devil, who was a 'murderer from the beginning' (8:44). Though they claimed to be 'the sons of Abraham' (8:37, 40), they were descended from the prince of darkness. John's hatred of the Jews was fierce. I often wonder whether he could possibly have been Jewish himself. Paul, in comparison, even with his occasional outbursts against his co-religionists (cf. 1 Thess. 2:14–16), appears almost tame.

The supreme head of the Jews, the high priest Caiaphas, like a good many political leaders before and since his time, was ready (according to the Fourth Gospel) to sacrifice Jesus for political expediency. He declared it preferable that one seemingly dangerous man should perish rather than the whole nation be destroyed (11:50). He is thus credited with the formulation of a legal principle which reappears later in the Talmud: 'It is better that this man should be slain rather than the community should perish on his account' (yTerumot 46b). However, the rabbis found the idea of handing over a trouble-maker to the state authorities unacceptable, and endeavoured instead to persuade revolutionaries sought by the Roman police to give themselves up in the interest of the community. Contradicting his earlier statements (5:16, 18) that Jesus was under threat from the start, John echoes the Synoptics (Mark 14:1; Matt. 26:3–4; Luke 22:2) in associating the ultimate murder plot against Jesus with this account of the high priest: 'So from that day they [the chief priests and the Pharisees, 11:47] took counsel how to put him to death' (11:53). The ruthlessness of the religious leaders seems to have known no bounds. Apparently they even sought to dispose of the resurrected Lazarus to prevent people

---

5. Mark and Matthew speak of an early plot by Pharisees and Herodians, or by Pharisees alone, to 'destroy' Jesus. In Luke, scribes and Pharisees merely wonder what they might do to Jesus. A parallel passage which seems more plausible mentions Pharisees and Herodians seeking a way to 'entrap Jesus in his talk' (Mark 12:13).

believing in Jesus on account of his raising his friend from the dead (12:9–10).

Nothing demonstrates better the singularity of John than his account of the last day in the life of Jesus (John 18–19). This section, which in many respects runs parallel with the Synoptics and now and again seems more reliable than their accounts, displays such notable divergences in essential aspects that any attempt at harmonization proves quite impossible. In particular, the two chronologies clash, with significant consequences. The Synoptics describe the last meal which Jesus shared with his apostles as a Passover supper, and in doing so present a historically untenable scenario. According to it, the interrogations of Jesus by the high priest and the council, as well as his condemnation and actual execution, all occur on 15 Nisan, the feast-day of Passover. But it is hardly conceivable that the religious leadership of the Jewish people should publicly break such basic rules as the prohibition of court hearings, and the pronouncement and execution of death sentences, on festive days and the Sabbath.

The Fourth Gospel, on the other hand, antedates these events by twenty-four hours. This is obvious from the remark about the Jewish notables' unwillingness to enter Pilate's residence. They sought to avoid contracting ritual defilement on 14 Nisan which would debar them from eating the Passover in the evening (John 18:28). This means that the *seder*-dinner had not yet taken place. Historically more probable than that of the Synoptics, the chronology adopted by John creates a theological snag. It excludes, or at least grossly diminishes, the possibility that the Last Supper was a Passover supper.[6] Yet the Passover identity of the meal is emphatically stated in Mark, Matthew and Luke.

And on the first day of the Unleavened Bread, when they sacrificed the Passover lamb, his disciples said to him, 'Where will you have us go and

6. Recently some scholars have surmised that Jesus followed not the mainstream Jewish calendar but the solar calendar of the Essenes, according to which the Passover always fell on a Wednesday. Consequently their Passover supper was held on a Tuesday, rather than the Thursday of the Synoptic tradition. This attempt still leaves the chronological problem of John unresolved. Besides, the assumption that Jesus observed the Essene calendar conflicts with the essentially non-Essene character of his teaching and behaviour.

prepare for you to eat the Passover?' . . . And the disciples . . . prepared the Passover. And when it was evening he came with the twelve. And . . . they were at the table eating . . . (Mark 14:12–17; cf. Matt. 26:17–21; Luke 22:7–14)

The anticipation by twenty-four hours of the meal by John annuls the sacrificial Passover symbolism of the Christian eucharist, implied in the Synoptics and heavily stressed by St Paul, who first formulated it (1 Cor. 5:7; 11:23–6). John shows no awareness of this idea. The symbolic message attached to the last meal which was consumed by Jesus and his disciples '*before* the feast of Passover' ( John 13:1) is not redemption through eating the body and drinking the blood of Jesus, the true Passover lamb,[7] but that of humility impressed on them by the master when he washed the feet of his disciples ( John 13:1–20).

Here ends my bird's-eye view of the distinguishing features setting apart John from the Synoptic Gospels. The differences are so telling that they turn John into an independent narrator, and render his story acceptable only to an audience unconnected with Jesus or his immediate disciples. In consequence, the picture of a supercelestial Christ sketched by this evangelist reflects the final stage of metamorphosis in the sequence of the changing faces of Jesus within the New Testament.

7. In John 6:35–59, in the context of Jesus being the manna, the bread of life descending from heaven, the shocking image of eating his flesh and *drinking his blood* symbolizes spiritual communion which leads to 'eternal life', because he who eats and thus absorbs him abides in Jesus, and Jesus in him (6:53–4). In brief, 'he who eats me will live because of me' (6:57). In Jesus' own society, profoundly rooted in blood taboo, the suggestion of drinking a man's blood would have filled his listeners with nausea. Even later, prospective Gentile Christians were obliged to abstain from blood (Acts 15:20, 29).

# 2

# The Jesus of John: Messiah figure or Stranger from heaven

The more often I re-read John, the more obvious it becomes that this Gospel consists of several portraits of Jesus superimposed on one another, and that three distinct approaches are needed for disentangling this complexity. All these portraits, even those which have their counterparts in the earlier Synoptic Gospels, display the theological hallmark of the Fourth Evangelist, and at the end of this chapter the reader will be in no doubt that the Jesus painted by John towers above the Jesus figure of the tradition represented by Mark, Matthew and Luke.

To begin with, the Fourth Gospel includes many passages which convey views about Jesus or attitudes towards him which the evangelist assigns to Jesus' Jewish contemporaries, among them friends and uncommitted observers as well as opponents and critics. The questions raised by them concern the role of Jesus: was he a prophet, the Messiah, the Son of God? The answers they provide shed precious light on the religious ideas current in Palestinian Judaism in the first century AD.

Next there are the texts, a mass of them, in which the evangelist makes Jesus speak of himself. The words which Jesus utters are mostly of John's own creation. The difference between the ideas of John's Jesus and the Jesus of the first three Gospels is particularly striking; they are indeed irreconcilable.

As far as the literary form is concerned, New Testament scholars generally agree that the Jesus of the Synoptic Gospels was not an orator delivering skilfully composed sermons. He communicated his teaching by means of pithy proverbs or sayings, and in colourful, highly express- ive but relatively short parables. Many of the utterances dealt with incidental questions put to the master by passers-by or by his followers, and Jesus' answers were unrehearsed responses, rather than planned and structured proclamations and exhortations. There are admittedly two larger pieces in the Synoptic Gospels, but neither the Sermon on the Mount (Matt. 5–7), which is vaguely echoed in Luke's briefer Sermon in the Plain (6:20–49), nor the Eschatological Discourse announcing the imminent end of the present era, marked by the destruction of Jerusalem (Matt. 24; Mark 13; Luke 21), strike the reader as organized rhetorical compositions. The Sermon on the Mount is an assemblage of unconnected sayings loosely stitched together by Matthew, a good many of which, though pronounced on diverse occasions, may ultimately go back to Jesus. But the 'Sermon' as it now stands was surely not intended for a single delivery. Bitty and disjointed, it would have confused the audience. As for the Eschatological Discourse, although it may include genuine words of Jesus (as will be shown in Chapter 6), in my view and in that of the majority of Gospel experts, as a whole it is a church creation which postdates the destruction of the Temple in AD 70 and uses the catastrophe as an indicator of the close proximity of Christ's return. To put it plainly, the Discourse was composed four decades after the time of Jesus as a prophecy after the fact.

Regarding their content, the Synoptic sayings of Jesus are centred on the heavenly Father, the imminent arrival of the Kingdom of God, and on the religious and moral requisites for people to enter the Kingdom through the gateway of repentance. This means that the teaching and religion of the Jesus of the Synoptics are not focused on himself, but on God. Even when he had to face straight questions relating to his role in the final events of the eschatological age, he was usually equivocal and evasive. When challenged whether he was the Messiah or the King of the Jews, his usual answer was not 'Yes', but 'This is what *you* say', or something similar.

Look now at the contrast when you open the Fourth Gospel. The Jesus of John is characterized by long, rambling, repetitive and often allegorical speeches. They are not primarily about God, and certainly show no preoccupation with the Kingdom of heaven. This key topic of the Jesus of the Synoptics figures on only one occasion – in the dialogue with Nicodemus (3:3–5) – in the whole of John. In the Fourth Gospel Jesus' sermons are all *self*-centred; they turn around *his* person, *his* teaching and *his* personal relation to God and to his followers. The style entails a lordly, elliptic delivery which often results in a lack of understanding by all and sundry. His words meet with the same uncomprehending reaction whether they address previously unknown individuals, such as the Jewish leader Nicodemus (chapter 3); or the Samaritan woman at Jacob's well in Sychar (chapter 4); or a hostile Jewish crowd by the Sea of Galilee, outraged by his teaching on the 'bread of life' (chapter 6); or dense and slow-witted groups of his own disciples who found his teaching 'hard' and impossible to understand (6:60). Even the intimate circle of the twelve apostles were often unable to grasp the meaning of his words. Impatient and sharp rejoinders by Jesus are not unusual. Nicodemus was rebuked: 'Are you a teacher of Israel, and yet you do not understand this?' (3:10). Not even the apostles could escape the annoyed remonstrance of the master: 'Have I been with you so long, and yet you do not know me, Philip?' (14:9). Unlike the Jesus of the Synoptics, the Jesus of the Fourth Gospel is a superior, authoritative and transcendent figure. He speaks down to people and shuns equivocation. When he is asked whether he is the Messiah or God's ambassador, he either firmly asserts that he is (4:26), or complains: 'I told you, and you do not believe' (10:25).

The Johannine Jesus is not the prophetic 'man of God', one who conveys divine teachings and precepts, with whom biblical and post-biblical Jewish tradition has made us familiar. He is a mysterious stranger, a celestial being in human disguise, who came from above and was to re-ascend to heaven. In contemporary jargon he could be called an ET. In John's idiom, he is the Son of God the Father in the full metaphysical sense and not just metaphorically, as the Bible and post-biblical literature apply the title 'son' of God first to every Jew, and later to pious Jews in general and to specially chosen individuals such as the prophets, the holy men and the Messiah.

The third source of the portrait of Jesus in the Fourth Gospel does not come from sayings attributed to contemporaries of Jesus or from John's words put in the mouth of 'the Son', but directly and openly from comments made by the evangelist himself. I refer above all to the Prologue (1:1–18), John's poetical and doctrinal masterpiece. This foreword, depicting the eternal Word (*Logos*) that was made flesh and became the manifestation of God on earth, provides in a nutshell the quintessence of Christology, or the doctrinal synthesis of Christ and his work of salvation. Out of this brilliant synopsis the essentials of Christian theology could be soundly reconstructed even if the rest of the evidence relating to the church and its teaching had been completely lost.

I hope that this brief outline of the structure of the Fourth Gospel affords an adequate insight into the aim of the evangelist in constructing his work. By crediting Jesus' contemporaries with the less developed traditional views on Jewish religion, John is able to bring into relief his beliefs relating to higher Christology, presented as coming directly from the mouth of the Son of God, and to give his own summary of these beliefs in the sublime Prologue to the Gospel.

# I
# JESUS IN THE EYES OF HIS CONTEMPORARIES

This heading does not imply that the excerpts designated as eye-witness accounts amount to reliable historical evidence. As I have said, the Fourth Gospel – perhaps with the exception of a few special details relating to the story of the crucifixion – cannot be accepted as a primary source of the life and teaching of Jesus. Nevertheless since the canvas is drawn with the help of titles given to Jesus in the Fourth Gospel, most of which appear also in the Synoptics, it is reasonable to presume that we are faced here with segments of common Gospel tradition already existent in written form when John set out to compose his story. Let us then meet Jesus the Teacher, the Prophet, the Messiah, the King, the Son of God, the Lord and the Lamb of God.

## Jesus the Teacher

To understand John's terminology, we must first inquire into the various connotations of 'teacher' in first-century Judaism. The word could point to an 'official' instructor, normally a priest, a scribe or a Pharisee. The Nicodemus of John belonged to the top layer of this category. He was a 'teacher of Israel' (3:10), possibly a member of the Sanhedrin, the supreme doctrinal and judicial body in Jerusalem (7:50). Clearly, Jesus did not belong to this stratum of Jewish society. Nor was he a 'rabbi' in the technical sense, despite being repeatedly addressed as such in John (1:38; 3:2; 20:16), since he was not an expert in Jewish traditional law and Bible interpretation. It is even questionable whether the term 'rabbi' in the specialized meaning was current in the early decades of the first century AD. The great Jewish masters who lived in the age of Jesus, Hillel, Shammai, Gamaliel, are all called 'elders', not 'rabbis'.

What kind of teacher, then, was the Jesus of the Fourth Gospel? John's narrative makes it plain that Jesus did not derive his doctrinal authority, as did the rabbis of the Mishnah and the Talmud, from years of study at the feet of an acknowledged master. That Jesus was not a trained teacher is indicated by the authorities' amazement at his wisdom: 'How is it that this man knows letters when he has never studied?' (7:15). The best outline of Jesus as a preacher in the Fourth Gospel is formulated in the words of Nicodemus: Jesus was a teacher commissioned by God, for no one can perform the works that he does unless God is with him (3:2). In other words, John portrayed him as a charismatic master whose message was confirmed by his mighty deeds.

While Jesus is made by John to concur with this assessment, referring to himself as 'Teacher and Lord' (13:13), the Fourth Gospel never gives him a chance to demonstrate by 'signs' that he is a God-sent Teacher. The Jesus of John prefers to prove his heavenly mandate from the fundamentally Father-centred nature of his ministry and from the fact that his words stem from God (7:16). Put differently, the truth of the message was revealed by the theocentric orientation of the messenger: 'He who speaks on his own seeks his own glory; but he who seeks the glory of him [i.e. God, the Father] who sent him is true, and in him there is no falsehood' (7:18).

## Jesus the Prophet

In common English idiom a prophet is someone who foretells the future. In the biblical language and the Judaeo-Christian terminology of the age of Jesus, the term can relate to a wonder-working prophet like Elijah or Elisha in the Old Testament Books of Kings, or to an inspired messenger of God and revealer of his secrets, such as Isaiah, Jeremiah or the other prophets who left books behind them.

The leading varieties of the prophetic figure in first-century Palestine, the prophet-teacher, the prophet-eschatologist who announces the events of the final age, and the prophet-thaumaturge or miracle-worker, are familiar representations of Jesus to be found in the Synoptic Gospels. To these we should add a further category, the so-called eschatological sign-prophet who heralds, in a context of miracles, the impending political liberation of the Jewish people. Such sign-prophets are well attested in the work of the first-century Jewish historian, Flavius Josephus. One of them, Theudas, announced to his followers in the mid-forties AD the onset of the final age of deliverance (*Jewish Antiquities* xx. 97–9). About ten years later, when Fadus (AD 52–60) was the procurator of Judaea, another 'prophet', called 'the Egyptian', led a group of credulous Jews to the Mount of Olives outside Jerusalem to show them the toppling of the walls of the holy city (*Ant.* xx. 169–72; *Jewish War* ii. 261–3). The Romans promptly quelled the two insurrections. Both Theudas, who was executed by them, and the Egyptian who escaped appear in the Acts of the Apostles (5:36; 21:38).

John, writing more than three decades after the fall of Jerusalem in AD 70, had obviously no intention of associating Jesus with a revolutionary type of prophet. It would have seriously harmed the progress of Christianity in the eastern Mediterranean provinces of the Roman empire if Jesus had been portrayed as a justly convicted enemy of the state. Generally speaking John minimizes both the prophetic role of Jesus and his function as charismatic teacher, no doubt because he has greatly reduced his importance as a healer and has kept dark his exorcistic activity. Nevertheless, two other facets of the prophetic image quietly emerge from the Fourth Gospel.

The first of these is the figure of the charismatic man of God who can read matters concealed in the heart and perform wonders (cf. Matt. 21:46; Luke 7:16; *Ant.* xviii. 63). Thus the blind man who was cured by Jesus recognized him as a prophet when he was asked by hostile Pharisees to identify the man who had healed him (9:17).

The second figure also appears in a miraculous context – Jesus feeding five thousand people with five barley loaves and two fishes – but goes beyond the image of the ordinary wonder-worker, as the spontaneous reaction of the beneficiaries of the 'sign' testifies: 'This is indeed the prophet who is to come into the world!' (6:14). The text speaks not of *a* prophet, but *the* prophet, a well-defined personality. Here the Fourth Gospel is a step ahead of the Synoptics, where Jesus is simply 'one of the prophets' (Matt. 16:14; Mark 8:28; Luke 9:19). John in fact takes on board the early Judaeo-Christian teaching about a messianic prophet formulated in the Acts of the Apostles (3:17–26; 7:37), which itself echoes an expectation attested in the Apocrypha and the Dead Sea Scrolls (cf. pp. 118, 191).

## Jesus the Messiah

If, in John's judgement, being called 'teacher' and 'prophet' was an underestimate of the dignity of Jesus, we may justifiably expect a more enthusiastic treatment for the notion of the Messiah.

The 'anointed one' (*Mashiah* in Hebrew, *Meshiha* in Aramaic and *Christos* in Greek) is among the most frequently occurring titles of Jesus in the New Testament, but ordinary readers may be surprised to learn that the meaning of these terms was much less clear in the age of Jesus than one might imagine today. The expression was applied not only to the king Messiah, but also to the priest Messiah, as the Dead Sea Scrolls and the Letter to the Hebrews indicate. Moreover the place and role of messianic expectation in Jewish thought are often misunderstood. Christians with no expert knowledge of Jewish religious history tend to conceive of the Messiah as the central figure in the theology of the Jews in the age of Jesus, a figure dominating every other hope of Judaism. In fact messianic fervour, far from being all-pervasive, was only sporadically attested in Jewish literature, mostly amid the political upheavals of the last two pre-Christian centuries and in the first century AD. The main messianic theme refers to the triumph of the future anointed king of the house of David, who was to restore the sovereignty of the Jewish people after bringing to an end centuries of foreign domination and overthrowing the mighty Roman empire.

The expectation of the *king* Messiah is a live issue in the New Testament. Jesus is linked to the Jewish royal dynasty in the messianic representation of the Synoptics: his genealogy is traced to David (Matt. 1; Luke 3), and he is addressed as 'Son of David' (Matt. 9:27; Mark 10:47–8; Luke 18:38–9). But by the time of the Fourth Gospel the Davidic ideology becomes rather muted. When the royal Messiah is alluded to, the applicability of this figure to Jesus is mostly denied by outsiders. Thus John makes hostile Jews assert that Jesus could not be the Davidic Messiah because they believed he was a Galilean, and did not come from Bethlehem where according to ancestral tradition the royal Christ was to be born (7:40–42). Another objection to recognition of the messianic status of Jesus arose from the belief in the secret origin of the Christ. He was supposed to appear suddenly, as it were from nowhere. In the eyes of many Jews Jesus did not fit this messianic requirement: 'We know where this man comes from; and when the Christ appears, no one will know where he comes from' (7:26–7).

Against these doubting voices John marshals a whole array of positive testimonies which give the impression that Jesus *qua* Messiah commanded a substantial following. In John, his messianic identity is not a secret as it is in the Synoptic Gospels. From the first moment of his manifestation in public, those who had eyes to see were able to perceive who he was. It started with John the Baptist, who knew straightaway that he faced the Messiah (1:32). Without preliminaries, Andrew, the future apostle, could confidently inform his brother Simon (Peter) that he had found 'the Messiah' (1:41). Such instant recognition meets with a plain acceptance on the part of the Jesus of John. To the Samaritan woman's hint, 'I know that the Messiah is coming', Jesus responds with 'I who speak to you am he' (4:25–6). Only the lack of messianic secrecy in the Fourth Gospel can explain Jesus' annoyance with those who kept on pestering him with questions. To 'How long will you keep us in suspense? If you are the Christ, tell us plainly', he wearily replied, 'I told you, and you do not believe me' (10:24–5).

Not only his friends were convinced that Jesus was the promised Christ, but according to John, so also were the Jewish crowds. This was primarily on account of the miraculous aura surrounding Jesus. We are told that in particular the raising of Lazarus from the dead produced a massive increase in the numbers of followers of Jesus (11:45). This growing sympathy for Jesus even engendered rumours that his official proclamation as Messiah might be imminent. The unwillingness by the high priests to restrain him was interpreted as a sign that even they were in two minds about him (7:26). We also learn that the officers dispatched by Jewish officialdom to arrest Jesus were afraid to lay hands on him because 'No man ever spoke like this man' (7:32, 7:46). In the view of the evangelist the Jerusalem authorities abstained from applying strong-arm methods because of Jesus' great popularity: 'You see that you can do nothing; look, the world has gone after him' (12:19).

John is, however, at pains to underline that Jesus' success was strongly resisted in high places. Not only did the chief priests and Pharisees envisage punitive action against those who sympathized with Jesus, excluding them from communal life (9:22),[1] but they were also ready to go so far as to plan the murder of Jesus in the national interest. 'What are we to do? For this man performs many signs. If we let him go on thus, everyone will believe in him, and the Romans will come and destroy both our holy place and our nation' (11:47–8). Hence John makes the high priest declare, 'It is expedient for you that one man should die for the people, and that the whole nation should not perish' (11:50). So the evangelist succeeds in offsetting the impression of great popular sympathy for Jesus by symbolically placing the guilt of the entire Jewish people on the shoulders of their official religious spokesmen.

1. This threat of a ban mentioned in the Fourth Gospel is often misinterpreted by Christian commentators as signifying an early formal separation between Judaism and Christianity. Synagogues were local places of worship, and in larger cities (let alone in Jerusalem, where the episode of the healing of the man born blind is located) there were many of them. So exclusion from one could easily be followed by joining another. The joke about the shipwrecked Jew building two synagogues on his desert island so as to have one where he never sets foot may express a timeless truth.

## Jesus the King

John also employs the titles 'King of Israel' and 'King of the Jews' in addition to that of 'Messiah'. To be more precise, 'King of the Jews' is always uttered by opponents with a political nuance attached to it, whereas 'King of Israel' has a religious meaning and issues from friendly lips.

The political usage of the term is the more frequent. It has nationalistic and even revolutionary overtones and does not find favour either with John or with his Jesus. The first example occurs in connection with the feeding of five thousand Galileans close to the Lake of Gennesaret (6:1–14). The instinctive reaction of the crowd at the sight of the miracle was to seize Jesus and proclaim him king. However, showing himself devoid of political ambitions, Jesus slipped away towards the solitude of the mountain (6:15).

The other allusions to kingship are attached by John to the account of the trial of Jesus. Pilate is said to have challenged Jesus whether he was the 'King of the Jews' (18:33, 37). We are told that he first gave an ambivalent answer: '*You* say that I am a king', but later he became more specific, 'My kingship is not from the world.' Jesus then made clear that his mission had no revolutionary aim: 'I have come into the world to bear witness to the truth. Everyone who is of the truth hears my voice' (18:33–7). The theologically unsubtle Pilate was lost and could only mutter, 'What is truth?' *Quid est veritas?* (18:38). He then condemned Jesus to death. The charge fixed to the cross read, 'Jesus of Nazareth, the King of the Jews' (19:19).

The religious use of the title 'King of Israel' appears in the ecstatic exclamation of Nathanael, friend of the apostle Philip, addressing Jesus: 'Rabbi, you are the Son of God! The King of Israel!' (1:49). The joint use of 'Son of God' and 'King of Israel' makes the messianic significance of the idiom unmistakable, recalling the declaration of Peter at Caesarea Philippi, 'You are the Christ, the Son of the living God' (Matt. 16:16). The same assessment applies to the chanting of 'Hosanna! Blessed is he who comes in the name of the Lord, *the King of Israel*!' (12:13) at Jesus' entry into Jerusalem. John, wishing to make the phrase plainly messianic but not warlike, appended a reworded version of Zechariah 9:9, 'Fear not, daughter of Zion; behold your *King* is coming, sitting on an ass's colt.' A bellicose Messiah would ride a horse; the irenic Jesus was mounted on a donkey.

## Jesus the Son of God

In the course of two millennia of Christian reflection on the figure of Jesus, the original Jewish meaning of the title 'son of God' has faded and the distinction between 'Son of God' and God has to all intents and purposes disappeared. In a Christian context, 'Son of God' is just another way of saying God. This was not so in the Old Testament and in intertestamental Judaism.

Starting at the top of the hierarchical ladder, the Hebrew Bible designates members of the heavenly court as 'sons of God' (Gen. 6:2; Deut. 32:8; Pss. 29:1; 89:6, etc.), interpreted as 'angels of God' in the Greek Septuagint translation of Scripture. A step or two further down comes the historical king of Israel of whom God declares, 'I will be his Father and he shall be my son' (2 Sam. 7:14). On the bottom rung stands every single Jew designated as a 'son of God' since the time of the exodus from Egypt, according to the words of the Bible: 'Thus says the Lord, Israel is my first-born son' (Exod. 4:22).

In post-biblical times, however, the honorific title 'son of God' began to be restricted to pious Jews only. Thus Jesus ben Sira declared in the apocryphal Book of Ecclesiasticus (early second century BC) that only the virtuous and merciful merited this epithet: 'Be a father to the fatherless and as a husband to widows, and God shall call you *son*' (4:10). Moreover, according to the writer of the Book of Jubilees, dating to the middle of the second century BC, the Israelites were reckoned 'the sons of the living God' provided that their hearts were circumcised and filled with the spirit of holiness (Jub. 1:24).

At about the same time 'son of God' also became the designation of the awaited royal Messiah. From the sixth century BC onwards, the descendants of David no longer ruled and the Jews were under Babylonian, Persian, Greek and finally Roman dominion. So the earlier promises to the reigning king were re-interpreted as applying to the last son of David. Thus for example, 'I will be his Father and he shall be my son', a divine assurance originally addressed to David's successor, King Solomon (2 Sam. 7:14), is expounded in a Dead Sea Scroll as referring to the final ruler of Israel: 'He is the Branch of David who shall arise ... in Zion [at the end] of time ...' (4Q174). Another Qumran text includes a badly preserved passage which seems to use the metaphor of God 'begetting' the Messiah (1QS$^a$ 2:11–12).[2]

So, depending on the context, 'Son of God' could point to any Jew, to a pious Jew, to a historical king or to the future Messiah. When they are considered together, all these designations display one element in common: they are all figures of speech. No biblical or post-biblical Jewish writer ever depicted a human being literally as divine, nor did Jewish religious culture agree to accommodate the Hellenistic notions of 'son of God' and 'divine man'. The designations, common in the terminology of ruler worship in imperial Rome and in the description of charismatic personalities in Hellenism,[3] remained taboo to Judaism. These concepts, coupled with the picture of children born of the union of Olympian gods and earthly women, known from classical mythology but divested of their pagan connotations, may have subconsciously played a part in the later Christian formulation of the divine sonship of Jesus within the thought world of Greek civilization.

In the light of these observations, what does 'son of God' signify when applied to Jesus by friendly speakers in the Fourth Gospel? We can be sure that it means more than just a pious Jew; more likely it is

2. An Aramaic text recently published by E. Puech ('4Q Apocryphe de Daniel ar' in *DJD* XXII, Oxford, 1996, 165–84), popularly known as the 'Son of God' document, is interpreted by several scholars as relating to the King Messiah because it contains the significant phrases, 'The *son of God* he will be proclaimed and the *son of the Most High* they will call him'. In my opinion, however, the person who calls himself 'son of God' is more likely to be the evil king of the last world empire, modelled on the Syrian Greek king Antiochus IV Epiphanes in the Book of Daniel. The surname 'Epiphanes', which appears on Antiochus' coins, is an abbreviation of 'Theos Epiphanes', the 'God who reveals himself'. This final wicked king is expected to be proclaimed and worshipped as a god: 'And the king ... shall exalt himself and magnify himself above every god ... he shall give no heed to any other god, for he shall magnify himself above all' (Dan. 11:36–7).

3. Best known among them is Apollonius of Tyana, a first-century AD neo-Pythagorean sage whose *Life* is recounted by Philostratus in the early third century. According to Philostratus, Apollonius was called 'son of Zeus' by the local people (*Life of Apollonius*, 1.6).

the equivalent of 'Messiah'. The only anomalous, i.e. literal, interpretation of the 'son of God' idiom is found on the lips of the Jewish authorities when they search for a capital charge against Jesus. Before the Roman governor, they claim that the phrase implies blasphemy. 'We have a law, and by that law he ought to die, because he has made himself the Son of God' (19:7). The accusation is baseless from the point of view of the Jewish traditional use of the idiom, and obviously meaningless to Pilate. For him this was just a quarrel between Jews about some nonsense of their superstition.[4]

## Jesus the Lord

'Lord' (*Kurios*) is the most frequently used title of Jesus in the Gospel of John. It occurs more than thirty times, and like its parallels in Jewish literature of the intertestamental period, it exhibits a great diversity of meanings.

On the lowest semantic level, 'Lord' is a polite form of address roughly corresponding to the English 'Sir'. It is used by a variety of persons in John, including the evangelist himself, and is regularly directed towards Jesus. But the same expression can be applied to anyone of some standing. For instance, a group of Jews from the Greek diaspora called the apostle Philip 'Lord' in Jerusalem (12:21). Again, Mary Magdalen, imagining that she was talking to the man in charge of the garden where Jesus had been entombed, addressed the unrecognized risen Christ, 'Lord, if you have carried him away, tell me where you have laid him' (20:15).

In connection with Jesus, the appellation 'Lord' may be used by a total stranger, like the Samaritan woman (4:11), the royal official (4:49), and 'people' who sympathized with him (6:34). Jesus is invoked as 'Lord' also by the apostles in contexts where the meaning seems to

4. While the evangelist, as we shall discover in the Prologue, personally believed in some kind of non-metaphorical divine sonship of Jesus, he was nevertheless aware that the 'son of God' formula could be employed without breaking the law. In fact, he makes his Jesus declare that the phrase was not to be taken literally. For if Scripture can indiscriminately call all the Jews 'gods' – 'I said, you are gods' (Ps. 82.6) – why should Jesus be reckoned a blasphemer for using that kind of language? (10:33–6).

be a reverential 'Sir' or 'Master' (i.e. teacher). Indeed, it is noteworthy that on the few occasions where the Jesus of John refers to himself as 'Lord', it is in the sense of Teacher or Master (13:13–14; 15:15, 20).

'*The* Lord', signifying Jesus, is endowed with a more elevated spiritual meaning in post-resurrection accounts, for example 'I have seen the Lord', or 'It is the Lord' (20:18; 21:7). Indeed, in the highly charged atmosphere of John's Gospel, 'Lord' imperceptibly rises from 'Sir' to greater heights. Not unexpectedly, though only once in the whole work, the intense spiritual excitement generated by an appearance of the risen Christ instinctively couples 'Lord' with 'God'. When touching the body of the revived Jesus, the previously doubting Thomas exclaims: 'My Lord and *my God*!' (20:28). Was this single occurrence just a slip of the tongue on the part of the evangelist? Perhaps not. It may have been the subconscious upsurge of the essence of his theology which is cleverly intimated in the opening verse of the Prologue, where Jesus, 'the Word', is clearly identified as 'God'.

Linguistic custom was instrumental in promoting this change. It is well known that the Jews employed 'Lord' as a synonym for God in their religious language. The various divine names, the sacrosanct and unpronounced YHWH ('Jehovah'), as well as the Hebrew *Adon* (Lord) and *Adonay* (my Lord) or the Aramaic *Mar* (Lord) are all translated into Greek by the same word, *Kurios* (Lord). We can be sure that Jews, whatever language they spoke, had no difficulty in distinguishing a divine 'Lord' from a human one. The hurdle which Hellenized Gentile Christians, like the members of the church of John, had to leap was considerably higher.

## Jesus the Lamb of God

The introduction of the title 'Lamb of God' is a landmark in John's creative contribution to the portrayal of his Jesus. The phrase, twice attributed to John the Baptist, is an unusual image in the New Testament. In the Fourth Gospel the baptism by John the Baptizer is referred to only incidentally (1:26, 33; 3:23) and there is no mention that Jesus himself was baptized by him. According to the evangelist, a divinely intended task of the Baptist was publicly to proclaim Jesus to the Jews as 'the Lamb of God who takes away the sins of the world' (1:29).

The metaphor 'Lamb ('*amnos*) of God' is exclusive to John in the Gospels. Admittedly, the Book of Revelation also speaks of 'the Lamb' but employs a different Greek noun ('*arnion*) and never uses 'Lamb of God'. The immediate religious symbolism of the phrase is associated with the animal victims regularly sacrificed for the expiation of sins in the Jerusalem Temple. While the Mosaic cult continued in the sanctuary until AD 70, the worshipper hoped to obtain divine forgiveness for his transgressions through spilling the blood and burning the body of a lamb by the officiating priest. Likewise the blood of the Passover lamb was believed to possess the saving power which had protected the Jewish people in Egypt in the time of Moses. So by applying to Jesus the title 'Lamb of God', John cleverly encapsulated in a single symbol the future Christian theology of universal expiation of sins through the sacrificial death of Jesus.

To grasp the significance of the idiom, it is important to realize that apart from this eloquent expression John is remarkably quiet on the subject of redemption of sins. Yet by adopting his peculiar chronology of the crucifixion (cf. pp. 20–21), John turned Jesus into a redeeming Passover lamb. For the Christ of John expired on the cross in the afternoon of the day *preceding* the Passover (19:14, 31), and thus his death exactly coincided with the slaughtering of the Passover lambs in the courtyard of the Temple of Jerusalem.

For a fuller understanding of the paschal symbolism of the 'Lamb of God' we must also remember an ancient Aramaic interpretation of Exodus 1:15 according to which Pharaoh's cruel decision to put to death all the male children born to the Jews in Egypt was inspired by a dream. In it he saw that a lamb, placed in one of the scales of a balance, outweighed the whole of Egypt lying in the other scale. The royal dream-interpreters explained to the king that a Jewish boy (Moses) about to be born would in due course destroy Egypt and liberate the Israelites. Hence the 'Lamb of God' typifies two saviours, Moses and Jesus.

The 'Lamb of God' metaphor carries a third symbolism: the sacrifice of Isaac, the 'lamb' of Abraham, narrated in Genesis 22. In Christian tradition traceable back to the New Testament and richly developed in the writings of the church fathers, the so-called 'binding' of Isaac, which according to some ancient Jewish sources happened on Passover day, symbolizes the death of Christ on the cross. I will return to this subject in connection with St Paul's portrayal of Jesus as the Saviour of mankind (cf. pp. 84–6).

This survey of the titles of Jesus in the Fourth Gospel has served a dual purpose.

In so far as the opinions of the friends and foes of Jesus represent the views contained in the earlier Gospel tradition, the titles enable us to get the feel of general Palestinian attitudes towards non-institutional religious masters (as opposed to priests and Levites), including the Messiah. But even from this point of view, compared with the Synoptic Gospels the titles in John often testify to a superior meaning. The concept of 'prophet' is sharpened, focusing on the final spokesman of God. 'Messiah' also undergoes a double mutation. On the one hand, its significance is diluted: no one knows from where he would come and his royal links are loosened. On the other hand, John paints a Jesus who openly admits that he is the Messiah and is recognized as such, with varying degrees of conviction, by practically the whole of Palestinian Jewry.

John's use of the traditional material in portraying Jesus is meant to supply a background against which he can bring into relief his theologically more developed ideas. These sophisticated notions first appear in the form of speeches, the words of which are lent by John to his Jesus. The main subjects he treats are the 'Son of Man' theology and the 'Son–Father' mysticism. They are followed by the evangelist's own magisterial depiction of the eternal and incarnate Word of God through whom all things were made, and who came to reveal the unseen Father.

## II
## THE 'SELF-PORTRAIT'
## OF THE JOHANNINE JESUS

The literary device chosen by the evangelist to imply that the great speeches of his Gospel reproduce Jesus' own words must not deceive readers. Since the teaching he transmits is entirely different from that of the other Gospels, and since John's account postdates Jesus by at least seventy years, the chances of hearing the genuine voice of the Galilean Master are minimal. It is more likely that the 'self-portrait' of Jesus, his reflections on himself and his mission, express the views of the evangelist. Thanks to the creative pen of the mystic John, the New Testament vision of Christ and of his relation to God undergoes a complete transformation, paving the way for the theology of the Christian church on the divine Trinity of Father, Son and Holy Spirit.

## Jesus the Son of Man[5]

The phrase 'the Son of Man' is a key feature in the portrait of Jesus in the Fourth Gospel. To grasp John's meaning, the reader will require some familiarity with the wider employment of the expression in ancient Judaism and elsewhere in the New Testament. I will try to reduce to intelligible essentials a convoluted subject which has made more than one contemporary scholar ask whether the 'Son of Man' problem will forever remain insoluble.

Here are some statistical data. In the Synoptic Gospels the expression 'son of Man' appears some sixty-five times and in John eleven times. In the rest of the New Testament it hardly figures: never in Paul, once in the Acts of the Apostles, and twice in Revelation in direct quotations from the Old Testament.

From the philological point of view it is generally accepted that the Greek formula *ho huios tou anthropou* ('the son of the man') translates an Aramaic idiom, *bar 'enasha* or *bar nasha*. In the Synoptic Gospels the phrase 'son of man' is found exclusively on the lips of Jesus, who speaks of himself. His use of the phrase appears to be intelligible as no one asks what he means. It is also perfectly acceptable to the listeners, upsetting no religious sensibilities.

Outside the New Testament, 'son of Man' is most commonly employed in the Aramaic language spoken by Jews either as a noun

---

5. For a fuller discussion of the 'son of Man' problem, see my *Jesus the Jew*, 160–91; *Jesus and the World of Judaism*, 88–99, 175–80; *Post-biblical Jewish Studies* (Brill, Leiden, 1975), 147–65.

('a man/the man'), or as the indefinite pronoun ('one/someone'), but neither of these usages is applicable to the Synoptic Gospels. Furthermore, in the Galilean dialect of Aramaic spoken by Jesus, 'son of man' sometimes appears in a monologue or dialogue as a circumlocutional reference to the speaker himself. It is not unlike the English figure of speech, 'yours truly', used in place of 'I'. For example, 'Who is the author of this splendid piece?' or 'Who is responsible for this horror?' may produce the modest or shamefaced reply, 'Yours truly.' The purpose of such a periphrastic style was to camouflage something fatal dreaded by the speaker or something that would sound boastful if directly asserted. So one would say in Aramaic, *the son of man* is going to die, or *the son of man* is about to become king, rather than *I* will die, or *I* will be proclaimed king.

There is also a non-literal, interpretative understanding of 'son of Man', displayed both within and outside the New Testament. It is based on the biblical Book of Daniel, 7:13. Chapter 7 of this book presents a dream of the sage Daniel in which four awesome animals symbolize the world empires of Babylonia, Media, Persia and Greece. Next follows a heavenly judgement scene with God, pictured as an old man, pronouncing the death sentence on the last beast and depriving the other three of their dominion. The climax of the dream in verse 13 contrasts the animals with a human being, 'one like a son of man', who is lifted from the earth by the clouds, and is granted eternal kingship by the heavenly judge. In the Book of Daniel 'one like a son of man' represents 'the saints of the Most High', that is to say, the Jewish people (Dan. 7:18, 22, 27), and this collective interpretation seems to have recently been confirmed by the first-century BC Aramaic Daniel Apocryphon from Qumran (cf. p. 33, n.2).

From the completion of the Book of Daniel in the 160s BC to the time of the destruction of Jerusalem in AD 70 there is no attestation in extant Jewish literature of the use of 'son of Man' as describing a religious function. However, in the decades following the first Jewish war against Rome which ended in AD 70, that is during the period of the composition of the Gospels, we possess independent literary evidence in which such a man-like figure is portrayed as a heavenly Messiah (4 Ezra 13), or a superterrestrial final Judge (Parables of Enoch, or 1 Enoch 37–71). A little later the famous Rabbi Akiba, who died as a martyr in AD 135, also recognized in 'one like a son of man' the Messiah, son of David (bHagigah 14a; bSanhedrin 38b).

As far as John is concerned, he reflects this richer messianic significance of 'son of Man', which in general he combines with the circumlocutional use reminiscent of the Synoptic Gospels. Hence in the Fourth Gospel it is not *I* ( Jesus), but *the son of Man* who gives eternal life or will be *lifted up*, i.e. crucified.

After these necessary preliminaries, we can now concentrate on the three central topics associated with 'son of Man' in the Fourth Gospel.

1. The first of these theological notions is that faith in the 'son of Man' bestows eternal life on the believer. We read: 'Do not labour for food which perishes, but for food which endures to *eternal life*, which the *son of Man* will give you' ( John 6:27).

2. The second topic links the giving of eternal life specifically to the 'lifting-up' of the 'son of Man'. 'As Moses lifted up the serpent in the wilderness, so must *the son of Man* be lifted up, that whoever believes in him may have *eternal life*' (3:14–15). The image arises from the Old Testament story of the brazen serpent which Moses was ordered to fix to a pole. A glance at it was enough to provide protection against snake bites in the wilderness of Sinai (Num. 21:6–9). In John's interpretation, however, the lifted-up serpent typified the crucified Jesus and the salvation promised to those who would look at the cross with faith. John gives here an interesting twist to the 'son of Man' imagery. He understands 'to lift up' in the sense of crucifixion,[6] and not in its normal figurative meaning of exaltation (12:32–3).

3. The third and perhaps the most important aspect of the Johannine representation of the 'son of Man' concerns his journeys between heaven and earth. The idea of the descent and ascent of the 'son of Man' originated in Daniel 7 and was further developed in the Synoptic Gospels before reaching its climax in John. The cloud was envisaged from the Book of Daniel onwards as the vehicle of heavenly transport. 'Behold, with the clouds of heaven there came one like a son of man' (Dan. 7:13). Here the movement appears to be upward, as it is in the

6. The same form of capital punishment by 'lifting up' is metaphorically described as 'hanging from the tree' in the Nahum Commentary and the Temple Scroll among the Dead Sea Scrolls, and in rabbinic literature.

account of Christ's ascension: 'He was lifted up, a cloud took him out of their sight' (Acts 1:9), and in the description of the meeting in mid-air of the resurrected souls and the still living faithful with Christ at the moment of the second coming: 'For the Lord himself will descend from heaven . . . And the dead in Christ will rise first; then we who are alive . . . shall be caught up together with them on the clouds to meet the Lord in the air' (1 Thess. 4:16–17).

In the Synoptic Gospels the return of the 'son of Man' on the clouds entails a descent from the heavenly regions (Matt. 24:30; Mark 13:26; Luke 21:27; Matt. 26:64; Mark 14:62). According to John the 'son of Man' travels in both directions: 'No one has ascended into heaven but he who descended from heaven, *the son of Man*' (3:13). In the Fourth Gospel the life-giving Redeemer is a heavenly traveller in temporary exile on earth who is longing to return to his real home.


## Jesus the Son

John does not need the 'son of Man' terminology to distinguish Jesus clearly from his Jewish listeners. His Jesus can speak plainly: 'You are from below, I am from above; you are of this world, I am not of this world' (8:23). This is indeed the nucleus of the central message of the Fourth Gospel: Jesus is 'the Son', the Son of God the Father. He proceeds from God (8:42; cf. 17:8) and goes to the Father (14:12): 'I came from the Father and have come into the world; again, I am leaving the world and going to the Father' (16:28; cf. 13:3). Having come down to earth from the celestial heights, he is getting ready to ascend again, but this is not the complete picture. In the discourse in chapter 14 yet another descent is intimated: 'In my Father's house there are many rooms . . . And when *I go* and prepare a place for you, *I will come again*' (14:2–3). However, this promised re-descent plays no real part in the drama of the Fourth Gospel and is insignificant compared with the apocalyptic representation of the return of Christ in Matthew and Paul. John was no longer an eschatological enthusiast but had a sedate spiritual outlook.

Jesus' explicit self-designation as *the* Son is a striking peculiarity of John and one of the most important expressions of his religious vision.

The message of his Jesus is that men must believe in the name of the only Son if they are to be saved (3:18); that the dead must listen to his voice if they want to live again (5:25); and that his audience must accept that he was consecrated and sent by God the Father (10:36). Unlike the previously discussed titles, *the* Son implies a unique standing in the hierarchy of beings. How does this Son define himself or, more precisely, how does John define him? In the first instance by means of his relation to the Father, and secondly by the mission he was to accomplish in the world.

According to the evangelist, the foremost distinguishing mark of the Son was his being *sent* by the Father. Recalling the notion of the descent from heaven of the 'son of Man', *the* Son was the celestial messenger commissioned by God to accomplish a special task among men: 'For God has *sent* the Son into the world . . . that the world might be saved through him' (3:17). Jesus proved by his words and deeds that he represented God. First, his teaching originated with the Father: 'For he whom God has sent utters the words of God' (3:34). Secondly, his deeds were modelled on, and imitated, the actions of the Father: 'I say to you, the Son can do nothing of his own accord, but only what he sees the Father doing; for whatever he [the Father] does, the Son can do likewise' (5:19). In short, the Father may be beyond the reach of human experience, but through the Son he speaks and acts, is heard and experienced in the world.

So the purpose of the mission of the Son was to grant 'eternal life' to those who had faith in him. 'He who believes in the Son has *eternal life*; he who does not obey the Son shall not see life' (3:36). The doctrine is stated not just in general terms as above, but also in the allegorical images of water and bread. 'Whoever drinks of the water that I shall give him will never thirst; the water that I shall give him will become a spring welling up to *eternal life*' (4:13–14; 7:37–8). 'I say to you, he who believes has *eternal life*. I am the *bread of life*' (6:47–8).

It is well known that the allegory of the bread of life descending from heaven is based on the Old Testament typology of manna, the miraculous food which sustained the Israelites during their long wandering in the wilderness after the exodus from Egypt (cf. Exod. 16). The Psalmist calls manna, this dew-like white edible substance, the 'bread of heaven' (Ps. 78:24, freely quoted in John 6:31). John's message is that, whereas the people of the exodus generation died despite consuming the manna, those who now mystically 'eat' Jesus, the 'bread of life' – that is to say, those who digest and absorb his teaching – will inherit eternal life. The main line of the allegory expresses the idea of the reciprocal indwelling of the Son in the believers and of the believers in the Son.

The allegory of the shepherd and the sheep is another image of the giving of life by Jesus. This biblical metaphor denotes the relationship first between God and Israel, and secondarily between the Davidic Messiah and the Jewish people (Gen. 49:24; Pss. 23:1; 80:1; Ezek. 34:23). According to John, the aim of the good shepherd was to provide security and abundant life for his flock (10:10). However, the religious and historical background of the imagery does not reflect the age of Jesus, but that of the evangelist. Jesus' job, and that of his own envoys, was to take care of the erring Jews, the 'lost sheep of the house of Israel' (Matt. 10:6; 15:24). The task of bringing alien sheep to his sheep-pen (10:16) shows that the mission of the Jesus of John was no longer confined to Jews; he also had strange sheep to look after, the Gentiles of John's community, and he had to ensure that 'there shall be one flock and one sheepfold' (10:16).

A final Johannine image relative to the granting of eternal life by the Son makes use of the traditional Pharisaic-Jewish concept of bodily resurrection (cf. pp. 84, 168, 170–81): 'For this is the will of my Father, that everyone who sees the Son and believes in him should have eternal life; and *I will raise him up* at the last day' (6:40; cf. 5:24). This statement on the benevolent ultimate mission of the Son apparently conflicts with the judicial function assigned to him elsewhere in John and requires closer consideration. John is adamant in affirming the judiciary role of the Son: 'For the Father judges no one, but has given *all judgement* to the Son' (5:22; cf. 5:26–7). But according to the familiar eschatological ideas of intertestamental Judaism, the final arbiter can either acquit or condemn.

There is no trace of such dark traits in the picture of the mission of the Son in John; he is all light. 'For God has sent the Son into the world, *not to condemn the world*, but that the world might *be saved* through him' (3:17). So how can he be a severe judge? Is it conceivable, therefore, that contrary to all expectation the Son as judge will condemn no one, but dispense only forgiveness and everlasting life? Does this mean that verses 26–7 in chapter 5 should be understood as revealing a merciful judge? 'For as the Father has life in himself, so he has granted the Son to have life in himself, and has given him authority to execute judgement' (that is to say, a judgement of life-giving acquittal).

What, then, will happen in John's neatly divided light–darkness world (cf. below, p. 51) to those who do not believe, in particular to all the wicked 'Jews'? (Those Jews who did believe created no problem because in John's eyes they automatically ceased to be Jews.) The answer is left to our imagination, namely that the unbelieving Jews need no condemnation as they have already condemned themselves. But one thing is certain: the Son is not seen as a dispenser of justice; he is, as he has appeared throughout, an instrument of vivification: 'I am the resurrection and the life' (11:25). And above all, he is a source of love.

Love is the dominating factor in John's Gospel, in the heavenly sphere, and on earth towards and among those who believe in the Son. The image of the Son is steeped in love. The Father loves the Son (3:35; 15:9) and the Son loves the Father (17:23); those who have faith in the Son love him and obey him. They are also loved by the Father and the Son (14:21; 16:27–8). Moreover, they have to love each other too, by virtue of a magnificent 'new commandment' given to them by Jesus 'that you love one another; even as I have loved you, that you also love one another' (13:34; 15:12, 17). This mutual love of the faithful is modelled on the love of the Son towards his own and is expected to be the distinguishing mark of Jesus' disciples (13:35).

The presumed novelty of the commandment to love is either a twist introduced by John, or more probably is attributable (like the need for translating into Greek common Semitic terms like 'rabbi') to the largely non-Jewish identity of the community addressed by the Fourth Gospel. The real Jesus of the Synoptics is well aware that the divine precept of brotherly love has been given to the ancients in the Old Testament: 'You shall love your neighbour as yourself: I am the Lord' (Lev. 19:18; cf. Matt. 5:43; 19:19; 22:39). His chief commandment enjoins in one breath the love of God and the love of one's fellow (Mark 12:29–31). John's Gentile Christians required a course for primary school pupils in which the simplest details had to be spelled out.

Next to eternal life and love, the notion of glorification and glory is the third unifying element linking the Father, the Son and the believers. At the highest level, glory is a timeless divine attribute shared by Father and Son since before the creation of the world, and it is specifically bestowed on the Son during his mission on earth: 'Father, glorify Thou me in Thine own presence with the glory which I had with Thee before the world was made' (17:5, 24). Considered from below, glorification is a recognition and proclamation of God's glory and connotes an element of gratitude. Both aspects are revealed in Jesus' prayer: 'Glorify Thy Son that the Son may glorify Thee' (17:1). This glorification of the Son by the Father is explained as the sequel of his being empowered to grant eternal life to all flesh (17:2). The process of glorification is completed by the believers' reaction of gratitude to the benevolence of the Son: 'Whatever you ask in my name, I will do it, that the Father may be glorified in the Son' (14:13). This glorification brings about a mystical participation in the divine glory of those attached to the Son and evolves into a universal 'deification' of the believers which is revealed to the world: 'The glory which Thou hast given me I have given to them, that they may be one even as we are one, I in them and Thou in me, that they may become perfectly one, so that the world may know that Thou hast sent me and hast loved them even as Thou hast loved me' (17:22–3). Here we are reaching the utmost depth of the Johannine idea of unity between Father and Son, the indwelling of the Son in the Father, and the consequential bond between Father and Son and the devotees of the closed esoterical-mystical fellowship of the Johannine church.

I have already used the term 'deification'. Indeed, the union between the Son and God the Father entails a sort of elevation of Jesus to a quasi divine status. To establish the significance of such an apotheosis, we have to subject to further scrutiny the relationship between Father and Son in the terminology of the Fourth Gospel. The brooding style of John is not conducive to clear-cut ideas, but I will try to throw as much light as possible on statements which sometimes seem to lack coherence and strict logic.

John follows three paths in describing the relationship between Father and Son.

1. Father and Son have knowledge and glory in common, and

believers pertain to both of them. These ideas are repeatedly stated. 'I am not praying for the world but for those whom Thou hast given me, for they are Thine; all mine are Thine, and Thine are mine' (17:9–10; cf. 16:15). The mutuality implied, especially 'mine is Thine, Thine is mine', points to equality. Here we are sailing in uncharted waters because no parallel concepts can be found in Judaism or for that matter elsewhere in the New Testament.

2. John's phenomenological representation envisages Jesus, the Son, as the mirror-image of the Father. The fisherman apostle Philip is told by Jesus: 'He who has seen me has seen the Father' (14:9). By this, John means that the words and deeds of Jesus the Son are prompted by, and reflect, those of the Father. Thus anyone who hears Jesus speaking or sees him acting witnesses the likeness of God's words and deeds. As is often the case, the Prologue sums up John's thought when it presents Jesus as the ultimate revealer of the invisible and consequently unseen Deity (1:18). The Jesus of John falls slightly short of declaring himself God, but implies that his teaching and his actions reflect and reveal the divine.

3. Quite frequently John's Gospel speaks of the actual oneness of Father and Son. The Synoptic evangelists would have had the cold shivers. In a prayer preserved in chapter 17 of John, Jesus begs the Father for the protection of his flock, which without his helping hand is bound to fall apart. The unity of God and the Son ensures that the flock will remain undivided: 'Holy Father, keep them in Thy name . . . that they may be one, even as we are one' (17:11). At its lowest level, this unity is that of a common mind and intention bonding several distinct personalities. The believers should be of one mind as the Father and the Son are always joined in thought, purpose and action. Elsewhere the level of communion seems to be much higher and the unity, instead of being moral and realized by a common purpose, is metaphysical and penetrates the very depth of being of the persons involved. The prayer of Jesus is not restricted to his current disciples, but embraces those in future generations 'that they may all be one; even as Thou, Father, art *in me*, and I *in Thee*, but they also may be *in us*. The glory which Thou hast given me I have given to them, that they may be one even as we are one, I in them and Thou in me, that they may become perfectly one' (17:21–3). It is hard to improve on this mystical intuition.

Employing allegorical imagery and representing Jesus as the true vine (15:1), John identifies the believers as the branches which cannot live if cut off from the plant: 'I am the vine, you are the branches. He who abides in me, and I in him, he it is that bears much fruit, for apart from me you can do nothing' (15:4–5).

This state of 'being in' or 'dwelling in' or 'abiding in' someone entails assimilation or absorption and recalls the image of eating and digesting the flesh and blood of Jesus (6:56). In modern religio-philosophical terminology we are faced here, if not with a pantheistic, at least with a restricted *panentheistic*[7] world in which Father, Son and the believers of all the ages reside in one another. The whole ideology reflects the dreamlike cogitation of a religious contemplative, possibly Jewish, addressing a Gentile confraternity nurtured on Hellenistic mysticism.

Here we penetrate once again the basic core of John's theology: the precise relationship between Jesus the Son and God the Father. There are two further specific passages in which John places the Son in the same category as the Father. The first of these is straightforward, at least at first sight. The blunt assertion of the Jesus of John that 'I and the Father are one' (10:30) is framed as an unequivocal affirmation of equality. It is very un-Jewish, and foreign to the Synoptic Gospels. Consideration of the context strengthens the impression that John meant real parity. The hostile Jews were unable to grab the sheep given to Jesus by God because Jesus and the Father 'are one' (10:27–30). The implied assertion is that the Father and the Son possess the same power and strength, that is to say that they are of the same stature. They are co-equal, to use the jargon of later Christian dogmatic theology.

The second crucial passage is more of a riddle. It belongs to the typical 'I am' (*ego eimi*) sayings of John's Jesus. In general the verb is followed by an allegorical predicate: 'I am the bread of life' (6:35); 'I am the resurrection and the life' (11:25); or 'I am the way, the truth and the life' (14:6). But in one case, and in a polemical context, 'I am' stands on its own.

The 'I am' passage in question occurs in an argument with a quarrel-

---

7. *Panentheism*, as distinct from pantheism (= all is divine), teaches that everything exists in God. Cf. A. Bullock and O. Stallybrass (eds.), *The Fontana Dictionary of Modern Thought* (London, 1977), 454.

some Jewish group which accused Jesus of being possessed by a demon. They found Jesus' claim that his followers would escape death (8:51) totally scandalous. After all, the heroes of the Old Testament had died, including Abraham, the father of Israel, and all the prophets. So how could Jesus promise immortality to his disciples? But Jesus retorted that he was not boasting; and that Abraham had rejoiced when he saw his (Jesus') day (8:52–6). The Jewish opponents were outraged: how could a man of less than fifty years old pretend he had seen Abraham (8:57)? Jesus' mysterious riposte, 'Before Abraham was, I am' (8:58), left them speechless. It seems that here we have once again John's frequently expressed idea of the pre-existence of the Son. In other words, Jesus' supertemporal existence, which according to the Prologue goes back to before the creation, began long before the age of Abraham. The Babylonian Talmud (Pesahim 54a) faintly echoes this concept when it states that the name, i.e. his ideal definition of the Messiah, was already in existence before God had set out to make the world. If so, the message of the provocative saying, 'Before Abraham was, I am', is that Jesus, the Son, in a mysterious way transcends the normal frontiers of time.

John, while tending to elevate Jesus to eternal heights, is nevertheless not altogether consistent. Many a time he allows it to be known that Jesus' oneness with the Father does not amount to strict equality. The Father is above the Son. The Father sends the Son; the Son does not send the Father. The Son can do nothing of his own accord but can only imitate the Father's actions (5:19). The teaching of the Son is not delivered of his own authority but comes from the Father (7:16). All this suggests lower status. At least on one occasion the inferiority of the Son is expressly admitted when Jesus declares that 'the Father is greater than I' (14:28). With this plain affirmation of the pre-eminence of the Father contradicting all the metaphors which suggest equality, John created a doctrinal problem the resolution of which kept the church, the councils, the bishops and the theologians fully occupied for several centuries.

## The personified Holy Spirit

A great doctrinal innovation of John which was to make a profound impact on later Christian dogma consisted in assigning a personal status to the Holy Spirit. To clarify this notion, it should be explained that in the Bible the spirit of holiness, or holy spirit, symbolizes the power through which God acts in the world. For example the spirit of prophecy inspires the prophets, the spirit of purity cleanses the unclean, and so forth. Likewise in the New Testament, it is through the holy spirit that God causes Mary miraculously to conceive Jesus (Luke 1:35). Jesus speaks of baptizing with fire and the holy spirit (Matt. 3:11). The same holy spirit enables the apostles to converse in tongues on the first day of Pentecost (Acts 2:4).

In John's particular slant the Holy Spirit brings to completion the work started by the Son. The shortness of his earthly ministry having prevented Jesus from delivering the full revelation of the words of the Father, the continuation of his unfinished enterprise was left to another heavenly being called in legal language the 'other Paraclete' (14:16), i.e. advocate or counsellor, the first 'Paraclete' being Jesus himself (1 John 2:1). This innovation shows that John was fully aware of the large gap which separated his message from teaching traceable to the age of Jesus, and that the gigantic doctrinal development contained in his Gospel required justification. He therefore devised a clever stratagem. A personified Holy Spirit was to perfect the revelation of the Son. This idea legitimized and furnished with divine authority all the doctrinal innovations, unknown to the Jesus of the Synoptics, which were initiated by John and afterwards taken over and further developed or even created by the church over the centuries.[8]

The Spirit was sent continuously to remind the believers of all the instructions they had received from Jesus (14:26). It was also to convey future messages entrusted to it by Jesus. Unlike Mark, Matthew and Luke, and in a sense unlike the church, John believed in an ongoing,

8. The most patent Christian dogmatic novelty of this sort, entirely lacking New Testament or even early patristic foundation, was the definition in 1950 by Pope Pius XII of the bodily assumption to heaven of the Virgin Mary immediately after her death.

self-renewing process of revelation. The Spirit animates the church. In the same way as the Father and the Son abide in the believers, so also does the Spirit (14:17). As the Son proceeds from the Father, so too does the Spirit (15:26). As the Son is sent by the Father, the Spirit is given by the Father (14:16) and is sent by the Son (15:26). Again, just as the Son transmits what has been confided to him by the Father and does not speak on his own authority, the Spirit communicates the words of the Father as it receives them from the Son (16:13). In John's dreamlike vision, revelation advances in a spiral movement mystically joining together Father, Son, Holy Spirit and the united body of believers.

## III

## THE WORD-*LOGOS* OF
## THE PROLOGUE OF JOHN

The portraits of Jesus sketched from the sayings attributed in the Fourth Gospel to his contemporaries, and from the reflections placed by John on the lips of the Son, are so complex that it was necessary to preface them by an introductory summary without which a full grasp of the message would have been almost impossible. The Prologue to the Gospel (1:1–18) is in fact such a summary. In 252 brilliantly chosen Greek words John manages to offer a pellucid abstract of the teaching laboriously conveyed in the speeches of Jesus in the pages of his Gospel.

All four evangelists supply an introduction to their works. However, while Mark chooses as the historical starting-point of his story Jesus' appearance on the public scene in the company of John the Baptist, and Matthew and Luke opt for a legendary account of the miraculous birth and early childhood of Christ, John takes us up on eagle's wings to the highest heaven to encounter the eternal Word of God. This Word-*Logos* was the instrument of creation long before being mystically united with the body of the Jewish man Jesus Christ. It came to bring light, grace and truth to the children of God in the world.

It is common knowledge that the Prologue deliberately imitates the opening of the Book of Genesis. Both start with the phrase, 'In the beginning'; both sketch a creation culminating in life; both envisage a dichotomy of light and darkness.

The contrast between light and darkness is an essential part of the teaching imagery of the Jesus of John (3:19–21; 8:12; 9:5; 12:35–6, 46). It recalls the corresponding dualism found in the Dead Sea Scrolls, in particular in the Community Rule with its Instruction on the two Spirits (1QS 3:13–4:26) and in the War of the Sons of Light against the Sons of Darkness. The actual phrase 'sons of light' figures once in John (12:36) and in two other places in the New Testament (Luke 16:8; 1 Thess. 5:5). However the similarities are not strong enough to suggest any direct link between Qumran and John-inspired Christianity, let alone to prove the Palestinian Jewish derivation of the Fourth Gospel. Curiously or significantly, the phrase 'sons of darkness' is never used in the New Testament.

In Genesis, chapter 1 the Old Testament describes the birth of the world below; John's eyes are fixed on the celestial mysteries above and he permits his readers to catch a furtive glimpse of the life within the Godhead. 'In the beginning was the Word [*Logos*], and the Word was with God, and the Word was God . . . All things were made through him [the *Logos*] . . . In him was life, and the life was the light of men. The light shines in the darkness . . .' (1:1–5).

The term *Logos*, the Word, plays an essential part in Greek philosophy and mysticism, with which John appears to have had some acquaintance. It is a pivotal concept in the theological elaboration of the Alexandrian Jewish philosopher Philo, and in the Hellenistic mystical speculation known as Hermetism which is attributed to the god Hermes Trismegistus (Hermes the Thrice-Greatest). Both are likely to have influenced Hellenistic Christianity. For Philo as for John, the *Logos* was God's tool in creating the world, a mediator figure between God and mankind. In Hermetic mysticism, which seeks the deification of man through knowledge, the *Logos* is called the 'son of God'. This phrase, echoed by 'the only Son in the bosom of the Father' in John, is the principle that brings form and order into the world. It is designated also in Greek religious philosophy as the Demiurge or 'Craftsman', a notion which will be much discussed in later Christianity.

However, since mystical speculation knew no frontiers, beneath the Greek garb of the *Logos* may also lurk the Jewish idea of the divine

Word, a device in God's hand in making the universe. It reminds one of the *Memra* (= Word) of the Aramaic paraphrases of Genesis 1:1 where we read: 'By the Word God created the heaven and the earth'. Four times repeated in verses 1–2 and 14 of the Prologue, the mysterious divine *Logos*, existing before the creation, dominates the opening of John's Gospel, never to recur in the later chapters, and only twice in the rest of the Johannine literature.[9] Placed in the first verse of the Gospel and culminating in 'and the Word was God', the *Logos* is patently meant to furnish the clue to the story of Jesus, a momentary but crucial phase in the eternal existence of the Son.

Unlike the Son in the main body of the Gospel, the divine Word was not *sent* by God, but came on his own initiative. He arrived as a source of light to overcome the reigning darkness and illuminate and raise to the dignity of children of God those men in the great cosmopolitan world who were ready to receive him and who, unlike his own people, believed in him. The identity of the Word's own people is left unspecified. Indirect hints at a Jewish connection are furnished first by the mention of John (the Baptist), a historical witness selected by God to identify Jesus in public as 'the light' (1:6). In a second allusion to the national-social context Jesus Christ is contrasted with Moses, the Israelite lawgiver. But the nation in question remains nameless, and the sinister word 'Jews', so common and so menacing in the story of the Fourth Gospel, was thought unworthy of a mention; it would have profaned the Prologue. John's outlook is essentially universal.

The Prologue is responsible also for the idea of 'incarnation', the most pivotal concept of Christianity. 'And the Word became flesh and dwelt among us' (1:14). The statement expresses the embodiment of the divine *Logos* (1:14) in the human person of Jesus. He, 'the only Son who is in the bosom of the Father' (1:18), descended to earth to make the invisible God visible, and his light, truth and grace accessible to those humans who react to the Son with faith.

A final glance at the Gospel of John through its Prologue reveals, under the opaque mask of the first-century Palestinian Jew Jesus, the

9. The First Letter of John begins: 'That which was from the beginning, which we have heard, which we have seen with our eyes, which we have looked upon and touched with our hands, concerning the *Logos* of life', and Revelation 19:13 calls the Rider on the White Horse 'the *Logos* of God'.

shining countenance of the only Son of God the Father. The idea of the divinity of Jesus was by then, at the opening of the second century AD, in the air among Hellenized Christians. It is not surprising therefore that in about AD 110 Ignatius, the bishop-martyr of Antioch, had no difficulty in crossing the final barrier when he referred to Jesus as '*our God*' (Letter to the Romans). At roughly the same time, Pliny the Younger, governor of Bithynia, characterized the Christians in a letter addressed to the emperor Trajan as a group accustomed to 'sing hymns to Christ *as god* [*Christo quasi deo*]' (Letter x. 96).

According to the Prologue, this Jesus, identical with the eternal creative *Logos*, overwhelmed and defeated the ( Jewish) forces of darkness: 'The light shines in the darkness, and the darkness has not overcome it' (1:5). In doing so he enabled his company of believers, and those multitudes of non-Jews who followed them under the guidance of the Spirit of truth, to behold in him through a glass darkly the image of God and enjoy for ever the unifying love and glory of the Father and the Son.

The Fourth Gospel reflects a composite picture of the face of Jesus in which the traditional elements, culminating in the figure of 'the Messiah, Son of God', are overlaid by the visionary discoveries of John the Divine. Looking ahead through his mystical lens, the evangelist was convinced that he had perceived in the by then distant person of the Galilean Jewish teacher Jesus, not only the Saviour of mankind, but also the Stranger from heaven in whom he recognized the reflected image of the countenance of the Father (1:18).

John left the church a rich, complex and often contradictory legacy about Jesus and his role on earth, and his relation in the sphere of the divine to the Father and the Paraclete. The evangelist's apparent aloofness from eschatological enthusiasm helped his church to overcome the crisis created in primitive Pauline Christianity by the delay of the return of Christ. The concept of a single body of believers, mystically united with the Father through the Son, eased the way for the church to take the place of the Kingdom of God, that central concept of the Jesus of the Synoptics and of Paul which John to all intents and purposes managed to obliterate.

The great doctrinal controversies of Christianity during the first millennium of its history and throughout the heated debates of its ecumenical councils from Nicaea (325) to Chalcedon (451) and Constantinople (553) mostly revolved around ideas first mooted in the pages of the Fourth Gospel. The orthodox doctrines relating to Christology – the one person and two natures of Jesus Christ – and to the Holy Triad or triune Deity, through which the various great heresies of the ancient church from Arianism to the *Filioque* controversy[10] were rebutted, all spring from the theology of the spiritual Gospel of John. However, he cannot be made responsible for Christianity as a whole because he has comparatively little to say about belief in redemption through the death of Christ. As we shall see, for the anthropological-theological features of the portrait of Jesus the primary source is provided by the letters of St Paul.

## POSTSCRIPT:
## THE FACE OF JESUS IN THE REST
## OF THE JOHANNINE LITERATURE

Church tradition assigns to John, the author of the Fourth Gospel, four further pieces of unequal length and significance, three letters and the Apocalypse or Book of Revelation. They have to be glanced at in order to round off the Johannine portrait of Jesus.

### The letters of John

None of the letters ascribed to John contains the name of an author. The first is totally anonymous and the other two stem from someone calling himself without further identification 'the presbyter' or elder.

10. Arianism was a heresy propounded by the Alexandrian deacon Arius (c. 250–336) who claimed that the Son was not eternal but created by the Father. It was condemned by the Council of Nicaea in 325. The *Filioque* ('And from the Son') debate sought to determine whether the Holy Spirit proceeded only from the Father or from the Father *and* from the Son. Rome championed the double procession from Father and Son against the Eastern Orthodox doctrine of the single procession from the Father alone.

The relationship between the Fourth Evangelist and the writer(s) of the letters is uncertain. There is general agreement that the brief notes known as the Second and Third Epistles of John come from the same pen. They all reflect the ideology of the Gospel of John in general and are believed to date from around AD 100 or later.

From the point of view of the portrayal of Jesus, the letters convey little that is new. On a more popular level than the Gospel they monotonously repeat characteristic Johannine doctrines, namely that Jesus is the Christ; that true religion consists in walking in the light away from the darkness, abiding in the Son and in the Father, and first and foremost loving one another, for without this no love of God is possible (1 John 4:20).

Nevertheless the letters comprise two doctrinal elements which are distinct from the Gospel. In discussing the work of the evangelist, I emphasized the decline of eschatological expectation. This is not so in 1 John, which stresses that the addressees of the letter live in 'the last hour' (1 John 2:18) and are awaiting the reappearance of Christ (3:2). Since this resurgence of fervour is explained by the activity of heretics in the community, it would be mistaken to conclude that 1 John represents a stage preceding the Gospel in the development of Johannine thinking. In fact, the false doctrine which the letters combat denies the reality of the incarnation: these heretics did not accept 'the coming of Jesus Christ in the flesh' (2 John 7; cf. 1 John 4:2). This early form of Gnosticism was opposed to the union of the divine *Logos* with the base matter of a human body, a type of doctrinal deviation that threatened the Greek-speaking church throughout the second century.

## The Book of Revelation

The Book of Revelation or Apocalypse purports to be the work of a visionary called John (Rev. 1:1, 4, 9; 22:8), recipient of revelations on the Aegean island of Patmos off the Asiatic Turkish coast. He belonged to the school of the author of the Fourth Gospel without being the selfsame person. The identity of the writer and the canonical character of the writing were the subject of a controversy which continued for some centuries in the early church, but finally the Book of Revelation ended up as part of the New Testament.

There are definite links between this work and the Gospel of John. Christ is commonly designated by the Johannine symbol of 'the Lamb' and is once called 'the Word of God' (Rev. 19:13). On the other hand, linguistically it is impossible to ascribe the two compositions to a single author and the general conceptual framework of Revelation is quite unlike the Gospel; it is Jewish apocalyptic writing adapted for believers in Jesus Christ. Its apocalyptic imagery often recalls the Dead Sea Scrolls. In both we have the blowing of trumpets, Gog and Magog, the ultimate foes, leading all the kings assembled for the final battle at Armageddon. Both grant a commanding role to the archangel Michael and his heavenly warriors. The floating down to earth of the heavenly Jerusalem, surveyed by an angel with a measuring rod, also appears in numerous manuscripts from Qumran describing the new holy City. One intriguing passage (Rev. 14:4) reminds one of the unmarried Essenes of Philo, Josephus and the Qumran Community Rule. It depicts the church redeemed by the Lamb as consisting of men 'who have not defiled themselves with women for they are virgins'.

Regarding the date of Revelation, a number of allusions to Christian martyrs and a definite hostility to Rome, described as the beast, the harlot or Babylon, point to a period after Nero, probably about AD 100 or later. There have been many attempts to determine the identity of the 'beast' by interpreting its number 666 (Rev. 13:18) with the help of *gematria* or use of the numerical value of Hebrew or Greek letters. They are as futile as they may be entertaining.[11]

Among the traditional features of Christ in Revelation is his portrayal as the Davidic King Messiah, 'the Lion of the tribe of Judah', the 'root and offspring of David' (Rev. 5:5; 22:16). The Johannine traits of 'the Lamb' and the '*Logos* of God' have already been mentioned, but there is a clear-cut distinction between God, who is the only one to be worshipped (Rev. 22:9), and the Messiah-Lamb-Word. From this point of view Revelation is considerably less theologically advanced than John.

11. Cf., for example, the Hebrew QSR NRWN (Emperor Nero) with Q = 100 + S = 60 + R = 200 + N = 50 + R = 200 + W = 6 + N = 50 = 666.

However, there are important novelties. The first of these is the presentation of a celestial *bellicose* Christ, riding on a white horse, with his robe dipped in blood, and as 'King of Kings and Lord of Lords' annihilating all the nations (Rev. 19:11–16). We are far removed here from the aura of love in which, according to John's Gospel, the Son and the Father dwell in one another and in the believers, and the believers in them. Compare this with the vision of Revelation 19:19–21: 'And I saw the beast and the kings of the earth with their armies gathered to make war against him who sits upon the horse and against his army. And the beast was captured and ... thrown alive into the lake of fire that burns with brimstone. And the rest were slain by the sword of him who sits upon the horse, the sword that issues from his mouth; and all the birds were gorged with their flesh.' That this Jesus is as distant from John's as he is from the real Jesus is clear from a study of the Synoptic Gospels.

The second novelty is the part assigned to the Lamb in the new world, after the passing away of 'the first heaven and the first earth' (Rev. 21). This Lamb-Christ is the celestial bridegroom of the radiant bride, the church, constituting the heavenly Jerusalem, inhabited only by those whose names are 'written in the Lamb's book of life'.

Finally, and most appropriately for this opening year of the third millennium, chapter 20 of the Book of Revelation is the New Testament source on which all the Christian millenarian speculations were based. Millenarianism implies that the return of Christ and the first resurrection which is granted only to Christians would be followed by a thousand-year reign of saints, during which Satan would be imprisoned. At the end of the millennium Satan would be let loose once more against the nations of the earth, only to be defeated for a second time by God's army. The fall of the rule of evil would be accompanied by another judgement and those found guilty would suffer a second death in the lake of fire. This notion of second death – meaning a situation out of which no further resurrection would provide an escape – also appears in Jewish texts, but only of a later vintage though it may have had a clandestine existence before first being expressed in Aramaic paraphrases of Deuteronomy, Isaiah and Jeremiah.

None of the peculiarities of the Jesus image produced by the Book of Revelation has made any deep impression on the religious thinking of the church, but they have provided a lasting source of inspiration for the images of heaven and hell in Christian literature and art over the centuries.

# 3

## Paul: the odd-man-out among the apostles

If John the mystic was responsible for the delineation of the divine *Logos*, the Word of God incarnate, and for the ensuing theological debates and speculations in the Greek-speaking church, the apostle Paul can be seen as the father of the Jesus figure which was to dominate Western European Christianity. He is hailed by independent scholars as the true founder of the Christian religion and its institutions, and even such a sound and solid publication as *The Oxford Dictionary of the Christian Church* describes Paul as 'the creator of the whole doctrinal and ecclesiastical system presupposed in his Epistles'.

Paul is the best known and probably the most controversial character in the New Testament. Unlike Jesus, he recorded his thoughts in writing and through his letters we learn a great deal about his life, ideas and personality. Of the fourteen letters attributed to him by church tradition, the authenticity of the epistle to the Hebrews is universally rejected by critical scholarship. The heading *To the Hebrews*, unlike all the other titles of writings associated with Paul, contains no mention of an author or sender. The so-called pastoral epistles (1 and 2 Timothy, and Titus) are generally thought to postdate Paul, though construed on his ideas. Ephesians and Colossians are probably apocryphal works of a later imitator of St Paul. However, more than half the collection, namely the letters to the Romans, 1 and 2 Corinthians, Galatians, Philippians, Philemon, 1 and probably 2 Thessalonians, are recognized (apart from occasional additions and glosses) by contemporary students of the New Testament as written by Paul as early as the fifties of the first century AD.[1]

1. While Paul's authentic letters predate the finished form of the Synoptic Gospels redacted between AD 70 and 100, the latter represent largely traditional material transmitted orally from the thirties and forties onwards, and at least partly traceable to the time of Jesus himself.

In addition to the general evidence furnished by an analysis of the genuine writings of Paul, some of the letters contain incidental autobiographical features which allow a deeper grasp of his mentality and motivation. Finally, about half the Acts of the Apostles is an account of the life and missionary activity of Paul, supplementing, sometimes confirming, but also contradicting, the information supplied by Paul himself. These data, luckily preserved, reveal to a careful and critical observer the inspiration underlying Paul's portrait of Jesus.

Who, then, was this true founder of Christianity? He always calls himself Paul, but in the Acts of the Apostles he is also known under the Jewish name of Saul. Acts 13:9 makes the identification explicit: 'Saul who is also called Paul'. According to the repeated testimony of Acts, he was born in the city of Tarsus in Cilicia (southern Turkey) and was a Roman citizen by birth. It was indeed from Tarsus that his fellow missionary, Barnabas, fetched him to come and preach Jesus in Antioch, the capital of northern Syria. Paul himself never refers in any of his letters to his birthplace or his citizenship; this silence is astonishing if these two factors played as important a part in Paul's story as the author of the Acts of the Apostles implies. The peculiar idea propagated by St Jerome in the fourth century that Paul was born in Palestine and later emigrated with his parents to Tarsus (*De viris illustribus* 5) deserves no credence.

The date of Paul's birth is nowhere given, but if it is correct that he was a young man at the time of the stoning of the deacon Stephen (Acts 7:58) in the mid-thirties of the first century, it would mean that he was born *c.* AD 10–15. At the end of Acts (chapter 28), i.e. in the early sixties, he was still alive and was awaiting trial in Rome. Christian tradition, dating to the fourth century, associates his death with Nero's persecution in AD 67.

Paul describes himself as a Jew of the tribe of Benjamin and an adherent of the religious party of the Pharisees (Rom. 11:1; 2 Cor. 11:22; Phil. 3:5). Acts 22:3 adds that he studied in Jerusalem 'at the feet of Gamaliel', one of the leaders of the Pharisees in the first half of the first century AD. Nevertheless, Paul's persistent silence on the subject adds a question mark to the validity of the information included in the Acts. A little boast (and he was certainly not averse to boasting), such as 'I am a former pupil of the famous Gamaliel', might have helped him in his disputes with Jewish legal authorities. His principles as a Pharisee cannot have been held very profoundly, bearing in mind how easily – unlike the Christian 'Judaizers' of the entourage of James – he could allow his Gentile followers (and himself) dispensation from observance of Jewish dietary rules and other Mosaic ritual precepts. He possessed two ascertainable Pharisaic features. He had an undeniable facility for argument, positively or negatively, from Bible texts. The letters to the Romans and Galatians are particularly rich in Old Testament quotations used as conclusive proof. Like the author of the Dead Sea Damascus Document, Paul was perfectly capable of turning the meaning of a scriptural passage topsy-turvy and arguing that the Jews were the children of Hagar, Abraham's concubine, and Christians the children of Sarah through Isaac (Gal. 4:21–31). Paul was also proud of his typically Pharisee belief in bodily resurrection, which he skilfully exploited in his polemical speech before the representatives of the Jewish high council in Jerusalem and in Caesarea, gaining the sympathy of its Pharisee members. 'When Paul perceived that one part were Sadducees and the other Pharisees, he cried out in the council, "Brethren, I am a Pharisee, a son of Pharisees; with respect to . . . the resurrection of the dead I am on trial"' (Acts 23:6–7; cf. 24:21).

He was a native Greek speaker, but if we can believe Acts 21:40 he could also improvise an address 'in the Hebrew dialect', in Aramaic. His letters were dictated in Greek, but he sometimes appended small sections, for instance the greetings in 1 Corinthians 16:21, in his own hand (cf. also Gal. 6:11; 2 Thess. 3:17; Philem. 19). He suffered from some disease which he calls 'a thorn in the flesh, a messenger of Satan' (2 Cor. 12:7) and which has been diagnosed variously as epilepsy, malaria, psychogenetic blindness (C. G. Jung), and the like. He was not an impressive personality. According to his Greek critics, his letters were 'weighty and strong, but his bodily presence weak, and his speech of no account' (2 Cor. 10:10). He himself admitted that he was not a great orator (2 Cor. 11:6). His success, mostly among uneducated Greeks, suggests a magnetic character with a charismatic message: 'I was with you in weakness and much fear and trembling; and my speech and message were not in plausible words of wisdom, but in demonstration of the spirit and of power' (1 Cor. 2:3–4).

Both his letters and the Acts of the Apostles depict him as at first intensely hostile towards the Jesus sect. Paul's own words are straight-forward: 'I persecuted the church of God' (1 Cor. 15:9). Or even more strongly, 'You have heard of my former life in Judaism, how I persecuted the church of God violently and tried to destroy it . . . extremely zealous for the traditions of my fathers' (Gal. 1:13–14). The Acts of the Apostles provide more colourful, but historically sometimes problem-atic, details. Paul is presented as a fanatic, determined to arrest and imprison members of the Jerusalem church who were no doubt con-sidered as troublemakers by the priestly authorities responsible for the maintenance of law and order. It has been conjectured, though without solid foundation, that Paul was a Temple policeman who on one occasion acted as the accredited envoy of the high priest to the Jewish synagogues of Damascus with a view to cleansing the local community from the followers of Jesus (Acts 8:3; 9:1–2). He is said to have taken a passive part – keeping an eye on the clothes of the executioners – in the stoning of Stephen in Jerusalem (Acts 7:58; 8:1; 26:9–11).

Then something extraordinary happened to Paul which occasioned a complete volte-face. His own account in Galatians 1:16 is very sober: God 'was pleased to reveal his Son to me'. The venue of the event is not identified but it is by implication Damascus (Gal. 1:17). The narrative provided by the Acts of the Apostles is enriched with legendary features: Paul, approaching Damascus, is blinded by a light from heaven and is addressed in Aramaic by a voice which identifies itself as that of Jesus (Acts 26:14). In a single instant, Paul the persecutor becomes an enthusiastic follower.

The next stage of the story differs depending on whether one follows the Acts or Paul's autobiographical reflections in Galatians. In the latter the purpose of Paul's vocation is immediately defined as the preaching of the gospel among the Gentiles (Gal. 1:16). However, in the Acts he at once confronts the Jews of Damascus and so incenses them by his teaching on Jesus that he has to escape the city by night, being lowered from the wall in a basket (Acts 9:20–25). The author of the Acts next implies that Paul straightaway joined the church in Jerusalem, introduced to the apostles by Barnabas; by arguing with the Hellenists or Greek-speaking Jews he made them so furious that to save his life the members of the church speedily spirited him away from Jerusalem to his home town, Tarsus (Acts 9:26–30). He reappeared again later in Antioch as the assistant of Barnabas, but in no time Paul took over the leading role. He always refers to himself before Barnabas (1 Cor. 9:6; Gal. 2:1, 9). Within a short time they twice clashed in Antioch and finally parted company (Gal. 2:13; Acts 15:36–40). Paul was not an easy partner unless he was the boss.

The account in the Acts of the Apostles of Paul's departure from Damascus and arrival in Jerusalem twice contradicts his own version of the story. First, Paul substitutes for the Acts' explanation of his sudden flight – urgent escape from a murderous Jewish mob – the need to elude the guards of the governor of Damascus appointed by the Nabataean king Aretas IV (9 BC–AD 40; cf. 2 Cor. 11:32–3). If so, the real reason for Paul's getaway was that his original task of arresting Jewish residents of Damascus was considered by the secular authority as a threat to law and order.[2] Secondly, Paul expressly denies that he went from Damascus to Jerusalem to visit the apostles; his destination, he says, was the Arabian desert in Transjordan (Gal. 1:17), where the mystical experiences described by him in 2 Corinthians 12:2–4 took place: 'I know of a man in Christ who fourteen years ago was caught up to the third heaven . . . And I know that this man was caught up into Paradise . . . and he heard things that cannot be told, which man may not utter.' From there he returned to Damascus (Gal. 1:17), and three years later his first brief meeting in Jerusalem with Peter (Cephas) and James, the brother of Jesus (but not with the other apostles or with the various churches of Judaea) came about. Then, after a fortnight spent with Peter and James, he departed for his mission in Syria and Cilicia (Gal. 1:18–21). If we accept Paul's first-hand account as correct, it must have a fundamental impact on our understanding of his self-awareness as the odd-man-out among the apostles, which would inevitably have influenced his depiction of Jesus.

2. In the eyes of the diaspora Jews as well as the zealots of Jerusalem Paul's provocative preaching and behaviour made him appear a troublemaker, to be controlled by legal means (communal imprisonment or flogging) or illegally by instant popular justice, stoning (cf. Acts 13:50; 14:2–5, 19; 17:5, 13; 20:3; 21:27–8; 21:30–31; 22:22; 23:12–24; 24:5; 25:2–7). Paul himself boasts of imprisonment and of countless beatings, receiving on five occasions thirty-nine lashes, the severest corporal punishment allowed in Jewish law; and of one (needless to say, unsuccessful) stoning (2 Cor. 11:23–5). In Philippi he was beaten and imprisoned by Greek magistrates (Acts 16:19–39).

Paul's Achilles' heel was the questionable nature of his status as an apostle. He himself was convinced that he was an 'apostle of Jesus Christ' (1 Cor. 1:1; 2 Cor. 1:1); 'a servant of Jesus Christ, called to be an apostle' (Rom. 1:1); one of the 'ambassadors for Christ' (2 Cor. 5:20), or more precisely 'a minister of Christ Jesus to the Gentiles' (Rom. 15:16). That this claim was contested by many in the church is made clear more than once by Paul's resentful polemic: 'Am I not an apostle?' he asked the Corinthians. 'If to others I am not an apostle, at least I am to you, for you are the seal of my apostleship' (1 Cor. 9:1–2). Elsewhere he denied any inferiority to those preachers he ironically called 'superlative apostles' (2 Cor. 11:5; 12:11). He was prepared to designate himself 'the least of the apostles' and in an off-guard moment to go as far as to declare that he was 'unfit to be called an apostle' (1 Cor. 15:9), yet in his heart of hearts he was ready to give his life for his apostolic title; despite paying lip service to humility, he did not hesitate to clash with his senior colleagues.

The opposition to Paul's apostolic dignity sprang from two sources. First, it came from the Judaizers, those Jewish members of the Palestinian church belonging to the faction headed by James, the brother of the Lord, who opposed Paul's willingness to offer dispensation to Gentile believers from the observance of Mosaic Law, and who considered him a self-promoting upstart. Secondly, it would seem that there existed in the primitive church a definition of apostleship with which Paul could not comply. When after the defection of Judas the eleven apostles were looking for a replacement, they laid down as a condition that the person should be someone who had 'accompanied us during all the time that the Lord Jesus went in and out among us, beginning from the baptism of John' (Acts 1:21–2). By this definition Paul, who had never set eyes on Jesus or John the Baptist, would have failed the qualifying examination.

Knowing that he could not designate himself an apostle along traditional lines, he emphasized instead that he had been directly chosen by the will of God (1 Cor. 1:1; 2 Cor. 1:1; Gal. 1:1), or through a supernatural vision: 'Am I not an apostle? Have I not seen Jesus our Lord?' (1 Cor. 9:1); and later, 'Last of all, as to one untimely born, [Christ] appeared also to me. For I am the least [i.e. the most recent] of the apostles' (1 Cor. 15:8–9). This vision must allude to the revelation at Damascus, which according to Galatians 1:16 entailed an order to become an apostle to the Gentiles.[3] As a result, Paul felt fully commissioned by Jesus, needing no appointment but only recognition by the earlier apostles. This would explain his insistence that his first visit to Jerusalem, a kind of courtesy call, was short and brought him into contact with only two apostles. When he returned there fourteen years later with Barnabas it was to inform the apostles of his gospel to the Gentiles, which entailed no compulsory circumcision and submission to the whole Torah as a precondition. He behaved like Peter's equal: 'I had been entrusted with the gospel to the uncircumcised just as Peter had been entrusted with the gospel to the circumcised' (Gal. 2:7). He firmly let it be known that he had received approval from the 'pillars' of the church, James, Cephas (Peter) and John (Gal. 2:1–9). As usual, the conciliatory author of the Acts of the Apostles offers a smoother representation of the conflict, referring to an apostolic synod culminating in a diplomatic settlement not mentioned by Paul. Gentile Christians were acknowledged as members of the church as long as they observed the so-called Noachic commandments which entailed abstention from meat sacrificed to idols, from the flesh of strangled animals and from the eating of blood, as well as from gross sexual immorality (Acts 15:1–29).

Not only did Paul consider himself Peter's equal, but in the famous incident in Antioch – recounted in the letter to the Galatians, but conveniently omitted by the author of the Acts – Paul 'opposed him to his face' and publicly reprimanded the head of the apostles for his cowardly and hypocritical behaviour. Peter's repeated denial of Jesus in the high priest's courtyard had already revealed his lack of guts (Mark 14:66–72, etc.). During a visit to the Gentile Christian community created by Paul and Barnabas in Antioch, Peter sat at their non-kosher table; but when a group of James's Torah-observing Jewish Christians turned up from Jerusalem, Peter, all the Jewish members of

3. The mystical experience described in 2 Cor. 12:2–3 was of a different kind, consisting in an assumption of Paul into Paradise, the third of the seven heavens of Chariot (Merkabah) mysticism of Jewish esoterical speculation from late antiquity to medieval Kabbalah. See Peter Schäfer, 'New Testament and Hekhalot Literature: The Journey into Heaven in Paul and in Merkavah Mysticism', *Journal of Jewish Studies* 35 (1984), 19–35.

the church of Antioch and even the spiritless Barnabas, 'fearing the circumcision party', turned their backs on their Gentile brethren. The furious Paul upbraided Peter in no uncertain terms for his duplicity in front of the whole community (Gal. 2:11–14). As his bad-tempered breach with Barnabas demonstrated (cf. p. 63), Paul was not exactly a forgiving character. Not surprisingly there is no mention of any further contact between him and Peter either in his writings or in the Acts of the Apostles.[4]

As a headstrong personality, Paul was often at the centre of conflicts throughout his missionary career. The church of Corinth founded by him soon split into competing factions. Some insisted that they belonged to Paul, others to Cephas or Apollos, and the rest, sickened by dissension, claimed to pertain to Christ (1 Cor. 1:12). There was internal strife, envy and rivalry in the church of Philippi, too, where opponents of Paul, whom he called dogs and evil-workers, preached in order to rile him (Phil. 1:15–17; 3:2). It seems that again and again he proved to be a rather harsh father to the offspring produced by his preaching of the gospel.

On the other hand, Paul's devotion to his mission knew no limits where the success of his gospel was at stake. He willingly suffered hunger, thirst, cold, exposure, dangerous journeys, shipwrecks, imprisonment, beatings and stoning (2 Cor. 11:23–7). He could also be calculating and ready to compromise: 'To the Jews I became as a Jew . . . to those under the law I became as one under the law . . . To those outside the law I became as one outside the law . . . *I have become all things to all men*' (1 Cor. 9:20–22). Or in short, 'I try to please all men in everything I do' (1 Cor. 10:33). Maybe Peter, in his unsophisticated way, was attempting to do the same thing in Antioch, but he met with the sharp edge of Paul's tongue.

\*

4. While no critical scholar would accept the genuineness of 2 Peter – some date it as late as AD 125–50 – it is worth noting that this letter tries to salvage the image of a lasting friendship between him and Paul, who is referred to as 'our beloved brother'. It is amusing to observe, however, that the author, representing the school of Peter, cannot help quietly administering a gibe in Paul's direction: his letters contain 'some things . . . hard to understand which the ignorant and the unstable twist to their own destruction' (2 Pet. 3:15; cf. also Jas. 2:14–26).

After this sketch of the life and character of Paul, of his position as leader of the Gentile mission and his self-knowledge when facing Peter, James and the other apostles, it is possible to go on with greater confidence and a more genuine insight to analyse and determine their impact on Paul's perception and portrayal of Jesus.

While trying to maintain that he had the full status of an apostle, the fact that he had to admit he was not one of them from the start – even from the days of John the Baptist – imposed on Paul a very serious handicap. He had no contact with the earthly Jesus; he did not hear his teaching or experience his spiritual presence and influence. Intelligent as he was, he bypassed this dangerous terrain and devised a new, non-historical approach to the Lord Jesus Christ which contained no obvious disadvantage for Paul himself.

To begin with the message of Jesus: Paul willingly admitted that some of the basic tenets came to him by word of mouth from those who preceded him in the church. In 1 Corinthians 15:3–7 he lists among the fundamentals the death and resurrection of Jesus. 'For I delivered to you as of first importance *what I also received*, that Christ died for our sins . . . that he was buried, that he was raised on the third day . . . and that he appeared to Cephas, and then to the twelve. Then he appeared to more than five hundred brethren at one time . . . Then he appeared to James, then to all the apostles.' The same tradition is implied in Paul's summary of 'the gospel of God' at the opening of the Epistle to the Romans: 'the gospel concerning his son, who was descended from David *according to the flesh* and designated Son of God in power *according to the spirit* of holiness' – according to the flesh and according to the spirit are essential notions in Paul – 'by his resurrection from the dead, Jesus Christ our Lord' (Rom. 1:3–4).

Only two further examples in the whole corpus of Paul's letters cite teachings of Jesus that had been handed down, no doubt through the channel of the oral tradition of the church. The first case concerns the absolute prohibition of divorce recorded in Mark 10:11–12, without the exception clause, 'save for fornication', mentioned in Matthew 5:32 and 19:9: 'To the married I give charge, not I but the Lord, that the wife should not separate from her husband . . . and that the husband should not divorce his wife' (1 Cor. 7:10–11). However, despite the belief that the precept originated with Jesus, Paul felt free to modify its application with the remark, 'I say, not the Lord' (1 Cor. 7:12). The case was that of a newly baptized, already married Gentile man or woman whose pagan spouse objected to the conversion; Paul permitted divorce, followed by the Christian partner's remarriage (1 Cor. 7:15). Known as the Pauline privilege, this exception is still part of the canon law of the Roman Catholic church (*Codex Iuris Canonici*, 1120–27).

Paul mentions as a second precept of Jesus transmitted by tradition the entitlement of the Christian preacher to be provided for by the faithful (cf. Luke 10:7): 'The Lord commanded that those who proclaim the gospel should get their living by the gospel' (1 Cor. 9:14). Once again for the sake of the success of his mission, Paul preferred not to avail himself of Jesus' authorization and opted for earning a living by manual work, apparently as a tentmaker (Acts 18:3). In this way his efforts to evangelize the non-Jewish world would not be jeopardized (1 Cor. 9:12).

There is a third case which, although considered by most scholars as belonging to the oral tradition, strikes me as more peculiar. It relates to Paul's account of the establishment of the eucharistic meal. He complained about division among members of the church of Corinth when they were partaking of the Lord's supper. Instead of sharing a common meal, the rich and the poor had recourse to their own provisions and as a result some remained hungry and others became drunk (1 Cor. 11:20–21). They should all share, Paul ordered, the same bread, symbolizing the body, and the same cup, symbolizing the blood of the Lord, making them contemplate the death of Christ until his return. Paul's eucharist is basically an allegorical or mystical reminder of Jesus' violent end. He does not dwell, however, as shockingly as John does (cf. above, p. 21, n.7) and even slightly less than the Synoptics (Matt. 26:26–9; Mark 14:22–5; Luke 22:15–20) on the *actual* identification of the bread and wine as his body and blood to be eaten and drunk. Paul has his own way of recounting the event both in 1 Cor. 11 and in 1 Cor. 10:16–17. He taught that the purpose of the mystical union or communion with the body and blood of Christ is symbolically to bind the many members of the church into a single whole.

Of course, it is conceivable that Paul re-edited the traditional version – except that even in the Synoptic Gospels there are no two accounts of the institution of the eucharist which are the same – and that John's last supper has nothing to do with the eucharist. But it would seem to me that Paul's introductory formula intimates that he meant to say something original and not just to reproduce an oft-repeated story. When handing down church tradition transmitted to him by anonymous agents, such as Jesus' death, burial, resurrection and later apparitions (1 Cor. 15:3–5), he prefaces his statement with 'I delivered to you . . . what I also received' (1 Cor. 15:3). In the case of the eucharist, however, his source is said to be Jesus, implying that it was directly *revealed* to him. 'I received *from the Lord* what I also delivered to you' (1 Cor. 11:23). If I am correct in interpreting this passage, it would mean that Paul's account stands apart from the tradition recorded some fifteen to forty-five years later in the Synoptic Gospels, since the first Epistle to the Corinthians was written *c.* AD 55. Consequently Paul's wording may have been the primary source for the New Testament formulation of the establishment of the eucharist. In other words, there is a good chance that the eucharistic interpretation of the communal meal of the church was due to Paul, and that the editors of Mark, Matthew and especially Luke, who follows Paul most closely, introduced it into their respective accounts in the Synoptic Gospels.

The doctrines which Paul quotes as traditional in origin are highly important, but quantitatively they do not amount to very much. Indeed, his gospel in no way resembles the account of the teaching and life of Jesus which in subsequent decades evolved into the Synoptic narratives. His preaching was not built on what Paul had heard from his predecessors; it relied on heavenly communications and visions. 'When he who had set me apart before I was born, and had called me through his grace, was pleased to reveal his Son to me, in order that I might preach him among the Gentiles, I did not confer with flesh and blood, nor did I go up to Jerusalem to those who were apostles before me' (Gal. 1:16–17). In other words, Paul did not solicit tutorials, convinced as he was that he knew all that he needed to know. Nor did he endeavour, as the evangelists did, to rehearse and reinterpret the story and the preaching of Jesus; his task was to reveal to the world the divinely designed meaning and purpose, and the achievements, of the crucified redeemer and saviour of humankind.

What would we know about Jesus if Paul's letters were the only evidence we possessed? After a meticulous combing of the whole corpus of his writings, the information relating to the prophet from Nazareth would add up to precious little. It would yield no chronological pointer of any kind. We would search for Galilee, its towns and villages, in vain; geography was of no interest to Paul. There is no mention of King Herod or his sons, of any of the high priests by name, not even Pontius Pilate. Mary and Joseph are ignored, though the brother of Jesus, James, is referred to twice in his apostolic capacity. John the Baptist is never alluded to. No apostle is named, apart from 'Cephas and James' on one occasion, and 'James, Cephas and John' on another, and Peter is said to be in charge of the 'gospel for the circumcision' as against Paul, whose remit is 'the gospel for the foreskin' (Gal. 2:7). Comparison with the detailed list of Paul's friends, colleagues, and companions proves that he did not live in an abstract dream world, and that his silence on Jesus' entourage was deliberate.

In fact everything seems to suggest that in order to emphasize the paramount importance of the Jesus revealed in visions, Paul deliberately turned his back on the historical figure, the Jesus according to the flesh, *kata sarka*. If we scour Pauline literature, all we discover there is that Jesus came from the Jewish nation, 'of their race according to the flesh is Christ' (Rom. 9:5); that he was the offspring of Abraham (Gal. 3:16) and belonged to the royal lineage of David 'according to the flesh' (Rom. 1:3).

Apart from these basic facts concerning the origins of Jesus and incidental allusions to his moral or liturgical injunctions, all we learn from Paul is that he was betrayed and died on the cross before rising from the dead and appearing first to his apostles and disciples, and finally to Paul. In brief, Paul's eyes were firmly averted from the living Galilean holy man about whom he had nothing original to say. The Jesus according to the flesh on whose behalf he could have acted only as a second-hand witness did not appeal to him. Polemically, and perhaps apologetically, he remarked that had he known Christ 'according to the flesh', he would prefer not to know him thus any longer (2 Cor. 5:16).

Instead, Paul focused on the dying and risen Christ, and his supernatural accomplishments on behalf of the faithful. At the same time he was continuously preoccupied with the shepherding of his Gentile

Christians who, unlike the Jewish adepts of Jesus, were religiously and morally untrained, and required strict control while awaiting the approaching second coming of the Lord.

Before turning to the reconstruction of the face of the Christ Jesus concealed in Paul's epistles, I would like to signal one feature of the church message originating with Jesus which perhaps unexpectedly entered and was developed by Paul's ideology: his expectation of the Kingdom of God simultaneously with the Parousia, the return of Christ. Notwithstanding his impetuosity and recurrent illogicality, Paul was a poetic and mystical genius capable of construing a multifarious, impressive and exciting theological complex. Without any doubt, Paul was the most imaginative and creative writer among the authors of the New Testament, even though his ingenuity often resulted in twisting and sometimes undoing the genuine message of Jesus. But he was also a brilliantly gifted organizer without whose contribution Christianity would not exist or would be something totally different.

To begin with an idea which echoes the belief of Jesus and of the primitive church, the imminent advent of the Kingdom of God still plays a notable role in Paul's thinking, reflected in his letters to the Thessalonians, Galatians, 1 Corinthians and Romans (written between AD 50 and 56). Paul's followers were called into God's Kingdom which no flesh and blood could inherit unless they were made worthy by their afflictions (1 Thess. 2:12; 1 Cor. 15:50; 2 Thess. 1:4–5). In regard to the impending onset of the eschatological age or 'the day of our Lord Jesus Christ' (Phil. 1:8; 2:16), Paul's hope differed only slightly from the expectation of Jesus. Urgency characterized both. Jesus saw the Kingdom of God lurking just round the corner, and showing itself from time to time. Similarly, Paul and his Thessalonian and Corinthian Christians were fired by the sure faith that the return of the Lord would occur at any moment, and certainly during their lifetime. Their conviction of the impending arrival of the Kingdom is manifest in statements such as 'the appointed time [had] grown very short' (1 Cor. 7:29) and that Christ would burst in suddenly 'like a thief in the night' (1 Thess. 5:2). 'For this we declare to you by the word of the Lord, that we who are alive . . . are left until the coming of the Lord . . .' (1 Thess. 4:15). The precision of the language precludes any explaining away of a literally imminent Parousia.

Paul's theology, which will be examined in the next chapter, and his eschatological ethics must be seen in this short time-span, which not surprisingly led to a few ephemeral oddities in the churches of Corinth and Thessalonica. Some members, anxious about the ultimate fate of their deceased friends and relations, introduced the custom of undergoing baptism on behalf of the dead (1 Cor. 15:29). Through this legal fiction, of which Paul did not disapprove, unbaptized pagans would vicariously gain Christian status and entitlement to resurrection as 'those who belong to Christ' (1 Cor. 15:23).

Even more curiously, in the early fifties AD rumours began to spread in the church of Thessalonica that Christ had already returned and that this event had been announced in a letter from Paul. As a result some Thessalonian Christians stopped working in the certainty of an instant manifestation of the Lord. Paul immediately intervened in this religiously and socially dangerous situation, denying the actual reappearance of Christ which, he declared, would not happen without a series of premonitions, and firmly admonishing the idle Thessalonians to go back to work (2 Thess. 2:1–8; 3:6–12).

Paul's faith in the fast-approaching second coming, so obvious in the letters to the Thessalonians and 1 Corinthians, affected not only his representation of Jesus Christ, but also the manner in which he instructed and led his flock.[5] Both Jesus and Paul lived through the same conditions of feverish insecurity, not knowing what would happen next, but they were surrounded by followers of different backgrounds. Jesus' disciples were Jews trained from childhood in how to behave and how to distinguish between good and evil in the light of centuries of Jewish religious tradition. All they had to learn was the meaning of absolute urgency, a total concentration on the needs of the present moment. While he was alive and leading his followers, Jesus did not need any specific communal organization.

Paul, on the other hand, had to care for freshly disciplined Gentile Christians who came from a totally different religious and moral environment. Despite the proximity of the day of the Lord, they needed

5. It seems that the only occasion when Paul, already a prisoner and awaiting trial for his life, envisaged the possibility that he might die before the return of Christ is in Phil. 1:21, probably written between AD 58 and 60.

constant guidance and supervision by their own leaders, bishops, presbyters and deacons, and when necessary, by Paul himself who, as the father of his churches, did not hesitate to intervene directly in serious matters. He unhesitatingly excommunicated a member of the Corinthian church because the man was living with his stepmother, a form of immorality which not even pagans could tolerate: 'You are to deliver this man to Satan for the destruction of the flesh' (1 Cor. 5:1–5). He also advised the congregation to keep away from the rather odd company of brethren who were unchaste, greedy, idolaters, revilers, drunkards or robbers and not to eat with them (1 Cor. 5:11). Like the Essenes, according to the Dead Sea Scrolls (CD 9:1), the Corinthians of Paul were forbidden to seek justice from a civil court (1 Cor. 6:1). He took a more elastic approach to the question of whether a Christian could eat meat purchased in the market which came from a sacrifice offered in a pagan temple. Those with a strong faith who knew that idols were as nothing were permitted to consume such meat, provided their behaviour would not cause the downfall of a weak brother (1 Cor. 8:1–12).

As for the lifestyle of church members during the short period leading to the second coming, Paul's overall rule of thumb was that if possible the members should remain as they were. Since the big change was imminent, they would have to put up with things. The circumcised man was to stay so and not seek to undergo an operation (known as *epispasm*) to conceal circumcision. The uncircumcised would keep his foreskin. Those who were slaves were to stay slaves, for they would soon be freed by Christ. A Christian freeman, on the other hand, should consider himself a slave of Christ (1 Cor. 7:22). The married person should preferably remain married and the unmarried single, but matrimony in itself was not sinful. However, because of the upheavals signalling the return of Christ it was convenient to be free of the troubles of marital responsibility. Indeed, even those who were married were to live as though they were single (1 Cor. 7:25–35). Being without a wife, unlike 'the other apostles and the brothers of the Lord and Cephas' (1 Cor. 9:5), Paul could offer them his own example. 'I wish that all were as I myself am,' he exhorted the faithful (1 Cor. 7:7). However, his argument for celibacy would have gained considerable strength if he had pointed out that Jesus, too, was wifeless. His refusal to touch the subject may derive from his unwillingness to know anything of Christ 'according to the flesh'.

Before turning to Paul's representation of Jesus, it would be useful to glance first at his overall theological canvas. Paul had a grandiose vision of the work of Jesus Christ in the history of salvation of both Jews and Gentiles. He saw the climax of this history in the form of an ultimate contest between compliant Gentiles and obdurate Jews, and he was also fully aware of the decisive role assigned to him personally in the divine plan to bring this conflict to a triumphant and happy ending.

In Paul's magnificent poetic-theological dialectic the salvation drama is played out by two stars, the first man, Adam, and Jesus Christ, or – in Paul's terminology – the first Adam and the last Adam (1 Cor. 15:45). This kernel of the central drama will be the subject of analysis in the next chapter, but two further aspects of it can serve as the conclusion of the present one.

The first of these is more concrete and down-to-earth than the 'last Adam' imagery. It is concerned with the actual reaction to the Christ phenomenon of Jews and Gentiles who, despite the disproportion in numbers, represented for Paul the two metaphysical halves of humanity. He developed this play magnificently in chapters 9 to 11 of his letter to the Romans. He found himself right in the middle of the conflict, being simultaneously a Jew and the apostle of Christ to the Gentiles.

The world had witnessed, Paul reckoned, God's ultimate gift, Jesus Christ. Yet nearly all Jews, to whom should 'belong the sonship, the glory, the covenants, the giving of the law, the worship, and the promises' (Rom. 9:4), displayed a baffling resistance, whereas the unprepared Gentiles showed themselves sensitive and receptive. Paul discovered a key to this puzzle in biblical history. In God's mysterious design, the order of precedence was sometimes unexpectedly reversed: the junior was preferred to the senior in the age of the biblical patriarchs, Isaac to Ishmael, Jacob to Esau. In this crucial moment the Gentiles were overtaking the Jews, or at least most of the Jews, because a little remnant, the community of Jewish believers in Christ, had already symbolically vindicated the divine promises to Israel. God did not reject his people; he simply allowed their unbelief to benefit the Gentiles and open to them the gate of salvation. But this Gentile success, the fruit of Paul's mission, would have a sting in the tail: it would kindle the jealousy of the Jews, or so Paul imagined. They would not contemplate passively a Gentile take-over of their spiritual patrimony. And once they decided to enter the competition, they would advance by leaps and bounds and catch up with the leaders so that not only the Gentile but also the Jewish world would enjoy salvation. 'I want you to understand this mystery, brethren: a hardening has come upon part of Israel, until the full number of the Gentiles come in, and so all Israel will be saved' (Rom. 11:25–6).

This brings us to the final aspect of Paul's eschatological dream, his own part in the fulfilment of this drama. To bring about the ultimate return of the Jews to Jesus Christ, his own specific mission must be achieved and 'the full number of the Gentiles' be brought into the church. During his various voyages he succeeded in planting the gospel in the hearts of Gentiles in many parts of the Mediterranean world, in Syria, Asia Minor and Greece; he hoped soon to travel to Italy and Rome. In reality, members of his churches may have amounted to no more than a few thousand, but they formed a significant element throughout the eastern half of the Roman empire. Paul probably knew that other apostolic missionaries were active in Egypt and northern Mesopotamia, and may have heard rumours that Christianity had reached as far east as India. But the west was still without the gospel; Paul felt it was up to him to carry the good news from Antioch on the eastern shore of the Mediterranean to the Pillars of Hercules (Gibraltar) where the sun set at the western extremity of the inhabited universe. After his planned visit to Rome he would rush to Spain (Rom. 15:24), no doubt expecting to hear, after a triumphant preaching mission, the trumpet signalling the great day of Christ's return, hailed by the mixed alleluia chorus of Jews and Gentiles.

As is often the case with beautiful dreams, they end before their climax is reached. Paul probably never arrived in Spain; Jews and Christians are still divided and two millennia have passed without the second coming. But Christianity still endures, and this is largely due to the theological vision of Jesus sketched by the odd-man-out among the apostles who never saw him in the flesh.

# 4

# The Christ of Paul: Son of God
# and universal Redeemer of mankind

## I
## PAUL AND THE
## TRADITIONAL TITLES OF JESUS

Paul, as I have noted, adopted a completely new stance in his attitude
to Jesus which distinguishes him not only from the more 'historical'
Mark, Matthew and Luke, but even from John. In ignoring the man
from Nazareth and his activities in Galilee and Jerusalem, Paul had
no need to incorporate into his synthesis traditional elements of the
portrayal of Jesus. For him, the history of Christ began with 'the night
of his betrayal' (1 Cor. 11:23) and ended three days later with his
resurrection. The term 'Jesus' on its own appears only about ten times
in the letters of Paul – excluding the inauthentic Hebrews, where it
figures nine times – and is invariably connected with the only aspects
of the earthly Jesus which were significant to Paul: his death and
resurrection. Neither did Paul use the Semitic title Messiah, encountered in John, although he was not averse to quoting Aramaic words
from Christian prayers, for instance *Abba*, 'Father' (Rom. 8:15;
Gal. 4:6), or *Maran atha*, 'The Lord has come' (1 Cor. 16:22).

Paul pays no attention to the biblical expectation of a king Messiah
or its fulfilment in Jesus the Christ apart from the vague mention of
his descent from David (Rom. 1:3, and 2 Tim. 2:8 in the post-Pauline
literature). The original Greek epithet, the Christ ('the anointed'),
qualifying Jesus as Messiah, fast evolves into a kind of double-barrelled
proper name, Jesus-Christ. Since his Gentile followers had no ground-
ing in the messianic hope of Judaism, Christ for them was a Saviour
figure who achieved his redeeming function not as the final occupant

of the royal throne of David who would defeat God's enemies and subject the world to the rule of divine justice, but in a totally idiosyncratic way through his death and resurrection. The biblically untrained Christians in Ephesus, Corinth or Rome were unaware that Paul was twisting the Jewish Messiah concept. For Jewish listeners, however, the message would have sounded inept: since the Messiah was not expected to die, there was no need for him to be raised from the dead.

Paul would never have dreamed of calling Jesus a 'prophet', which was not sufficiently grand to fit Christ. And predictably the title 'Son of man', often used with different meanings in the Synoptic Gospels and in John, is completely foreign to him.[1] As will be shown in Chapter 6, 'son of Man' as a title first emerged in the Synoptic tradition, in combination with 'one like a son of man' (Daniel 7), in the decades that followed Paul's literary activity; so of all the pre-existing traditional designations of Jesus only 'Son of God' and 'Lord' continued to flourish in Paul's writings.

## The Son of God in Paul

Unlike the Synoptics and John, in which the public manifestation of Jesus as Son of God is chronologically linked to the prominent figure of John the Baptist, Paul makes no attempt whatever to anchor Christ in history. In fact he never mentions the Baptist in any of his authentic writings; the historical sermon attributed to him in Acts 13 in which John is referred to follows the teaching pattern of Palestinian Christianity rather than Paul's own style. Again, the story of Paul's encounter with prospective Christians in Ephesus, who knew nothing about Christian baptism but were familiar with the baptism of John (Acts 18:25; 19:3), derives from the not always reliable author of the Acts of the Apostles. All that Paul tells us about Jesus' arrival into the

---

1. However, a reshaped form of son of man (= a man) appears as a self-reference by the speaker. Paul, alluding to his own mystical experience in Arabia (Transjordan), out of modesty writes in a circumlocutional style: 'I know *a man* in Christ who ... was caught up to the third heaven ... And I know that *this man* was caught up into Paradise' (2 Cor. 12:2–3).

world is that he was born of an unnamed Jewish woman – this is all
we learn from Paul about the mother of Jesus – and that this occurred
in the fullness of time, at the most important moment in history. 'When
the time had fully come, God sent forth his Son, born of woman, born
under the law' (Gal. 4:4).

Leaving for a later discussion the significance of the mission of the
Son – atonement, redemption, bestowal of divine sonship on believers
– our main concern at this moment is to determine his status and his
relationship to God the Father in Paul's thought. Did he anticipate
John and consider Father and Son as co-equal?

On two occasions it would seem that he may have done so. The first
example of the promotion of Jesus Christ to a quasi-divine status
occurs in Philippians 2:6–11. The passage comes from a hymn which
is quoted to support Paul's exhortation to the Philippians to live in
harmony.

> Have this mind among yourselves,
> which you have in Christ Jesus, who,
> though he was in the form of God,
> did not count equality with God a thing to be grasped,
> but emptied himself, taking the form of a servant,
> being born in the likeness of men.
> And being found in human form, he humbled himself
> and became obedient unto death, even death on a cross.
> Therefore God has highly exalted him
> and bestowed on him the name which is above every name,
> that at the name of Jesus every knee should bow,
> in heaven and on earth and under the earth,
> and every tongue confess that Jesus Christ is Lord,
> to the glory of God the Father.

The expressions 'in the form of God', 'grasping equality from God',
and 'emptying himself' echo mythological concepts familiar from the
Gospel of John and from later heretical Gnostic speculation. If so,
chronologically they point to the early second century AD rather than
the age of Paul. The hymn makes much better sense if it is taken as an
existing liturgical composition inserted into the letter to the Philippians
not by Paul himself but by a later editor. The fact that this poem

can be removed without spoiling the general meaning of the chapter strongly favours the theory of its post-Pauline origin.

The second example is furnished by Romans 9:5. Depending on its punctuation – and of course ancient Greek manuscripts were not punctuated – this verse can have two totally different meanings. The significance revolves around the identity of the addressee of the final blessing: is it aimed at Christ or God? 'To them [the Jews] belong the patriarchs and of their race according to the flesh is the Christ *the one over all God blessed for ever amen*' (Rom. 9:5). Now if the doxology or liturgical praise is attached to Christ, i.e. 'Of their race is ... the Christ, who is over all God blessed for ever. Amen' (so the Authorized Version), there is no mistaking that Paul identifies Christ with God. But the alternative punctuation, preferred by modern translators and commentators, places a full stop after Christ, thus treating the doxology as independent and clearly referring to God: 'Of their race ... is the Christ. God who is over all be blessed for ever. Amen' (Revised Standard Version, New English Bible, etc.). As it stands, the Greek text can be read as though the blessing were addressed to Christ; but this, as well as any direct deification of the Son of God, is unsupported in the authentic letters of Paul.[2]

To begin with, we have substantial and unanimous evidence that Paul's prayers and liturgical blessings are regularly addressed to God or the Father, and not to, though often through, Jesus Christ. As a result, Christ is neatly distinguished from God. The matter being of great importance, I include a detailed list of prayers and doxologies from Paul's letters.

## PRAYERS

'We cry *Abba! Father!*' (Rom. 8:15; cf. Gal. 4:6).

'I appeal to you, brethren, by our Lord Jesus Christ ... to strive together with me in your prayers to *God*' (Rom. 15:30).

---

2. The deutero-Pauline Titus 2:13 reads: 'the appearing of the glory of our great God and Saviour Jesus Christ'. However, in the light of Paul's writings as a whole, most contemporary scholars suggest the reading, 'the appearing of the glory of *the* great God and *our* Saviour Jesus Christ'. Cf. the alternative reading in the RSV, the NEB, the Nestle-Aland Greek–English New Testament, etc.

'I give thanks to *God* always for you' (1 Cor. 1:4).

'I thank *God* that I speak in tongues more than you all' (1 Cor. 14:18).

'He will worship *God*' (1 Cor. 14:25).

'Thanks be to *God* who gives us the victory through our Lord Jesus Christ' (1 Cor. 15:57).

'Thanks be to *God* who in Christ always leads us in triumph' (2 Cor. 2:14; cf. 8:16; 9:15).

'We pray *God* that you may not do wrong' (2 Cor. 13:7).

'We give thanks to *God* always for you all . . . remembering before our *God* and *Father* your work of faith' (1 Thess. 1:2–3).

'For what thanksgiving can we render to *God* for you' (1 Thess. 3:9).

'May the *God* of peace himself sanctify you' (1 Thess. 5:23).

'We are bound to give thanks to *God* always for you' (2 Thess. 1:3).

## DOXOLOGIES

'From him (*God*) and through him and to him are all things. To him be glory for ever. Amen' (Rom. 11:36).

'To the only wise *God* be glory for evermore through Jesus Christ. Amen' (Rom. 16:27).

'Blessed be the *God* and *Father* of our Lord Jesus Christ' (2 Cor. 1:3).

'The *God* and *Father* of our Lord Jesus Christ, he who is blessed for ever' (2 Cor. 11:31; cf. Rom. 9:5).

'To our *God* and *Father* be glory for ever and ever. Amen' (Phil. 4:20).

These examples clearly show that when it came to some of the most essential aspects of religious activity such as prayer, thanksgiving and blessing, Paul's subconscious Jewish mind instinctively distinguished between God the Father and the Son of God. His prayers are automatically addressed to the Father either directly or through the mediation of the Christ Jesus, the Son, who is above ordinary mortals, but indubitably below the transcendent deity.

Paul is categorical in proclaiming a hierarchical order by virtue of which Christ and God do not belong in the same category. Taking the husband–wife relationship as his model, Paul argues that just as the man is superior to the woman, so is Christ superior to humans, but God is above Christ. 'The head of every man is Christ, the head of a woman is her husband, and the head of Christ is God' (1 Cor. 11:3). The true relationship between the Son and the Father will be made clear at the climax of the cosmic drama. At the moment of the second coming, having destroyed the power of evil and even death, Christ will submit himself to God the Father. 'When all things are subjected to him [Christ], then the Son himself will be subjected to him [the Father] who put all things under him, that God may be everything to every one' (1 Cor. 15:24–8).

Paul goes even further. In contrast to John, who sees in Jesus Christ the temporary incarnation of the eternal divine Word – 'the Word was with God and the Word was God; and the Word became flesh' (John 1:1, 14, 18) – Paul specifies the historical, or rather the meta-historical, moment when a Jewish man descended from King David was elevated to the dignity of God's Son. In the opening verses of the letter to the Romans, he momentously proclaims that Jesus Christ was '*designated* Son of God in power according to the spirit of holiness *by his resurrection* from the dead' (Rom. 1:4). In other words, Jesus of Nazareth was not the Son of God before the morning of the first Easter. In this instance the religious vision of Paul does not equal the loftiness of the theology of John.

Instead of the Johannine metaphysical definition of the relationship (co-eternity, co-equality) between Father and Son, Paul's understanding of Jesus Christ is existential and entirely depends on the effect on believing mankind of his crucifixion and resurrection.

Paul makes plain the purpose of the coming of the Son of God: through him and his vicarious suffering and death on behalf of mankind, God declared sin defeated and gave a chance to every human being to inherit the image of his Son. In simple terms, the aims pursued by the Son of God were atonement, i.e. redemption from sin, and eternal salvation. 'For God has done what the law . . . could not do: sending his Son in the likeness of sinful flesh and for sin, he condemned sin in the flesh' (Rom. 8:3). Surpassing Abraham, who placed Isaac on the altar but was stopped short of completing the deed (cf. below, pp. 84–6), God went so far as actually to sacrifice his Son on behalf of humanity to 'give us all things with him' (Rom. 8:32). These 'all things' are again and again defined by Paul. In his spiritual perception, redeemed men and women mysteriously inherit the status of 'the

Son' and, 'conformed to [his] image' (Rom. 8:29), themselves become symbolically children of the heavenly Father. 'In Christ Jesus,' Paul asserts, 'you are all sons of God through faith' (Gal. 3:26).

## The Lord in Paul

The title 'Lord', so multifaceted in the Synoptics and even in John, is employed less variably in Paul's letters. Here its most common Synoptic use, the polite form of address, 'Sir', is completely absent: as best he could, Paul shut his eyes to the historical Jesus. Nevertheless he was unable to avoid the ordinary Christian terminology when he called James and other siblings of Jesus the brother, or brothers, of *the Lord* (Gal. 1:19; 1 Cor. 9:5). The occasional hint at a traditionally transmitted teaching as one coming from *the Lord* also points to the pre-Golgotha Jesus, but it may also be conceived as issuing from the lips of the resurrected Christ who revealed himself to Paul: 'To the married I give charge, not I but the Lord' (1 Cor. 7:10), or 'We declare to you by the word of the Lord, that we who are alive . . . shall not precede those who have fallen asleep' (1 Thess. 4:15).

Paul also inherited from primitive Christianity a confession formula, usually a single-sentence proclamation, declaring the lordship of Jesus: 'No one can say Jesus is Lord except by the holy spirit' (1 Cor. 12:3). 'What we preach is not ourselves but Jesus Christ as Lord' (2 Cor. 4:5). 'Every tongue [shall] confess that Jesus Christ is Lord to the glory of God the Father' (the editor of Phil. 2:11, citing an early Christian hymn). This proclamation can be developed into a rudimentary creed, such as 'If you confess with your lips that Jesus is Lord . . . you will be saved' (Rom. 10:9), or into one which is a little more elaborate, like 'There is only one God, the Father, from whom are all things and for whom we exist, and one Lord Jesus Christ through whom are all things and through whom we exist' (1 Cor. 8:6). In Paul's post-Easter world universal instrumentality is ascribed to Christ, while universal causality remains with the Father.

In the thinking of Paul, as one would expect, the designation 'Lord' most frequently applies to Christ who died and rose again; that is to say, the only Christ the apostle of the Gentiles was willing to acknowledge and preach, and whose destiny is eloquently summarized by Paul in one sentence: 'For this end, Christ died and lived again, that he might be Lord of both the dead and the living' (Rom. 14:9).

## II
## THE CHRIST OF PAUL

### The mystery of Christ's death and resurrection

Paul's conviction that he was liberated from sin and engulfed in the love of God was founded on his belief that Christ 'died, yes . . . was raised from the dead . . . is at the right hand of God . . . indeed intercedes for us' (Rom. 8:34). Ultimately this amounts to a myth-drama of salvation. I do not use 'myth' in any pejorative sense, but as an interpretative concept entailing what is often a poetic explanation attached to death, burial, life, revival, etc. The Pauline myths understood in this sense do not depend on what Jesus taught or even on what he did, but on the consequences, assumed to be providential, of what happened to him. In this respect, Paul's perception is unique and is clearly distinguished from that of the Synoptic evangelists and John. In the Gospels Jesus is a teacher who delivers a message to his followers; in the epistles he is the object of the message devised and disseminated by Paul, with the exception of the few examples where he claims to transmit 'the words of the Lord'. Nevertheless, though he was aware of being the father of his Gentile spiritual children, Paul was fully conscious that he was not their saviour. 'Was Paul crucified for you? Or were you baptized in the name of Paul?' he asked the Corinthians (1 Cor. 1:13).

In Paul's portrait of Jesus the two most essential features are, negatively, that of a deliverer from sin and death through the cross and, positively, that of an agent of justification and rebirth through his resurrection from the dead. Further elements are the Law, typified in a polemical context by circumcision, and the tomb of Jesus, venue of the resurrection, which is symbolized by the baptismal pool of water. Once the significance of these constituents of the picture have been determined, it is possible to focus on the grand design, Paul's overarching mythical/mystical mural of man's salvation starting with the creation and culminating in the Parousia, or second coming.

To understand Paul's mind, one has to be familiar with some of the presuppositions of his Jewish religious culture. Both in the Bible and in early post-biblical Judaism, sin was seen as a rebellion against God, punished by sickness and ultimately by death. Virtue was the result of obedience to God, rewarded by health and a long happy life, and by the time of Jesus and Paul by the prospect of eternal life or renewed existence in a resurrected body. The latter belief was championed by the Pharisees (to whose party Paul claimed to belong), but not by other religious groups such as the Sadducees who rejected the idea of an afterlife, and the Essenes who, according to Flavius Josephus, believed only in the survival of the soul. The evidence of the Dead Sea Scrolls in this respect is equivocal, and in any case possible allusions to bodily resurrection are few and far between. But while in the Gentile milieu of his ministry Paul had no great difficulty in abandoning other Pharisee teachings, such as the centrality of the strict observance of the Torah (circumcision, ritual laws, etc.), the doctrine of bodily resurrection became an indispensable part of his majestic mystery drama.

A second major underlying factor in Paul's understanding of the cross as a redemptive sacrifice is the account of the intended but unrealized immolation of Isaac by his father Abraham. The cruel story is preserved in chapter 22 of Genesis, but what is more important is its reinterpretation in the intertestamental period, and later in the age of the rabbis, then known as the tale of the Binding (or *Akedah*) of Isaac. The Bible recounts the story of the heroic and blind faith of Abraham who without hesitation follows the inexplicable and perplexing divine command to sacrifice his only son, miraculously born to him when he was a centenarian and to his ninety-year-old wife, Sarah. The father and the young son set out on a three-day journey to Mount Moriah, identified in later Jewish and Christian tradition as a mountain in Jerusalem on which both the Jewish Temple and the cross of Jesus would stand. There Abraham built an altar and placed his unsuspecting child on it, but God through the intervention of an angel prevented the execution of the terrible act.

The fundamental difference between the biblical report and the account reshaped by Jewish teachers from the second century BC onwards – in the Book of Jubilees, the Dead Sea Scrolls, Josephus, Pseudo-Philo and rabbinic literature – concerns the active role of Isaac in the drama.[3] Instead of being a young boy, unaware of what was happening, Isaac is portrayed as an adult – aged twenty-five in Josephus, thirty-seven according to the rabbis – who was told by his father of God's order. Isaac gladly consented, and ran joyfully to the altar; he asked Abraham to tie his hands and feet and stretched out his neck towards the knife of the slaughterer. Thus the sacrifice which Abraham was to offer also became *a fortiori* the (unaccomplished) self-immolation of Isaac.

Jewish tradition supplies two further details unknown to the Bible, but of major significance. The first concerns the effect of Isaac's self-offering. Every future deliverance of the Jewish people and their final messianic salvation would be seen as resulting from the merit of the sacrificial event of the *Akedah*. Each time God recalled the Binding of Isaac, he would show mercy to his children. The idea expressed in a later prayer was certainly familiar among first-century Jews: 'If the Jews are guilty and are on the point of being slain, remember Isaac their father who stretched out his neck on the altar to be slain for your name's sake. May his immolation take the place of the immolation of his children' (Exodus Rabbah 44:5). In other words, Isaac's willingness to be sacrificed was transformed in Jewish religious thought into a redeeming act of permanent validity for all his children until the arrival of the Messiah.

The second new element inserted into the story as early as the second century BC (Jubilees 17:15; 18:3) is the date, determined by month and day, of the Binding of Isaac. It happened on the fifteenth day of the first month (Nisan), the date on which the Law of Moses would subsequently ordain the celebration of Passover.

Because the reshaped version of the sacrifice of Isaac was a familiar idea among first-century Jews, Paul was able to formulate his teaching about Jesus' death on the cross, freely suffered, as the perfect fulfilment of the redeeming self-offering of Isaac. But in Paul's eyes the main distinguishing mark of the sacrifice of Christ was its universal effect.

3. Cf. G. Vermes, *Scripture and Tradition in Judaism* (Leiden, 1961), 193–227; 'New Light on the Aqedah from 4Q 225', *Journal of Jewish Studies* 47 (1996), 140–46.

It affected the whole of mankind and not only (or primarily) the Jews as the Binding of Isaac was expected to do.

Indeed, it is hard not to see in certain passages of Paul allusions to the reinterpreted Abraham–Isaac narrative of Genesis 22. Paul's statement in the letter to the Romans, 'If God is for us, who shall be against us? He who did not spare his own Son, but surrendered him for us, will he not grant us every favour with him?' (8:31–2) depends on Genesis 22:16, 'By myself I have sworn, says the Lord, because you have done this and have not spared your son, your only son, I will indeed bless you.' The Greek verb 'to spare' used by Paul in connection with God and Christ is the same as the word employed in the Septuagint version of Genesis 22:16 apropos of Abraham and Isaac; this was in fact recognized in the third century by Origen, the greatest Christian Bible expert in antiquity. Again, 'Christ redeemed us . . . so that by Christ Jesus the blessing of Abraham might come upon the nations' (Gal. 3:13–14) echoes Genesis 22:18, 'and through your seed [Isaac] shall all the nations of the earth be blessed'. This obvious influence of the recast Isaac story on Paul's imaginative mind seems to justify the surmise that Genesis 22 was the text hinted at by him without quoting chapter and verse: 'Christ died for our sins *in accordance with the Scriptures*' (1 Cor. 15:3). This also accounts for the predilection of the ancient church fathers, among them Tertullian, Cyril of Alexandria and Augustine, for seeing in Isaac a prefiguration or typology of Jesus.

Having discovered the mould which Paul used to shape his theology regarding the atoning death of Jesus, his thinking becomes easier to follow. In Paul's view 'the wages of sin is death' (Rom. 6:23), and since death has always been and will remain the fate of man – 'death is the final enemy' (1 Cor. 15:26) – it follows that every human being must have sinned. But this sin–death syndrome took an entirely new shape and significance because of the death of Christ on the cross. To Paul the obedient and *sinless* Son of God appeared in the likeness of 'sinful flesh' and he was 'made to be sin who knew no sin' (2 Cor. 5:21). The purpose of God in this cruel drama was to condemn 'sin in the flesh' (Rom. 8:3) through subjecting Jesus to death on the cross. There the crucified Christ would first agree to 'become a curse for us', and then redeem us 'from the curse of the law' (Gal. 3:13–14) by giving himself for our sins and thus delivering us (Gal. 1:4). So every Christian who by faith unites himself to the death of Christ mystically participates in his death and resurrection. In Paul's own words, 'We are convinced that one has died for all; therefore all have died. And he died for all, that those who live might live . . . for him who died for their sake' (2 Cor. 5:14–15).

Perplexing though these statements may appear to detached or uninvolved readers, for believers who see them through the eyes of faith they are full of meaning. For them, the crucifixion of Christ is a 'mythical' event which needs no explanatory detail. Paul does not even specify by whom and for what reason Jesus was killed. Nevertheless Golgotha is placed in the centre of world history, and accounts for Paul's insistence on preaching nothing but 'Christ crucified' (1 Cor. 1:22). The focusing is absolute: the primary concern of Paul is not the risen and glorified Lord, but the Jesus who expired on the cross. 'I decided to know nothing among you except Jesus Christ and him crucified' (1 Cor. 2:2).

How did the death of Christ benefit others? Here again the Pauline belief is simple and powerful, more assertive than explicative. Christ died for all sinners (Rom. 5:8), redeeming them and so potentially saving them. To convert potential salvation to reality, they need a faith that applies to the individual the merits of redemption by Jesus. Occasionally, and superficially, Paul recalls the biblical idea of atoning sacrifice, an animal victim figuratively representing sinful man and expiating his transgression. To satisfy the Jewish theological principle that 'without blood there is no atonement' (bYoma 5a; Heb. 9:22), it is explicitly stated that Christ offered universal 'expiation by his blood' (Rom. 3:25). Moreover Paul on one occasion associates the death of Jesus more specifically with the saving role of the Passover lamb: 'Christ, our paschal lamb, has been sacrificed' (1 Cor. 5:7). But Paul was not really sacrificially-minded; he seems to have been more profoundly influenced by the story of the spiritual self-oblation of Isaac than the blood-shedding ceremonies in the Temple of Jerusalem. In his mystical vision, it is God-given faith that unites believers with the crucified Christ and allows them to appropriate for themselves the fruit of the cross. Such spiritual communion with the death of Jesus allegorically terminates sinful existence and opens the door to a new life. 'We know that our old self was crucified with him [Christ] so that the sinful body be destroyed and we might no longer be enslaved to sin' (Rom. 6:6).

Paul repeatedly stresses the personal, subjective aspect of faith by formulating his statements, negative and positive, in the first person. 'Far be it for me to glory except in the cross of our Lord Jesus Christ, by which the world has been crucified for me, and I to the world' (Gal. 6:14). And again, 'I have been crucified with Christ; it is no longer I who live, but Christ who lives in me' (Gal. 2:20). He also uses the first person plural: 'If we have died with Christ, we believe that we shall also live with him' (Rom. 6:6, 8). We, formerly enemies of God, have been reconciled to him 'by the death of his Son' (Rom. 5:10).

Death and resurrection, liberation from sin and sharing the new life imparted by the Redeemer are facets of the same spiritual reality in Paul's theological contemplation. And although at the end the glory of the resurrection outshines the despondency of the cross, the cross must precede it; the resurrection of Christ is seen as the necessary sequel and vindication of his death.

My statement must not be misinterpreted; it would be foolish to imply that for Paul the resurrection of Jesus was only of secondary importance. Without it his splendid doctrinal edifice would have collapsed like the walls of Jericho at the sound of Joshua's trumpets. Reacting to doubts circulating among Corinthians about the reality of the resurrection itself, Paul vehemently voiced his outrage: 'Now if Christ is preached as raised from the dead, how can some of you say that there is no resurrection of the dead? But if there is no resurrection of the dead, then Christ has not been raised; if Christ has not been raised, then our preaching is in vain and your faith is vain' (1 Cor. 15:12–14).

In Paul's eyes, resurrection is the straight counterpart of the cross: the Lord Jesus was put to death for mankind and raised for mankind (Rom. 4:25). His rising from the dead symbolically disclosed his absolute triumph over the grave: 'Christ being raised from the dead will never die again; death no longer has dominion over him' (Rom. 6:9). But beyond the detached image of life overcoming death, the risen Son of God is seen by Paul as the source of rebirth for the believer: in Christ all shall be made alive (1 Cor. 15:22).

This revival has a twofold meaning: the first is symbolical or in church jargon sacramental, the second eschatologically real, that is to say, it is expected actually to happen at the second coming. In this connection, Paul's imagery presupposes a tomb (1 Cor. 15:4) out of which the dead Christ is believed to have been raised by God. No one knows exactly what Paul thought had happened, but he stressed that the risen body of Christ (or any risen body) was not physical and earthly, but spiritual and heavenly (1 Cor. 15:42–9). Nevertheless this spiritual body is visible, as it has been seen by apostles, disciples and finally by Paul himself (1 Cor. 15:5–8). He does not know or explain where the body of the risen Christ has gone; after a series of apparitions in the early days, weeks or months after the resurrection it was no longer thought to be on earth. Indeed, it may be deduced from Paul's accounts of the second coming that the risen Christ ascended to heaven, to return later as 'the first fruit of those who have fallen asleep' (1 Cor. 15:23), leading the splendid procession of those belonging to him.

Put more simply, for Paul and his Christians the resurrection of Jesus signified the availability of a spiritual renaissance for spiritually dead sinners, for those who through their union with Christ's death inherited a share in his new life. By means of a simple yet highly expressive ritual, reinterpreted by Paul, this mystical union could turn into reality for each believer. This ritual was baptism as conceived by Paul, which echoed the Oriental mystery cults widespread in the Graeco-Roman world of that era.

The primary imagery of baptism, originally a Jewish immersion rite, points towards cleansing, both physical and spiritual. It was a common and as a rule repeatable and repeated religious practice. It was prescribed for the ritual purification of Jews, priests, Levites and lay Israelites, before they could enter the sanctuary of Jerusalem and participate in Temple worship. On a more practical level, ceremonial bathing combined hygiene with allegorical lustration aimed at forms of uncleanness. It was imposed to mark the end of certain contagious diseases, such as dermatological and genital disorders designated by the umbrella terms of 'leprosy' and 'flux'. A ritual bath also restored a state of purity after contact with a dead body, after sexual intercourse for both sexes, and after menstruation and childbirth in the case of women.

Some specific forms of Jewish baptism were performed only once. Such was the baptism of penitence preached by John the Baptist, which was meant to wash away the impurity of sin and indicate the turning towards a holy life leading to the Kingdom of God. It seems that the Qumran Essenes underwent a special ritual bath bound to spiritual renewal during the ceremony of entry into the sectarian covenant (1QS 5:13–14). Rabbinic Judaism, relying on a custom which probably goes back to the first century AD, also compelled both male and female Gentiles who wished to convert to Judaism to undergo the so-called proselyte baptism in addition to circumcision in the case of men. However, whether reiterated or unique, Jewish baptism always retained its primary symbolism of bathing or cleansing by water.

In general, Paul shows no interest in Jewish ritual and if he uses the notion of impurity it is always in the moral sense. Baptism for him is endowed with an allegorical significance which has nothing to do with washing. The pool in which it takes place symbolizes first and foremost the tomb from which Jesus rose at Easter. So when those undergoing the initiation ceremony into the Christian mystery were immersed (i.e. buried) in the baptismal water, allegorically they embraced the death of Christ when they joined him in his grave; and when they were lifted up, they re-enacted and mystically communed with Christ's resurrection. Henceforward they belonged to him. The drama is outlined by Paul in a few poignant words. 'All of us who have been baptized into Christ Jesus were baptized into his death. We were buried therefore with him by baptism into his death, so that as Christ was raised from the dead by the glory of the Father, we too might walk in newness of life' (Rom. 6:3–4). So by reinterpreting the original imagery of the baptismal rite, Paul offered Christians a means to make their own the virtue of both the cross and the resurrection. Needless to say, when with the generalized introduction of infant baptism aspersion was substituted for immersion in the administration of the sacrament, which originally was reserved only for adult initiates and performed at Easter, the powerful Pauline symbolism was killed stone dead.

In addition to the immediate result of this mystical union with the risen Lord which Paul envisaged as a substitution of a life in God's service 'through Jesus Christ' for a sinful existence, the symbolic baptismal resurrection also provided the neophyte or fresh initiate with as it were a ticket for participation in the final real resurrection. As we know (cf. p. 71), the prospect of the ultimate triumph of Christ and of his adepts was not, in Paul's theology, an event belonging to a far distant future; it was expected within the lifetime of the apostle and his own generation. Indeed, Paul repeatedly outlined the scenario of the concluding ceremony.

Every detail was known to him. Christ, surrounded by his angelic guard, would descend from the highest heaven. The archangel, no doubt Michael – head of the heavenly host not only here, but also in the Pseudepigrapha and the Dead Sea Scrolls – would blow the trumpet to call to life the baptized dead. They would be joined by Paul and all the living Christians, their frames of flesh and blood transformed into spiritual bodies, and lifted up towards the Lord in the clouds. 'Lo! I tell you a mystery. We shall not all sleep [= die], but we shall all be changed, in a moment, in the twinkling of an eye, at the last trumpet. For the trumpet will sound, and the dead will be raised imperishable, and we shall be changed' (1 Cor. 15:51–2). Finally the triumphant and risen Lord to whom God had subjected everything, even death, will make obeisance to the Father so that 'God may be everything to every one' (1 Cor. 15:28). To quote Paul further, 'The Lord himself would descend from heaven . . . And the dead in Christ will rise first; then we who are alive, who are left, shall be caught up together with them in the clouds to meet the Lord in the air; and so we shall always be with the Lord' (1 Thess. 4:16–17). The baptismal rising from the dead leads directly to the eschatological triumph of Christ and the Christians. In fact, the two coalesce, thanks to Paul's masterly brush, in one monumental fresco painted on the backcloth of the clouds of heaven.

After a moment of admiration in front of Paul's masterpiece, unease begins to creep into one's mind. The picture is incomplete. After this meeting with the Lord in mid-air, what will happen to the faithful? Will they all continue their journey on the cloud towards the seven heavens, or will they return to earth as citizens of a Jerusalem from above after it has descended to replace the earthly Zion? And what will happen to those who are not 'in Christ'? Paul breathes not a word about them. Will they vanish or be annihilated?

Paul's picture of the end in Thessalonians contains no judgement scene. Here, as not infrequently in his writings, Paul is simply inconsequential. In Romans 2:16 he declares that according to his gospel

'God judges the secrets of men by Jesus Christ', without specifying when and how. Elsewhere he refers to the judgement seat of Christ before which all will appear (2 Cor. 5:10). Even more explicit and harsh is his description of 'the Lord Jesus revealed from heaven with his mighty angels in flaming fire, inflicting vengeance upon those who . . . do not obey the gospel of our Lord Jesus. They shall suffer the punishment of eternal destruction' (2 Thess. 1:7–9). On the other hand, from other statements one might assume that Paul hoped for a universal conversion by the time of the arrival of the Lord. Christ will 'bring to light the things now hidden in darkness . . . Then every man will receive his commendation from God' (1 Cor. 4:5). It does not seem that Paul has made up his mind and his view oscillates between ultimate divine benevolence, a resurrection reserved only for the faithful, and the traditional division of the flock into sheep and goats with their appropriate reward and punishment.

## Jesus, the last Adam

Even more impressive than Paul's myth of the dying and resurrected Christ is his monumental mystery drama of salvation which starts with the creation and culminates in the eschatological glorification of the Lord Jesus. He has two leading actors, the first Adam and the last Adam, with several quasi-personified religious ideas (sin, death, the Law, etc.) playing supporting roles. The plot and the denouement are developed in the letters to the Romans and 1 Corinthians. On this mystery drama depends the doctrine of original sin and justification (i.e. how sin is replaced by righteousness); out of it arose both Catholicism in the wake of Augustine and Protestantism in the Lutheran mould.

For Paul it all began with the first man in Paradise. Through disobeying God's command Adam brought sin and its reward, death, on himself and his progeny (Rom. 5:12–14). Through the crucifixion and resurrection of the last Adam (Jesus), death introduced into the world by the first man was defeated and eternal life made available to those mythically united to Christ. Between the two Paul's conjuror-like handling places the Law of Moses, which he manages to depict both as a blessing and as a curse. Paul sees the mystery play of human destiny acted out by two universal protagonists, each embodying and typifying mankind as a whole, Adam and Christ.

To understand the distinctiveness of Paul's vision, it may be useful to look again at the story of Adam and Eve and so-called original sin. Genesis, chapter 3, is understood by contemporary scholarship as an explanation of how death entered the human realm. Whereas in Mesopotamian mythology man's mortality was attributed to the caprice of the gods who were unwilling to share their immortality, the Jewish Bible presented death in a framework of morality. Adam and Eve, created by God in a golden age, might have been spared the grave. It was the sin of disobedience, engineered by the principle of evil in the guise of the serpent, that led man astray through the woman, and the transgression brought with it the sentence of death for the first couple and for posterity.

Jewish tradition stoically accepted mortality as part of human destiny. While religious souls dreamed of an afterlife in which access to God remained open even beyond the grave, it was not until the second century BC and the experience by Jews of religious martyrdom under Antiochus Epiphanes' enforced Hellenization that a clearly formulated belief in eternal life first appeared. It is found in the form of bodily resurrection in chapters 7 and 10 of the Second Book of the Maccabees. Early post-biblical teachers occasionally commented on the origin of death, and as befits male chauvinists they sought to excuse Adam. The Book of Ecclesiasticus, or Wisdom of Jesus ben Sira, of the early second century BC, declares Eve to be the guilty party: 'From a woman sin has its beginning, and because of her we all die' (Ecclus. 25:24). The Greek Book of Wisdom, originating in the same century, puts the blame on the devil (identified as the serpent of Genesis): 'For God created man for incorruption, and made him in the image of his own eternity [or nature], but through the devil's envy death entered the world' (Wisd. 2:23–4). There is no trace, however, of the idea of *transmitted* sin. For Jewish thinkers sin was just part of the human make-up. The Fourth Book of Ezra, dating from the end of the first century AD, attributes to Adam an evil heart (*cor malignum*), prompting him to sin. Rabbinic literature, too, speaks of an evil inclination (*yetzer ra'*) and a good inclination (*yetzer tov*). It was the tendency towards disobedience and not actual sin that was inherited by the descendants of the first man. Likewise in the Instruction on the two Spirits in the Qumran Community Rule, antedating Paul by about one hundred and fifty years, each human being is governed by a 'spirit of truth and a spirit of injustice' (1QS 3:18–19). But again this is a hereditary impulse rather than an inherited sin, and in all three sources even the evil inclination was created by God. Consequently, none of the Jewish parallels could properly explain Paul's vision.

His grand design develops the contrast between Adam, the ancestor, and Jesus Christ, the saviour of the human race. Reduced to its simplest formulation, the first Adam is responsible for every evil affecting mankind and the last Adam for everything good. In Paul's words, 'As by one man came death, by a man has come also the resurrection of the dead. For as in Adam all die, so also in Christ shall all be made alive' (1 Cor. 15:21–2). In the Epistle to the Romans, he is more specific: 'Sin came into the world through one man and death through sin' (Rom. 5:12). Adam's sin inflicted death on him and his children – death being the punishment of sin; in other words, if every human is mortal, this is because all have sinned.

But Paul's logic works differently because he had a particular forensic or legal understanding of sin. Sin for him is the breach of a commandment, so there is no sin without the existence of a law. Adam indeed transgressed by disobeying the explicit order of God not to eat the fruit of the tree of knowledge. But until the time of the gift of the Torah on Mount Sinai more than two millennia later (according to traditional reckoning attested in the Book of Jubilees) his descendants faced no law, so they could not formally transgress. Nevertheless they all died before the promulgation of the Mosaic legislation, even the righteous like Abraham and the other patriarchs. 'Sin indeed was in the world before the Law was given, but sin is not counted where there is no law. Yet death reigned from Adam to Moses, even over those whose sins were not like the transgression of Adam' (Rom. 5:13–14). Hence in Paul's idiosyncratic perception, distinct from the general Jewish understanding of the consequences of the Paradise story, the first man's sin actually affected the nature of his descendants. To be remedied, this fundamental flaw needed more than a code of law, even a divinely dictated Law. It demanded a change in the very constitution of man. This change was effected by Christ who in his own person allegorically brought to an end 'the likeness of sinful flesh' (Rom. 8:3), i.e. the human body spiritually debilitated by Adam's transgression, and opened the era of a 'new creation' (2 Cor. 5:17; Gal. 6:15).

Why did Paul complicate the neat antithesis of the two Adams by the inclusion of the Law? It would seem that he tried to kill several birds with one stone. In the first instance, he made a theological statement proclaiming the termination of the old dispensation of sin and death and its replacement by righteousness, resurrection and life. Furthermore, he underscored the difference between the Law which demanded but did not automatically produce 'works', and 'faith' that bore the fruits of 'righteousness' both before and after the death and resurrection of the last Adam. By declaring the Law inadequate to bring about righteousness without faith, Paul theoretically justified his *political* struggle against the Jewish-Christianity of Peter and James in favour of freedom for his Gentile-Christian churches. They were liberated from the (non-moral) Mosaic commandments, and especially from circumcision, which for Paul was the epitome of the Law.

What, then, is Paul's attitude to the Law? It is equivocal throughout as he is torn between two extreme attitudes, one inherited from ancestral Judaism and the other arising from his exclusively pro-Christ, anti-legalistic, anti-Jewish (or Judaeo-Christian) polemic. His Jewish subconscious prompts him openly to declare the Law 'holy', 'spiritual', and 'good' (Rom. 7:12,14,16). However, in his debate about justification Paul speaks of 'the curse of the Law', of a 'dispensation of death carved in letters on stone', of letters that 'kill', having aroused 'sinful passions', and having turned into 'the Law of sin and death' (Gal. 3:13; 2 Cor. 3:6–7; Rom. 7:5; 8:2).

With the exception of the incidental allusion to the Law of Moses as a 'pedagogue' (a Graeco-Roman slave who accompanied a child to and from school), that is, a guide 'until Christ came' (Gal. 3:24), the Torah is generally represented as fulfilling an essentially negative role in Paul's large canvas of salvation history. To begin with, by telling man what is wrong, what he should not do, the Law informs him about sin. By instructing him that he should *not* covet, it sows the seed of covetousness in his heart and thus unwittingly induces him to sin (Rom. 7:7–11). Paul's concern was that while the Law is clear about what the Jew should avoid (or indeed perform), it does not empower him to keep away from wrongdoing (or to act justly). He faces his Jewish or Judaeo-Christian opponents with a series of questions: 'You who teach others, will you not teach yourself? While you preach against stealing, do you steal? You who say that one must not commit adultery, do you commit adultery? . . . You who boast in the Law, do you dishonour God by breaking the Law?' (Rom. 2:21–3). For him these are rhetorical questions to which the answer is a resounding yes, yes, yes.

So, contrary to the real Jesus who found in the Torah of God his supreme source of religious inspiration, Paul's judgement of the Law is mostly critical. What is more, even the Law's positive aspects, which inspired Jews to attempt to live a godly life, are described as lacking the force to transform cold commandments into holy deeds. The mere knowledge of the duty to love one's neighbour does not necessarily lead to charitable behaviour. For Paul, righteousness and justification primarily spring not from doing but from believing, not from 'works' but from faith. Or as he states with a kind of self-mocking pride, 'We . . . who are Jews by birth and not Gentile sinners, yet who know that a man is not justified by works of the Law but through faith in Jesus Christ, even we have believed in Christ Jesus, in order to be justified by faith in Christ, and not by works of the Law' (Gal. 2:15–16).

Paul found in his interpretation of the story of Abraham the ultimate proof that faith-trust – the biblical *emunah*, reliance on divine benevolence and mercy – and not 'works' makes a man acceptable to God (Rom. 4:1–3). It was because of the Patriarch's total confidence in the implausible divine promise of a son in his and his wife's extreme old age that he was reckoned righteous, and not on account of the observance of some precept. Of course, there cannot be question here of commandments of the Mosaic Law as Abraham lived half a millennium before Moses. In fact, what Paul seeks to exclude from consideration is the quintessential 'work' of the Law, circumcision, the *bête noire* of his anti-Judaizing polemic. It was not the later act of severing his foreskin, however painfully meritorious in a man aged ninety-nine years (Gen. 17:24), that made him just, but his earlier unconditional trust in God's word (Gen. 15:6). Paul could not be more repetitively emphatic. 'We say that faith was reckoned to Abraham as righteousness. How then was it reckoned to him? Was it *before* or after he was circumcised? It was not after, but *before* he was circumcised. He received circumcision as a sign or seal of the righteousness which he had by faith while he was still uncircumcised. The purpose was to make him the father of all who believe without being circumcised . . . and likewise the father of the circumcised who are not merely circumcised but also follow the example of the faith which our father Abraham had *before* he was circumcised' (Rom. 4:9–12).

From Moses to the last Adam, Paul argues, there was the mostly inefficient interim regime of the Law. By the time of the redeeming death and resurrection of Christ this Law had run its course. In Paul's words, 'Christ is the end of the Law that everyone who has faith may be justified' (Rom. 10:4). In a summary of his complex imagery, he manages to make his meandering reasoning run its full course: 'As one man's trespass led to condemnation for all men, so one man's act of righteousness leads to acquittal and life for all men . . . Law came in, to increase the trespass; but where sin increased, grace abounded all the more, so that, as sin reigned in death, grace also might reign through righteousness to eternal life through Jesus Christ our Lord' (Rom. 5:18–21).

## Christ and worship in Paul

The Pauline myth of redemption, though consistently structured, is essentially supra-rational, and although designed with vaguely historical strokes as the culmination of a salvation mystery, the last Adam repairing the harm caused by the first, it is painted with faint, almost indistinguishable colours. The Jesus of Paul has no earthly identity, he is without human face or character. And since no evidence whatever is extant to suggest that his Christians had a Gospel or Gospels at their disposal – our written Gospels are all post-Pauline – Paul and his church members could seek only a spiritual-mystical encounter with the death and resurrection of a superterrestrial, meta-historical being.

How, then, does this Christ fit into the worship of Paul's churches? He is not the object of prayer; prayer is always addressed to God (cf. above pp. 79–80). Christ is rather the channel which carries the Christians' supplications or thank-offerings to the Father; he is as it were the powerhouse of Pauline piety. Paul quotes the proclamation *Kurios Iesous*, 'Jesus is Lord', and himself uses the Aramaic eschatological exclamation *Maran atha*, 'Our Lord has come' or *Marana ta*, 'Come, our Lord' (1 Cor. 12:3; 16:22; cf. Rev. 22:20), which is also included in the first-century AD liturgical work, the *Didache* or Doctrine of the Twelve Apostles (10:6).

Luckily a fairly detailed description of worship in the church of Corinth founded by Paul has survived, and it can no doubt be safely applied to worship organized by Paul in house churches, homes of better-off Christians such as Aquila and Prisca, Gaius and Nympha (Rom. 16:5,23; Col. 4:15), in his various communities in Asia Minor, Greece and Rome. Its framework was a communal meal during which the participants recalled the death of Christ in the form of a symbolical re-enactment of the Lord's supper in remembrance of him. Without indicating how frequently this ritual was performed, Paul clarified its aim, which was to 'proclaim the Lord's death until he comes' (1 Cor. 11:23–6), i.e. that the eucharistic meal was endowed with the significance of an eschatological reminder. He also insisted on good order as well as on an appropriate religious atmosphere, and castigated shortcomings on both counts.

In the first instance Paul had to legislate about headgear. It may surprise present-day Jewish readers that Paul ordered male worshippers to be bare-headed when praying in the church (1 Cor. 11:7). In fact for many centuries Jewish custom varied, and the compulsory covering of the head among the Orthodox did not become a general rule until the Middle Ages. By contrast, Paul would not tolerate a woman in church without a headdress; he considered a female person without a veil similar to one whose hair had been shaved off (1 Cor. 11:6). In addition to constituting an impropriety in human society, a woman's fully displayed hair was condemned as a potential temptation for susceptible angels (1 Cor. 11:10)! It would seem that the old myth preserved in Genesis, chapter 6, and in the Book of Enoch about heavenly beings ('sons of god' = angels) falling for the charms of pretty women still had a meaning for Paul, who as is well known was rather neurotic in matters relating to sex. He also strictly forbade women to open their mouths in church; if they needed some information, they could always ask their husbands (1 Cor. 14:34–5). It never occurred to him that the holy spirit might also inspire a female worshipper.

He had unexpectedly harsh words to say about the behaviour of the congregation at the common table. Instead of partaking in one and the same meal served for all, groups tended to form separate companies and have their own food and drink. So the rich showed off and humiliated the poor. Some even overindulged ('one is hungry and another is *drunk*', 1 Cor. 11:21). This was scandalous and disrespectful retrospectively towards the death, and prospectively towards the second coming of the Lord.

It is noteworthy that at these gatherings we discover no hint of the Jewish custom of reading extracts of Holy Scripture followed by a sermon or homily, so commonly attested in synagogues (see Chapter 5). Additional rules of good conduct reveal further facets of the worship performed in the primitive church. Apart from the communal meal already outlined, the cult assembly described by Paul in 1 Corinthians 12 and 14 is a kind of cross, if I may use contemporary terms of comparison, between a Pentecostal service and a Quaker meeting. The various acts of worship were charismatic, consisting of inspirational utterances of wisdom, knowledge and faith. The gift of discrimination between the words of the spirit of God and the evil spirit reminds one of the Instruction on the two spirits in the Dead Sea Scrolls (1QS 3:12–4:25) listing the works of truth and the works of falsehood. Healings and miracles, so prominent in the Gospels and in the Acts, are underemphasized by Paul, although according to the Acts of the Apostles he himself is credited with charismatic cures and exorcisms.

The two chief spiritual gifts which preoccupied him were prophecy, i.e. inspired, improvised and intelligible teaching of which he approved, and *glossolalia* or incomprehensible 'speaking in tongues', which was impressive, popular, but in Paul's judgement unproductive unless it was explained by another charismatic who had the gift of interpretation. The kind of *glossolalia* to which Paul refers was different from the 'speaking in other tongues' mentioned in Acts in connection with the apostles preaching on the first Pentecost (Acts 2:4–11). The *glossolalia* in the Pauline churches consisted of ecstatic noises presumed to be prayers to God, possibly 'in the tongue of angels' (1 Cor. 13:1), but meaningless to the uninitiated. It was a cause of disturbance to other worshippers and of possible scandal to visiting outsiders. 'If ...

unbelievers enter, will they not say that you are mad?' (1 Cor. 14:23). Hence Paul decided to reduce *glossolalia* to a minimum of two or three performances at one meeting and on condition that an interpreter was available. Otherwise 'let each of them keep silence in church and speak to himself and to God' (1 Cor. 14:28). Finally, as a sensible pastor, in preference to showy exhibitions Paul recommended to the faithful the basic virtues of faith, hope and especially love (1 Cor. 13:13). By love he meant the love of the neighbour which is 'not jealous or boastful . . . arrogant or rude . . . irritable or resentful' but is 'patient and kind', 'bears all things, believes in all things, hopes all things, endures all things' (1 Cor. 13:4–7). In short, Paul quite naturally fell back on essential religious attitudes taught by Judaism and by Jesus.

As an appendix to Paul's outline of primitive Christian worship, it should be noted that his perception of Jesus, and *a fortiori* of God the Father, in not too anthropomorphic terms accounts for a twist in his religious orientation which distances him from the teaching and practice of Jesus and his immediate followers.

The fundamental direction of the religion observed and taught by Jesus was theocentric: in the traditional Jewish mould, he and his Galilean disciples endeavoured to be imitators of God. 'Be perfect as your heavenly Father is perfect' (Matt. 5:48), Jesus enjoined them. With a single exception in the inauthentic Epistle to the Ephesians (5:1), such direct imitation of God is absent from the letters of Paul. As next best he could have advised his followers to copy the example of Christ, but since there is little concrete about the Jesus of Paul, he instructed his novice Gentile Christians to follow his own example or the example of his close companions, who modelled themselves on Paul (1 Thess. 1:6). In the first letter to the Corinthians Paul set himself as the focal point: 'Be imitators of me, as I am of Christ' (1 Cor. 11:1), and with even more emphasis he exhorted the faithful, 'I urge you then, be imitators of me' (1 Cor. 4:16).

Although pedagogically this was sound counsel to give the religiously untrained Corinthians, Paul's recommendation to them to do as he himself did established a new religious stance in which the worshipper found himself at one remove from Christ and at two removes from God. With a distant Father and a faceless Christ Paul's advice was reassuring for diffident new Christians; they could observe at close quarters someone they could trust. Thus began a trend, still conspicuous in Catholic and Orthodox Christianity, to introduce models, mediators and intercessors between the believer and God. These intermediaries were Christ and Paul, and later (under Johannine inspiration) Mary, the mother of Jesus, who in some popular quarters of Christendom tended to be treated as a quasi goddess, almost as a fourth person of a holy quaternity.[4] They were joined in the early centuries of the church by the martyrs, and subsequently by the ever increasing number of saints. Of the latter, Pope John Paul II alone has managed to add about a thousand new names to their register, turning the Vatican, as one wit remarked, into a beatification and canonization factory. Incidentally, it is quite amusing that St Paul, the bastion of the Reformation (surely we must not call him its patron saint!), appears to be responsible for the legitimization of go-betweens, leading to that pet hatred of the Protestants, the cult of saints, and above all to 'Mariolatry', reckoned by them to be the worst corruption of 'popery'.

Having considered the bond in Paul's thought between Christ and divine worship, we can examine the manner in which he connected Jesus to the church and to individual church members. By now readers will have guessed that the relationship envisaged by Paul was of an allegorical, symbolical and mystical character. His understanding of the eucharist provides the most helpful point of departure. The bread of the communal meal, the symbolical body of Christ, allegorically transforms the many who eat it in the church into a single mystical body (1 Cor. 10:17).

When he had to correct excesses, Paul was able to handle his people in a practical and down-to-earth manner, recommending in the famous hymn to charity the old-fashioned biblical love of the neighbour as the ultimate yardstick of genuine piety; yet in his visionary mind he always sought a deeper, 'mythical' solution to the complexities of religious existence. His meditation on the fate of Christ did not induce in him primarily a moral reshaping of the self, but rather a mystical re-enactment of the destiny of Jesus in one's own body. For Paul, life

---

4. Sarcasm apart, two of the latest *ex cathedra* doctrinal definitions of the Roman Catholic church relate to Mary: the dogmas of the Immaculate Conception (1870) and the Assumption (1950).

was lived as a recurrent mythical dying and rising with Christ every day (1 Cor. 15:30–32).

So the aim of ordinary daily existence, as well as of the special rites of baptism and the eucharist, was to effect a mystical union between the body of the faithful and that of Christ on two levels. 'Do you not know that your bodies are members of Christ?' (1 Cor. 6:15). Mysteriously, individual Christians were seen as coalescing into the one spiritual frame of the Lord. No doubt for the non-believer in antiquity or in any age Paul's talk sounded like empty words, but the Pauline 'myth' has always had an extraordinary power to move those who are inspired by faith. The outcome of this mystical union with the Lord was that Christians belonged to Jesus Christ, first allegorically as babes, then as children and finally as adults (Rom. 1:6; 1 Cor. 3:1; 13:11). They had the mind and the spirit of Christ and emitted his 'aroma' (1 Cor. 2:16; Rom. 8:9; 2 Cor. 2:15). In simple terms, through pertaining to Christ they belonged to God: 'You are the body of Christ and individually members of it' (1 Cor. 12:27); 'You are Christ's and Christ is God's' (1 Cor. 3:23). This is the first level of mystical union.

The second level is the corollary of the first. By becoming mythically part of the body of Christ, the baptized are also united to each other and form the spiritual body of the church. The relationship between the body and its members is one of Paul's familiar metaphors. 'For just as the body is one and has many members, and all the members of the body, though many, are one body, so it is with Christ. For by one spirit we were all baptized into one body' (1 Cor. 12:12–13). This union of believers as members of Christ's body once and for all dispenses with such basic distinctions as Jew and Gentile, free man and slave, man and woman. In more practical terms Paul deduced from it a moral lesson, namely that irrespective of their status in secular society Christians were of equal importance before God and had to treat each other as such. 'God has so composed the body, giving the greater honour to the inferior part, that there may be no discord in the body, but that the members may have the same care for one another. If one member suffers, all suffer; if one member is honoured, all rejoice together' (1 Cor. 12:24–6). Thus the necessity of harmony and love among members of the community springs from their forming simultaneously the body of Christ and the body of the church. Indeed, using yet another metaphor, Paul compares the connection between the members of the church and Christ to the marriage bond: 'I betrothed you to Christ to present you as a pure bride to her one husband' (2 Cor. 11:2).[5]

Paul like John stresses the symbolical union between believers, Christ and God, but their approaches are very different. For John the basis of the union rests on the 'equality' of Father and Son, and their mutual indwelling in which Christians secondarily participate: Father, Son and the faithful all being in one another. For Paul, on the other hand, the bond between Jesus and the members of the church resides in the participation in Christ's death and resurrection. Through his rising from the dead Jesus was elevated to the dignity of Son of God and through their faith in the Son of God his followers became the adoptive children of the Father.

## The church of Christ according to Paul

Judged by ordinary human wisdom the abstract and mystical-mythical theology of Paul combined with his ardent belief in the imminence of the return of Christ had only a very limited chance of succeeding, especially as it was addressed to a religiously unsophisticated Greek audience which, apart from a small number of better-off merchants and artisans, and the odd official like Eratus, the city treasurer of Corinth (Rom. 16:23), was largely recruited from the lower classes of society. Yet compared with the ultimately failed ministry of Peter, James and the other apostles among the Jews, Paul's Gentile Christian-

---

5. The marriage metaphor is developed more fully in the deutero-Pauline letter to the Ephesians in order to emphasize the importance of marital love among Christians. 'Husbands should love their wives as their own bodies . . . For no man hates his own flesh, but nourishes and cherishes it, as Christ does the church, because we are members of his body. For this reason a man shall leave his father and mother and be joined to his wife, and the two shall become one flesh. This mystery is a profound one, and I am saying that it refers to Christ and the church' (Eph. 5:25-32). The same epistle includes further 'church–body' metaphors of which Eph. 2:19-20 is the most striking: 'You are fellow citizens with the saints [angels] and members of the household of God, built upon the foundation of the apostles and prophets, Christ Jesus being the chief cornerstone in whom the whole structure is joined together.'

ity turned out to be a lasting success. The secret of this success lies, I believe, in the influence of the Pauline 'myth' seen as a spiritual liberation by Christ and as an equal treatment granted to the redeemed, whether great or humble, by their divine Father in the name of the Lord Jesus Christ. Though impervious to rational proof, Paul's gospel made a greater impact than the Judaeo-Christian attempt at demonstrating from biblical exegesis that Jesus was the Messiah promised to the people of Israel.

However, the powerful impact on simple souls of Paul's mystery of salvation would not account by itself, especially in an atmosphere of a burning eschatological expectation, for the consolidation, growth and lasting survival of infant Christianity in the uncongenial surroundings of the Graeco-Roman world. For this we have to admire the organizational talent and pastoral zeal of Paul and his companions. Two of these, Timothy, Paul's favourite disciple, and Titus, are the addressees of the pastoral letters usually held to be deutero-Pauline, i.e. written after the death of Paul. The others – unless the Luke referred to in the letters to Philemon and 2 Timothy is actually the author of the third Gospel and the Acts of the Apostles – are slightly more than names. Silvanus was an early companion, mentioned in the letters to the Thessalonians; Sosthenes, Apollos and Aquila figure in 1 Corinthians, and Mark, Aristarchos and Demas in Philemon. Christianity is probably more indebted to these shadowy co-workers of Paul than most people imagine.

Apart from an incidental allusion to the existence of bishops and deacons in a church founded by Paul (Phil. 1:1), we learn nothing about such officials in the authentic corpus of his writings. However, from the post-Pauline first Epistle to Timothy and the letter to Titus, we gain a useful insight into the qualities required of bishops, presbyters (or priests), deacons and widows or deaconesses, and into their respective duties. Since the detailed organization described in the pastoral letters is likely to belong to a period in which eschatological expectation was already on the wane, it probably corresponds to the decades which followed the death of Paul in the late sixties (cf. 1 Tim. 3:1–10; 5:9–12; Titus 1:5–11).

The functions of the various church leaders can be only approximately determined. It is odd that not a single word is said about their role in conducting the Christian cult. But perhaps in those early days the eucharist was genuinely a community celebration in which there was no need for specific clergy to take part. Baptism could be administered by any Christian. Paul emphatically stated that he was not sent by Christ to baptize, but to preach the gospel, and that he administered baptism only to two men, Crispus and Gaius, and also, he suddenly remembered, to the household of Stephanas (1 Cor. 1:14, 16).

We learn that a bishop, described as 'God's steward' (Titus 1:7), had a double obligation. First of all he had to be an 'apt teacher' of 'sound doctrine' and a skilful polemist against 'empty talkers and deceivers' (1 Tim. 3:2; Titus 1:9). Surprisingly, the chief culprits in this group came not from the ranks of heretics or Gnostics, but from Jewish Christians, ironically referred to as the 'circumcision party', insisting on the strict observance of the Mosaic Law even by baptized non-Jews (Titus 1:10). The bishop's second job was to 'care for God's church' (1 Tim. 3:5) as pastor or shepherd. Since Jewish communities were governed by a council of elders, for the nearest parallel to such an individual religious superior we have to look at the description of the Essene overseer or guardian in the Qumran Damascus Document. 'This is the rule for the Guardian of the camp. He shall instruct the Congregation in the works of God. He shall cause them to consider His mighty deeds and shall recount all the happenings of eternity to them [according to] their [ex]planation. He shall love them as a father loves his children, and shall carry them in all their distress like a shepherd his sheep. He shall loosen all the fetters that bind them that in his Congregation there may be none that are oppressed or broken' (CD xiii. 7–10). It is quite possible that the office of the Pauline bishop was modelled on such an Essene spiritual leader.

The next figure in the ecclesiastical hierarchy is the presbyter, whose explicit function was to preach and teach (1 Tim. 5:17); but implicitly he was also in charge of the pastoral care of the local congregation (Titus 1:6). The presbyters (or priests) seem to have been the helpers of the bishop.

The third male office was occupied by the deacons. They are not given a clear job description in 1 Timothy. According to the Acts of the Apostles, deacons were charity workers in the church (Acts 6:2).

The mention of a deaconess, Phoebe (Rom. 16:1), would suggest that formal involvement in the field of good works was open to women. Indeed, it is likely that the widows described in 1 Timothy represent a specific group of older ladies chosen, it seems, to look after the needs of the humbler members of the community since only those who had previously excelled in every kind of good deed could be selected for this role (1 Tim. 5:10). These 'church' widows, as distinct from ordinary ones, had to pledge themselves not to remarry.

No one was eligible for a church appointment unless he or she was found to possess certain moral qualities. Curiously, celibacy was not among them despite the fact that Paul himself boasted that unlike Peter and the other apostles, he had preached the gospel without being accompanied by a wife (1 Cor. 9:5). Bishop, presbyter and deacon had to be the 'husband of one wife', and the widow 'the [former] wife of one husband'; since polygamy was out of the question in Christian circles this must mean that they were married only once. The fact of having successfully run a family, raised children and kept them under control was seen as a guarantee that they would be competent shepherds, ministers and helpers in the church (1 Tim. 3:2, 12; 5:9; Titus 1:6). A positive requirement for male candidates was first and foremost a hospitable temperament, as well as a sensible, blameless, dignified, upright and holy personality capable of exercising self-control in tense situations. In the case of the widows, they had to be over sixty years of age and noted for their devotion to good deeds and charitable actions, such as 'washing the feet of the saints' and bringing relief to the afflicted. Younger widows were excluded: they were thought to be too fickle: 'When they grow wanton against Christ they desire to marry' (1 Tim. 5:11)!

Negatively, those in charge of selecting bishops and deacons had to make sure that candidates known as drunkards were rejected. As their exclusion is mentioned several times (1 Tim. 3:3, 8; Titus 1:7), addiction to 'too much wine' must have been widespread, as one might deduce from Paul's mention of inebriated partakers of the eucharistic meal in Corinth. Other negative traits to watch out for were quick temper, violence, quarrelsomeness and arrogance, and also – bearing in mind that bishops handled charitable funds – love of money.

The solid, carefully planned infrastructure which the builders of the Pauline communities devised and put into practice accounts without any doubt for the smooth development and enduring success of Paul's Gentile church in the Graeco-Roman world. Divorced from Judaism and even in a sense from the piety of Jesus, this well-organized institution dominated by the image of Paul's otherworldly Christ-Redeemer in time blended with the more subtle and lofty Johannine ideal of the 'divinization' of mankind. This new religion soon disposed of what remained of Paul's and Jesus' eschatological enthusiasm and evolved in the centuries that followed into a church run by bishops and councils to form the Christianity of late antiquity, the Middle Ages and modern times.

# APPENDIX:
## SPECIAL FEATURES OF JESUS IN THE DEUTERO-PAULINE LETTERS

To complete the broader 'Pauline' portrait of Jesus, I will sketch some of the additional features garnered from letters which most scholars consider as inauthentic, that is to say not written by Paul himself but by his disciples and heirs, such as the letters to the Ephesians and the Colossians, and especially the Epistle to the Hebrews.

## Christ as high priest

The author of the Epistle to the Hebrews breaks new ground by describing Jesus as high priest. Paul, while aware of Temple sacrifice imagery such as expiation by the blood of an animal, preferred in dealing with the death of Christ on the cross to envisage it in terms of human typology. His explicit thought followed the first and the last Adam, but implicitly he also took his inspiration from the self-offering of Isaac.

The Epistle to the Hebrews makes of Christ a heavenly spiritual pontiff, elevated far above the Jewish high priests who officiated in the earthly sanctuary in Jerusalem. Jesus is said to resemble the mysterious Melchizedek, the priest-king of Salem (Gen. 14), who was superior to Abraham whom he blessed, who lacked 'father or mother or genealogy' (Heb. 7:3) – Genesis being silent on his family tree – and who was expected to remain a priest for ever.

As Christ was superior to the Jewish high priests, his sacrifice was also incomparably greater than those performed at the altar in Jerusalem. Being the supreme expiator for sin, he officiated on the eschatological Day of Atonement. That the writer of Hebrews had the sacrosanct feast of Yom Kippur in mind is obvious from his remark concerning the high priest entering the inner shrine (Heb. 6:19–20), which he did once a year on that particular day. The author emphasized that Jesus, the high priest, offered expiation for the whole of mankind, and not only for the Jews, and did so not with 'the blood of goats and calves but his own blood' (Heb. 9:12). Moreover, this sacrificial offering took place in the heavenly sanctuary, not in a man-made temple, and unlike the ceremony of the Day of Atonement which had to be repeated year after year, Christ's sacrifice was made only once (Heb. 9:24–5).

While the idea of an eternally effective redemptive act is genuinely Paul's, the detailed Temple symbolism is peculiar to the writer of Hebrews. Some of the features pre-existed in intertestamental Judaism. The pontifical figure and the introduction of a parentless Melchizedek possess their parallels in the Dead Sea Scrolls in the Messiah of Aaron or Priest Messiah, as well as the heavenly Melchizedek, an angelic character with a redemptive role who was linked to the Day of Atonement (cf. 1QS 9:11; 11Q Melch). They may have influenced the author of Hebrews.

In spite of its brilliance from the literary point of view, the general ideology of the Epistle to the Hebrews has left no deep mark on later New Testament thought or on Christian theology in general. The doctrine of the church on atonement echoes the genuine Paul rather than the stylish writer of Hebrews.

## Steps towards the deification of Christ

As I have stressed, Paul stops short of declaring Jesus divine. It was his resurrection from the dead that caused the Jewish man Jesus to be appointed, named and designated Son of God. The deutero-Pauline writers do their best to surpass Paul and reach out towards Johannine heights.

Paul described Christ as the 'likeness', or icon, of God (2 Cor. 4:4), but while he no doubt used the term significantly, it cannot be taken as being anywhere close to inferring divinity; strictly speaking it can be applied to the first Adam created in the image and likeness of God (Gen. 1:26–7). But Paul's heirs far exceeded their master, granting Christ a pre-existence from eternity and associating him with the work of the creation.

The opening verses of the Epistle to the Hebrews, which – unlike the other letters of Paul – plainly addressed a Hellenistic *Jewish* audience, express themselves so clearly that commentary is almost superfluous. 'In many and various ways God spoke of old to our fathers by the prophets; but in these last days he has spoken to us by a Son, whom he appointed the heir of all things, *through whom also he created the world*. He reflects *the glory of God* and bears *the very stamp of his nature, upholding the universe by his word of power*' (Heb. 1:1–3).

The writer of the letter to the Colossians, who was fighting against early Gnostic tendencies, sketched a similar picture, mystical in tone. 'He [God] has delivered us from the dominion of darkness and transferred us to the kingdom of his beloved Son, in whom we have redemption and forgiveness of sins.' Here follows a hymnic exaltation (Col. 1:13–19):

> 'He is the *image of the invisible God*,
> the *first-born of all the creation*;
> for *in him all things were created*,
> in heaven and on earth,
> visible and invisible,
> whether thrones or dominions
> or principalities or authorities.
> All things were created through him and for him.
> He is before all things
> and *in him all things hold together* . . .
> For in him all the *fullness of God* was pleased to dwell.

It is impossible not to recognize the similarity between these descriptions and the prologue of the Fourth Gospel. But it is equally impossible in the present state of New Testament research to determine with any degree of certainty whether these post-Pauline authors, writing at the turn of the first century, slightly anticipate and so possibly influence John, or whether they echo ideas which are on the point of being, or have just been, crystallized in the Fourth Gospel.

## Postscript: The Jesus image in the letters of Jude, Peter and James

Of the seven so-called 'catholic' or universal letters, that is, apostolic circulars addressed to churches in general and not to any named person or community, the three Johannine epistles have already been discussed. None of the remaining four, Jude, 1 and 2 Peter, and James, includes anything substantial or novel concerning the representation of Jesus. Since they are all post-Pauline, and in two of them Paul is mentioned either explicitly or implicitly, I hope I will be excused for treating these epistles summarily as a postscript to this chapter devoted to Paul.

The *Letter of Jude* claims to be written by 'Jude, a servant of Jesus Christ and brother of James', i.e. another of the four brothers of Jesus listed in the Synoptic Gospels (Mark 6:3; Matt. 13:55). Nothing in the brief note confirms this claim, and in an age in which pseudonyms were fashionable the use of a pen name by no means counted as a lie. The letter, generally dated to *c.* AD 100 and intended as a polemic against false teachers, is more famous for its uncommon interest in non-biblical Jewish literature (it cites the first Book of Enoch and the Assumption of Moses) than for its concern with the portrait of Jesus to which in fact it contributes nothing.

The *First Letter of Peter*, addressed to persecuted Christian communities, is also held by almost every New Testament expert to be pseudonymous, that is to say, not to be the work of the apostle Peter. By the turn of the first century AD apostolic authorship, real or fictitious, was a must if a text were to acquire authoritative status. Hence the dubious Johns, Judes, Peters and Jameses. But the Greek of 1 Peter gives the game away: it is far too good to be the work of an 'uneducated and common' Galilean fisherman (Acts 4:13). Further, the persecution presupposed in it cannot have taken place before the reign of the emperor Domitian (AD 81–96), by which time according to church tradition Simon-Peter-Cephas was no longer alive. He is believed to have been martyred under Nero, i.e. before AD 68. 1 Peter repeats Paul's doctrine of redemption by the blood of Christ (1:2, 19) and even echoes the Johannine idea of pre-existence in asserting that Christ was 'destined before the foundation of the world but was made manifest at the end of the times' (1:20).

The letter adds one extraordinary detail to the story of Jesus. Half-mythically, half-exegetically it refers to a journey 'in spirit' of the crucified Christ to the underworld to preach to the 'spirits in prison' who had been languishing there since the time of Noah's flood! So like Orpheus in Greek mythology, Christ too paid a visit to Hades. Where does this curious idea spring from? The Bible (Gen. 6) and related Jewish interpretative traditions report that the general wickedness of the inhabitants of the earth which was punished by the flood was brought about by the fallen angels, or 'sons of God', and their semi-human offspring, the 'giants'. However, divine justice would not destroy even this worst-ever generation without giving it a last chance to mend its ways. So God appointed Noah as a preacher or 'herald of righteousness' (2 Pet. 2:5) to summon everyone to conversion. However, apart from his own family, no one would listen; they all perished except Noah and his wife, their three sons and three daughters-in-law who entered the ark. Nevertheless, with the gospel proclaimed to them by Christ before his resurrection, the gaoled spirits were granted a second chance to repent (1 Pet. 3:18–21; 4:6).

This strange account of Jesus' visit to the nether world gained unexpected entry into Christian belief through the Western form of the Apostles' Creed which in its original Latin formulation runs: '*crucifixus, mortuus et sepultus, descendit ad infera*' – crucified, dead and buried, he descended to hell. However, despite the clear meaning of 1 Peter, theologians found unpalatable the idea that Christ liberated souls from hell. Therefore they transformed the infernal prison into a neutral territory of limbo, where the saints of the Old Testament, the patriarchs and the prophets, had been relegated until the good news of their redemption was announced to them by Christ.

The *Second Letter of Peter*, far from being the work of the senior apostle of Jesus, is probably the most recent composition in the New

Testament, dating to AD 125 if not later. Literary analysis shows that it was composed *after* the Letter of Jude (written around AD 100) on which it visibly depends. Furthermore the document testifies to a conspicuous disenchantment in the ranks of the faithful caused by the prolonged delay of the return of Christ. The author himself did not expect to witness the Parousia (2 Pet. 1:14–15). The allusions to a mass of false teachings hint at the growth of Gnosticism, which points to the second century. Finally, the letters of Paul, already forming a literary corpus, are referred to as 'Scripture' (3:15–16). In all the other books of the New Testament, and even in later Christianity, only the Old Testament bears this title.

2 Peter adds nothing more to the New Testament image of Christ. Its negative input to a better understanding of the changing faces of Jesus consists in pouring cold water on, and practically extinguishing, the last cinders of eschatological urgency so characteristic of the religion of the Galilean master. The author, writing about a hundred years after Jesus, was persuaded to venture into this slippery arena because of the sarcastic remarks made by Christian sceptics of his time: 'Where is the promise of his [Christ's] coming? For ever since the fathers fell asleep, all things have continued as they were from the beginning of the creation' (2 Pet. 3:4). Pseudo-Peter offers a twofold evasive answer: that on the one hand time seen from God's point of view differs from human reckoning, and that on the other hand the postponement of the return of Christ should be seen as a favour, an extra period granted for turning away from sin. 'But do not ignore this one fact, beloved, that with the Lord one day is as a thousand years, and a thousand years as one day. The Lord is not slow about his promise as some count slowness, but is forbearing toward you, not wishing that any should perish, but that all should reach repentance. But the day of the Lord will come like a thief . . .' (2 Pet. 3:8–10). This justification is similar to the argument put forward by the author of the Qumran Commentary on Habakkuk, writing to sectarians tired of waiting for the day of the Lord to come, also about a century after the Teacher of Righteousness of the Dead Sea sect. Explaining Habakkuk 2:3, 'If it [the end] tarries, wait for it, for it shall surely come and not be late', he wrote: 'Interpreted, this concerns the men of truth who keep the Law, whose hands shall not slacken in the service of truth when the

final age is prolonged. For all the ages of God reach their appointed end as he determines for them in the mysteries of his wisdom' (1QpHab 7:9–14). Intense eschatological expectation could not be sustained for any length of time in a closed religious community, whether the Essene sect or the Christian church. Apocalyptic fervour gave way to institutional certainty, or, if I may quote freely Alfred Loisy's half-witty, half-serious remark, 'The first Christians expected the return of Christ, but it was the church that arrived instead.'

The *Letter of James* has given many a headache to Christian interpreters from the time of the Reformation to the present day. James, 'a servant of God and of the Lord Jesus Christ', is generally taken to be James 'the brother of the Lord', the leading Jewish-Christian apostle according to the book of Acts. For most critical scholars James is a pseudonym and they date the epistle to the end of the first century AD. Their refusal to attribute it to the brother of Jesus is based on the excellent Greek of the author and on the absence of any mention of compulsory circumcision and of Jewish ritual observances among Christians, the hallmarks of James and his 'circumcision party' according to Paul and his circle. In fact, the author of the letter emphasizes only the moral precepts of the Ten Commandments, which he describes as the law of liberty granted by the divine King (Jas. 2:8–13). Be this as it may, the epistle which is likely to have originated in the last third of the first century AD, can at best indirectly be ascribed to James, who was stoned to death in AD 62. Although it yields hardly any information regarding Jesus himself, it is nevertheless highly significant for our inquiry because it provides a bridge linking the Johannine-Pauline religion devised for Gentile believers to the Judaeo-Christianity of Acts and the Synoptic Gospels.

It should be underlined that James's message is entirely God-centred: Jesus stands very much in the background. The prayers are directed to God the Father; it is he who is blessed, and to whom the believer submits himself. The God of James bears the 'honourable name' of the God of Judaism (Jas. 2:7; cf. 1QS 6:27); he *is* the God of Judaism. His pure and undefiled worship is defined throughout the letter in ethical terms: visiting orphans and widows in their affliction, and living a good life in the meekness of wisdom (Jas. 1:27; 3:13). All this is performed in the framework of 'the faith of our Lord Jesus Christ, the

Lord of glory' and intensified by the lively prospect of his impending return (5:7–9). Healing the sick by means of oil (cf. Mark 6:13) in the name of Jesus, accompanied by the forgiveness of sins (Jas. 5:13–15) represents a piety characterized by efficient (miracle-working) prayer. Typical of Judaeo-Christianity, it is the prophet Elijah who is proposed as the example to contemplate: 'He prayed fervently that it might not rain and for three years and six months it did not rain. Then he prayed again and the heaven gave rain, and the earth brought forth its fruit' (Jas. 5:17–18). As we shall see, James echoes here the early Jewish-Christians in Acts and beyond them the Jesus of the Synoptic Gospels.

It is hardly surprising that the letter of James has always filled theologians with unease. In near desperation, some have argued that it is really a Jewish document which was later revised and superficially glossed over by a Christian editor. The main thorn in the interpreters' flesh is James's diatribe against one of the main teachings of Paul, although he does not actually name him. Here again – and this truly shows the magnitude of the unease – contemporary ecclesiastical spokesmen make hopeless efforts to alleviate the problem by suggesting that James's criticism is directed against a distorted version of Pauline theology propounded by heretics, and not against the genuine teaching of Paul, namely that justification comes from faith and not from the practice of the Law.

But look at James's argument. 'What does it profit, my brethren, if a man say he has faith but has no work? Can his faith save him? If a brother or sister is ill-clad and in lack of daily food, and one of you says to them, "Go in peace, be warmed and filled", without giving them the things needed for the body, what does it profit? *So faith, by itself, if it has no works, is dead* ... Was not Abraham our father justified by works, when he offered his son Isaac upon the altar? You see that faith was active along with his works, and faith was completed by works, and the Scripture was fulfilled which says, "Abraham believed in God, and it was reckoned to him as righteousness"; and he was called the friend of God. *You see that a man is justified by works and not by faith alone*' (Jas. 2:14–24).

In the past, Luther found this flimsy ('strawy') letter intolerable on account of its teaching. Today many Christian biblical scholars cannot stomach the idea of an open doctrinal conflict in Holy Scripture between two apostles of Christ. But we know from Paul that his conflict with the Judaizers, the 'circumcision party', was all too genuine, and we shall learn more about it when examining the account of the real beginnings of the Christian church given in the Acts of the Apostles.

# 5

# The Jesus of the Acts of the Apostles:
# Prophet, Lord and Christ

If we move away from John's mystical vision of the divine Christ, and from Paul's mystery drama of salvation, so familiar to those whose image of Jesus is conditioned by traditional Christianity, and look rather for the way the early adherents of the Jesus movement conceived of their crucified Master, our perspective undergoes a stupendous sea change. Instead of John's eternal Son temporarily manifest in a first-century Jew, or of Paul's dying and resurrected Saviour redeeming and vivifying mankind, we encounter in the Acts of the Apostles a Galilean prophet elevated by God to the dignity of Lord and Christ after raising him from the dead.

Let me mention by way of introductory comment that the Acts of the Apostles forms the second half of a historical narrative which starts with the life of Jesus in the third Gospel. The Gospel of Luke ends with the ascension of the risen Jesus to heaven on Easter Sunday, the very day of his resurrection. The author of the Acts picks up the thread left by Luke, but dates the Ascension forty days later (Luke 24:50–51; Acts 1:6–11). Both writings are dedicated to the same person, the otherwise unknown Theophilus (Luke 1:3; Acts 1:1), and Acts 1:1 qualifies the Gospel as 'the first book' (of Luke). The Acts furnishes a fairly detailed report on the progress of the Jesus movement from about AD 30 to the early sixties in Palestine and Syria, where the members of the new group were first given the name of Messianists or *Christians* (11:26),[1] and on the evangelizing mission of Paul through

---

1. Later we read that King Agrippa II semi-jokingly remarked to Paul, 'In a short time you think to make me a Christian!' (26:28). The only other use of the term outside the Acts occurs in 1 Peter 4:16, 'If one suffers as a Christian'.

Asia Minor and parts of Greece. The story finishes with Paul's arrival in Rome as a prisoner and his two years spent waiting for his case to be heard by the imperial tribunal, but it abruptly breaks off at that point without reporting his trial and execution which, according to Christian tradition, took place during the final years of the reign of Nero, who ruled the empire from AD 54 to 68.

Both the third Gospel and the Acts are attributed by the church to Luke, but neither book contains any direct evidence to support the tradition. The earliest attestation that a Gospel and the Acts of the Apostles were written by a physician called Luke comes from the so-called Muratorian canon, probably the most ancient catalogue of the books of the New Testament, of about AD 180. Since the only physician called Luke mentioned in the New Testament is an otherwise rather obscure companion of Paul (Col. 4:14), he has in the absence of a stronger candidate been recognized as the writer of the third Gospel and the Acts. There are serious objections to this attribution. The difficulties arise partly from the many clashes in the story, relating to Paul, between the Acts and the autobiographical accounts in the Pauline letters (cf. pp. 60–63), and from the absence of any noticeable impact of the teaching of Paul on the theology of either of the two writings. One would have expected an associate of Paul to do better than that. Be this as it may, as far as the dating is concerned it is obvious that the Acts of the Apostles follows the Gospel, which it calls 'the first book'. Since Luke's Gospel is generally held to have been written after AD 80, the Acts of the Apostles must have originated somewhere between AD 90 and 100, i.e. roughly within half a century of the events reported in it. Though historically not always reliable, chronologically Acts proves to be useful in understanding the formation of the primitive Christian church, faith and practice in the second half of the first century.

## THE TITLES OF JESUS IN
## THE ACTS OF THE APOSTLES

To follow the pattern established in our search for the image of Jesus in John and Paul, I shall start with a survey of the titles given to Christ in the Acts of the Apostles. These designations show at once that the author of the Acts intended to place Jesus lower than the Christ of Paul and John, but above the Jesus of the Synoptic Gospels.

We owe to the Acts a fresh epithet, the 'Servant' or the 'holy Servant' of God (3:13, 26; 4:27), an ephemeral designation of Jesus which disappeared from the later writings of the New Testament. This is a biblical and post-biblical title borne by Abraham, Moses and David and other such saintly characters in the intertestamental age. In the Dead Sea Scrolls the prophets are regularly referred to as God's servants. 'Servant' is an honorific appellation which does not, however, confer a unique distinction on its holder, and in a prayer attributed to Peter it is simultaneously applied to the apostles and to Jesus: 'Lord ... grant to thy servants to speak thy word with all boldness, while ... signs and wonders are performed through the name of thy holy servant Jesus' (4:29–30). This special terminological innovation of the Acts of the Apostles thus firmly located Jesus within Jewish tradition, among the holy men of biblical and intertestamental past. The same can also be said of the label 'the Righteous One' (3:14; 7:52; 22:14), a common designation of a man of God.

The relatively low-ranking theological title 'teacher' is absent from the Acts, but the teaching role of Christ is indirectly implied in the expression 'disciples of the Lord', and in references to remembered 'words of the Lord', some of which are preserved in the Gospels (cf. Acts 11:16) though others are unattested (cf. 20:35).

Jesus is further identified as a prophet in the earliest layer of Palestinian Jewish-Christian testimonies. The Acts represents here the tradition familiar to the Synoptic Gospels and to John (see above, p. 28), but unknown to Paul. In fact the view later expressed in John that Jesus was *the* prophet, the decisive, ultimate, eschatological prophet, is already foreshadowed in a speech attributed to Peter in which Christ is the second Moses, whose arrival would coincide with the onset of the messianic age. Indeed Jesus is proclaimed the realization of the words of Moses: 'The Lord God will raise up for you a prophet from your brethren as he raised me up. You shall listen to him' (3:22, citing Deut. 18:18; cf. the Qumran Testimonia or 4Q175).

'Son of Man' and 'Son of God', the two more advanced titles of Jesus in John, hardly make their presence felt in Acts. The former occurs once in the climax of a sermon apparently delivered before the great Sanhedrin by the Hellenist deacon Stephen: 'Behold, I see the heavens opened, and the son of Man standing at the right hand of God' (7:56). The vision mirrors Jesus' purported prophecy before the high priest, 'From now on the son of Man shall be seated at the right hand of the power of God' (Luke 22:69). But whereas in the Synoptic Gospels the expression is spoken by Jesus and the reference is to himself, on Stephen's lips it becomes a name of Jesus. For this reason, and because it is used by a Hellenistic Jew, this single occurrence of 'son of Man' in Acts is unlikely to reflect the ideology of the primitive Jewish church of Jerusalem. A more detailed discussion of the phrase will follow in Chapter 6.

The expression 'Son of God', so central in the Gospels and in Paul, hardly fares better than 'son of Man' in the Acts. The only direct usage is attributed to Paul, who in speeches in the synagogues of Damascus proclaimed Jesus the 'Son of God' (9:20). A second indirect use appears in a sermon of Paul in the synagogue of Antioch in Pisidia where he interpreted Psalm 2:7, 'Thou art my Son, today I have begotten thee' (13:33), as fulfilled in Jesus.

'Lord' is the most frequently used designation of Jesus by the primitive church in the Acts. It was applied to him as a form of address spoken by the apostles before his ascension: 'Lord, will you at this time restore the kingdom of Israel?' (1:6). This is how the visionary proto-martyr Stephen and Paul on the way to Damascus invoked the heavenly Christ: 'Lord Jesus, receive my spirit' (7:59), and 'Who are you, Lord?' (9:5). In most other cases, however, 'Lord' has a reverential descriptive function without a clearly defined meaning. Nevertheless – and this is why the use of the title in the Acts shows an advance on the Synoptic Gospels – in a number of passages its bearer is depicted as risen from the dead in conformity with prophecy (2:31; 4:33), as the object of religious faith accompanied by the gift of the spirit, and as the source of salvation (11:17; 16:31; 20:21).

The Paul of the Acts received his ministry from the Lord Jesus (20:24); in his Roman captivity, he devoted himself to 'teaching about the Lord Jesus Christ', for whose name he was prepared to die (21:13). Once 'Lord' is given as the equivalent of 'Christ', i.e. the Anointed One (2:36), the primitive Jesus movement is definitely placed within a messianic, though non-royal, framework. It is significant that on the only occasion when the writer of the Acts tried to define what he meant by Messiah, he clearly portrayed Jesus as a charismatic miracle-worker: 'God anointed Jesus of Nazareth with the holy Spirit and with power . . . [and] he went about doing good and healing all that were oppressed by the devil' (10:38).

The specific lordship of Jesus derives from his being proclaimed Christ by God. This proclamation, like his designation as 'Son of God in power' in Paul's terminology (Rom. 1:3), follows his resurrection and exaltation. 'This Jesus God raised up . . . Let all the house of Israel therefore know assuredly that God has made him both Lord and Christ' (2:32–6). This implies that Christhood and lordship in the complete sense are associated not with the earthly, but with the glorified Jesus sitting next to the Father in the celestial throne-room. It is from heaven that he will return as the Messiah 'appointed for you [the Jews]' at the time determined by God (3:20–21). The author of the Acts viewed the career of Jesus as consisting of two halves: his exalted state from the resurrection to his second coming was preceded by the historical mission of the *man of Nazareth*, distinguished by 'mighty works and wonders and signs' (2:22), and marked by an inglorious end.

This idea of a non-royal and non-triumphant Jesus coming before the glorified Christ constituted a major stumbling-block to ordinary Jews, and the main thrust of the early preaching of the apostles was aimed at explaining and justifying the suffering, death and resurrection of Jesus, which were not part of the common Jewish messianic expectation. In fact the author of the Acts makes both Peter and Paul emphatically assert that the tragic end of the Christ followed by triumph was part of the prophetic heritage, even though Jews seemed to have forgotten it. 'God foretold . . . that his Christ should suffer' and 'it was necessary for the Christ to suffer and to rise from the dead' (3:18; 17:3; 26:23).

## HOW THE JEWISH CHURCH TRIED TO PROVE THAT JESUS WAS THE MESSIAH

The best way to grasp the primitive Christians' picture of Jesus is by reconstructing the contents and style of their preaching. How did they present their gospel, and how did they endeavour to convince their first listeners, variously addressed as 'Men of Judaea and all who dwell in Jerusalem' (2:14), 'Israelite men' (2:22; 3:12) and 'House of Israel' (2:36)? The approach they adopted seems to have been substantially the same, whether the message was delivered in Jerusalem or in the very different setting of the Gentile mission of Paul, who usually began to preach the gospel in diaspora synagogues attended both by Jews and by Greek sympathizers of Judaism.

There is one totally discrepant case in the Acts: Paul's speech in the Areopagus of Athens, where the audience had no synagogue connection whatever (17:16–32). After Paul's earlier attempts to engage Greeks in religious debate in the market place or agora, Epicurean and Stoic philosophers are said to have invited him to explain his message concerning Jesus and his resurrection, which at first hearing had struck them as inconsequential chatter. In reply, Paul set out to reveal to these intellectuals his gospel about the 'unknown God' to whom they, the 'very religious' Athenians, had erected an altar. This God, he told them, was the creator of the universe and of all the nations; he desired to be sought and found by mankind and as Greek philosophers and poets had correctly perceived, every human being was the offspring of this unknown deity. He was the God who dwelt in heaven; he was not to be confused with man-made statues in earthly shrines. Paul concluded by exhorting the Athenians to repent in view of the imminent judgement of the whole world, which was already entrusted to a man raised by God from the dead. Unsurprisingly, this mixture of superficial Greek religious philosophy and traditional Jewish misconceptions regarding paganism – the Gentiles were assumed to worship lifeless stone and wood – ended in an almost total fiasco. The mention of resurrection from the dead was bound to provoke a smile. Except for two individuals, the sophisticated audience lost interest and politely dismissed Paul (17:16–32). As we have seen, the successful appeal of his message to less demanding Greeks followed a non-intellectual, mystical-mythical path.

Apart from this one exception, reports of Christian preaching in the book of Acts vary from the one-sentence flat statement to greater elaboration. At their simplest, addresses delivered in Jerusalem and in Samaria speak of 'teaching and preaching Jesus as the Christ' (the apostles in the Temple, 5:42) or the 'proclamation of the Christ' (Philip in Samaria, 8:5). Occasionally slightly more detail is given. In Jerusalem the apostles announced through Jesus the resurrection from the dead (4:2), and Philip preached to the Samaritans the good news about the kingdom of God and the name of Jesus Christ (8:12). Peter's instruction of the Roman Cornelius in Caesarea mentions John's baptism, Jesus' preaching, healing and exorcizing activity in Galilee, his death and resurrection, and his return as judge, all being presented as foretold by the prophets (10:36–43).

Outside Palestine the scene of the activity was usually situated in a diaspora synagogue. In Damascus and Corinth Paul declared Jesus to be 'the Son of God' or 'the Christ' (9:20; 18:5). In Cyprus and Antioch Barnabas and Paul preached 'the word of God' or 'the word of the Lord' (13:5; 15:35) and Paul taught 'the kingdom of God' in Ephesus, Miletus and Rome (19:8; 20:25; 28:23, 30). When the Jewish audience proved unreceptive, the gospel was directly offered to the Gentiles (11:20; 13:46; 18:6; 28:28).

In a Jewish setting, whether in Palestine or the diaspora, apostolic teaching about Jesus took the form of an argument based on the Bible, interpreting and seeking to demonstrate that in Jesus the scriptural prophecies found their fulfilment. Quite often the message is reported in general terms. Thus we learn that Paul entered the synagogue in Thessalonica, and 'as was his custom . . . argued with [the Jews] from the scriptures' (17:1–2; cf. 17:10–11; 18:4–5, 26–7). Although on one occasion it is specified that he proved his case both from the Law and from the Prophets (28:23), explicit references to the Torah itself figure very infrequently in the New Testament in regard to Jesus. Most of the doctrinal demonstrations are construed on prophetic passages or on the Psalms.

Most speeches in the Acts seem to reflect a common pattern of preaching. To start with Peter's address to the Jewish crowd in

Jerusalem on the first Pentecost, the argument runs as follows. Jesus of Nazareth, whom in conformity with God's providential plan the Jews had crucified, was raised from the dead as foretold by the prophets, and subsequently was made into Lord and Messiah. The listeners must repent and be baptized in order to receive the gift of the holy Spirit (2:22–38). The message is validated by an 'intellectual' biblical argument, followed by an 'existential and experimental' confirmation through charismatic manifestations.

## Jewish Bible interpretation

To understand the argument from Scripture in the New Testament, and in particular in the Acts, a brief outline of ancient Jewish biblical exegesis may be helpful. During the last two or three centuries of the Second Temple period, say between 200 BC and AD 100, Bible interpretation was developed by Jews into a fine art. By the middle of the second century BC Palestinian Jews possessed a collection or canon of holy scriptures arranged in three divisions: the Law, the Prophets, which also include the historical books from Joshua to Kings, and the Writings, viz. poetic and wisdom compositions as well as the late arrivals in the Old Testament, Esther, Ezra-Nehemiah, Chronicles and Daniel. The Law of Moses was the most influential of the three sections, but all the volumes contained in the Hebrew Bible enjoyed authoritative status and generated a whole body of explanatory literature. The commentaries served partly to clarify the meaning and partly to further develop the message recorded in Scripture.[2]

One of the various types of exposition was particularly concerned with the interpretation of prophecies relating to the 'end time'. This genre was highly significant in those Jewish groups which expected the onset of the final age in, or close to, their own time. Next to the primitive church, the best-known community preoccupied with the

2. See G. Vermes, 'Bible and Midrash', in the *Cambridge History of the Bible* I (1970), 199–231 (reprinted in Vermes, *Post-biblical Jewish Studies* (1975); G. Vermes, *Scripture and Tradition in Judaism* (1961); 'Bible Interpretation at Qumran', *Eretz-Israel* XX (1989), 184*–191*; 'Biblical Proof-Texts in Qumran Literature', *Journal of Semitic Studies* 34 (1989), 493–508.

contemporary application of prophecy was the religious brotherhood of the Essenes which bequeathed to us the Dead Sea Scrolls. Now and again, however, the same type of Bible commentary is found in rabbinic literature too.

The most remarkable type of exegesis at Qumran is known under the technical title of *pesher*. This Hebrew word literally means explanation, but it is used to designate a kind of fulfilment interpretation. It may be applied to individual passages and to groups of extracts selected from various biblical books, or even to a whole chapter or an entire book.

The significance of a prophetic, or presumed to be prophetic, text is determined by identifying persons roughly contemporaneous with the commentator as individuals in whom the ancient prediction is thought to have been realized. For instance in the Commentary on Habakkuk, discovered in Qumran Cave 1 and dating to the middle of the first century BC, the Chaldaeans or Babylonians, the final enemies of the Jews according to the prophet Habakkuk of the seventh century BC, were assumed by the author of the scroll to represent the Kittim or Romans of his own age who in the first century BC began their successful conquest of the Near East by subjugating Syria and Palestine. Mention of 'the righteous' and 'the wicked' by Habakkuk persuaded the commentator that the prophecy was aimed at 'the Teacher of Righteousness', the founder of his community, and at 'the Wicked Priest', the mortal enemy of the Teacher. The famous rabbi of the second century AD, Akiba ben Joseph, introduced the same kind of interpretative reasoning when he asserted that the messianic prophecy of Numbers 24:17, 'A star shall come forth out of Jacob', was realized in the leader of the second Jewish war against Rome, Simeon bar Kosiba, to whom Akiba punningly referred as the Son of the Star or Bar Kokhba (yTaanit 68d).

When Qumran commentators or later rabbis had recourse to this sort of *pesher*, they tried to kill two birds with one stone. Not only did they provide a definite meaning for a vague prediction, but simultaneously declared the person or the event of the fulfilled prophecy ordained by God. In this way the chosen individuals and members of the group associated with them were both divinely predestined and approved. Thus St Paul's favourite verse of Habakkuk (2:4), 'The righteous shall live by his faith', which he saw fulfilled in those who believed in Christ (Rom. 1:17; Gal. 3:11), was understood by the Qumran interpreter as applying to faith in their Teacher of Righteousness; so the commentator demonstrated from Scripture that the election of their Master and his community was divinely predetermined. 'Interpreted, this concerns those who observe the Law in the House of Juda [namely the Qumran Community], whom God will deliver from the House of Judgement because of their suffering and their faith in the Teacher of Righteousness' (1QpHab 8:1–3).

## Bible interpretation in the Acts

In addition to the generic scriptural proof that Jesus was the Christ, the book of Acts contains many individual prophecies which the church believed came true in the career of Jesus. The majority of these relate to the topic most in need of justification: his rising from the dead and subsequent exaltation. Thus in his first speech Peter argued that the 'prophet' David (2:30) had foretold the resurrection of Christ in Psalm 16:8–11. On the other hand, convincing prophetic quotations came less easily to hand in regard to the main scandal connected with Jesus, the suffering and death of the Messiah. In fact, what for the modern reader appears to be the most telling passage, Isaiah's description of the suffering and death of the servant of the Lord (Isa. 53:7–8), was not one directly chosen by a Christian preacher, but happened to be the text which an Ethiopian Jewish proselyte had read without being able to understand it (8:27). The evangelist Philip, whom he met on the way, interpreted it for him as applying to Jesus (8:34–5).

The early Christian *pesher*, like the Qumran *pesher*, was not primarily an interpretative exercise. Its aim was to furnish biblical sanction to disturbing details in the life of Jesus and of his associates. It also sought to demonstrate that these details fitted into, and were an integral part of, a chain of happenings arranged by God for the salvation of the Jews (and of mankind). This second form of argument is exemplified in Acts by two historical sermons which will be examined later.

Let us begin with individual cases reported in the Acts; they tend to illuminate the mentality which produced the Jesus portrait of the early

Palestinian church. As I have pointed out, Peter 'proved' in his first speech to Jewish bystanders in Jerusalem that the resurrection of Jesus came as the fulfilment of Psalm 16, verse 10, 'For thou wilt not abandon my soul to Hades, nor let thy Holy One see corruption'. The reasoning goes like this. The purported author of this 'prophecy', King David, could not possibly speak of his own resurrection. It was common knowledge that he was dead and buried, and the tomb containing his bones was still publicly venerated in Peter's day. Consequently David must have envisaged the rising from the dead of someone else, namely the future Messiah (Acts 2:25–31). Again (Acts 4:10–12), the crucifixion and resurrection of Christ verified the words of another Psalm (118:22), 'The stone which the builders rejected has become the chief cornerstone'. The stone was Jesus; the builders who rejected and killed him were the Jews; and the cornerstone holding up the whole building was the risen Christ, the source of universal salvation. As for the glorification and heavenly enthronement of Christ, they resulted from a divine decree promulgated in Psalm 110:1, 'The Lord [God] said to my Lord, Sit at my right hand', for since David did not go up to the heavens, the Lord referred to in the second place must be his descendant, the Messiah (Acts 2:34).

Fulfilment interpretation, though most commonly used to convince Jews who shared the same principles in regard to the nature of holy Scripture, could also serve as a 'rational' back-up to the faith of the apostles and disciples themselves. In a prayer, Psalm 2:1–2 – 'Why did the Gentiles rage, and the peoples imagine vain things? The kings of the earth set themselves in array, and the rulers were gathered together, against the Lord and against his Anointed' – is made to account for the plot against Jesus in Jerusalem which brought together Herod Antipas and Pilate (Luke 23:6–12), i.e. kings and rulers, the representatives of the Jews and of the pagan nations (= the peoples) (Acts 4:24–8). Considered from a psychological point of view, this type of internal apology probably anticipated the form of proof used to convince outsiders.

Other occurrences of *pesher* in the Acts relate to figures associated with Jesus. It is first employed to explain the ecstatic behaviour of the apostles on the day of the first Pentecost, their 'speaking in tongues'. Sarcastic onlookers ascribed the strange happenings to too much alcohol: 'They are filled with new wine' (Acts 2:13). But Peter advised them rather to celebrate in the event the realization of the words of the prophet Joel: 'In the last days . . . I will pour out my spirit upon all flesh, and your sons and daughters shall prophesy, and your young men shall see visions, and your old men shall dream dreams; yea, and on my menservants and maidservants in those days I will pour out my spirit; and they shall prophesy' (2:17–18). Another *pesher* concerns various acts of Judas, his betrayal of Jesus, the purchase of a plot of land called 'Field of Blood' with the thirty pieces of silver received from the high priests, his death,[3] and his replacement by Matthias in the college of the apostles. They are presented as the fulfilment of Psalms 69:25 and 109:8, 'Let his habitation become desolate, and let there be no one to live in it', and 'His office let another take' (1:16–20).

Furthermore, the rejection of Paul's preaching by the Roman Jews (Acts 28:24–7) was predicted by the prophecy of Isaiah, 'You shall indeed hear but never understand, and you shall indeed see but never perceive. For this people's heart has grown dull, and their ears are heavy of hearing, and their eyes they have closed . . .' (Isa. 6:7–9). As for the choice of the Gentiles, it was foretold according to James, the brother of the Lord, by a combined quotation of Jeremiah 12:15, Amos 9:11–12 and Isaiah 45:21, 'After this I will return, and I will rebuild the dwelling of David, which has fallen; I will rebuild its ruins, and I will set it up, *that the rest of men may seek the Lord, and all the Gentiles who are called by my name*, says the Lord, who has made these things known of old' (Acts 15:16–18).[4]

All the *pesher* arguments so far cited are casual, that is to say, they refer to odd verses in Scripture. A more consequential biblical proof is developed in the form of a missionary sermon giving an abridged

3. Judas fell and his abdomen burst open, allowing his bowels to gush out (1:18). This description of the death of the traitor clashes with Matthew 27:5 where Judas is said to have hanged himself.

4. This argument is based on the Greek version of Amos. The words in the Hebrew text corresponding to the italicized passage have a totally different meaning: 'that they (the Jews) may possess the remnants of Edom and all the nations who are called by my name'. Since it is unlikely that James, the leader of the Judaizers, used the Septuagint rather than the Hebrew Bible, one must assume that the version in the Acts is a later Gentile-Christian fabrication.

version of the religious history of the Jews from Abraham to Jesus. One of two surviving examples, it is said to have been delivered before the high priest and the council in Jerusalem. It is presented as the self-defence of the deacon Stephen, accused of preaching against the Temple and the Law of Moses. But Stephen's speech is a clumsy and ineffectual construction. If, as we are told in the Acts, it was addressed to the high priest and the Sanhedrin, the speaker was guilty of a colossal misjudgement. With his long-winded elementary account of the story of the Patriarchs and Moses he first bored his learned audience to death, and then he infuriated them with an unjustified attack on the Jerusalem Temple. Instead of steadily building up his pleading towards a climax in Jesus, he lost his temper and burst out in vituperation – 'You stiff-necked people . . . you always resist the holy Spirit . . .' (Acts 7:51) – and perhaps inevitably he ended up being lynched (7:57–60).

The second example is given as a sermon preached by Paul in a city in Asia Minor at the invitation of the president of the local synagogue and is perhaps more apposite in revealing how the primitive church understood the role of Jesus in biblical history (13:16–37). It appears to be, in fact, an early Christian model of catechism. The line of the argument is as follows. God chose the Jewish people, led them out of Egypt, protected them in the wilderness for forty years, and gave them the land of Canaan. Judges and kings, above all King David, were granted to them. Jesus, the offspring of David, was introduced and proclaimed as the promised Messiah by John the Baptist. Yet the Jews in Jerusalem, and especially their leaders, failed to understand the prophets, although their words were read in public every sabbath; despite their inability to find a capital charge against Jesus, they urged Pilate to put him to death. Crucified and buried, he was raised from the dead by God as witnessed by his apostles and foretold by David in two of his psalms. The first, 'Thou art my Son, today I have begotten thee' (Ps. 2:7), proves that he was the Christ, the Son of God, and the second, 'Thou wilt not let thy Holy One see corruption' (Ps. 16:10), predicts his death and resurrection – provided that the listeners agree with the presuppositions of the preacher.

The examples set out here illustrate the basic problems facing the earliest propagators of the message about Jesus. Focusing not on peripheral issues but on the heart of the matter, the preachers had to provide an explanation for the disconcerting suffering and crucifixion of the Messiah and for the subsequent miraculous revival of Jesus, who for them was still 'a *man* attested by God' (Acts 2:22). As for the larger canvas of the historical sermon, the purpose was to stress that the whole destiny of the Jewish people was geared towards the universal salvation to be brought about by the same Jesus of Nazareth.

As the subsequent history of early Christian preaching proves, the New Testament *pesher* was more effective in the Greek world unaccustomed to this kind of argument and impressed by its mysterious strangeness than among Jews who were used to the vagaries of sectarian Bible exegesis. Many of them must have found the demonstration from Scripture used by Christians whimsical and unconvincing.

## WORSHIP AND RELIGION IN THE PRIMITIVE JESUS MOVEMENT

### The Palestinian church

Before we can properly confront the problem of the primitive church and its religion two preliminary questions must be raised and resolved. First, did the new Christian movement consider itself an independent and autonomous institution in relation to 'official' Judaism, that is to say a Judaism with a Temple and Sanhedrin, with a high priest and priests, with schools and teachers? Secondly, did this church consciously turn its hero, Jesus, into a figure of worship?

Regarding the second question, all the elements point towards an answer in the negative. Jesus of Nazareth was acknowledged as the performer of mighty deeds, but he was and remained during his lifetime a man destined to impart to the Jewish people the good news of peace and redemption. His elevation to a superhuman status of Lord and Christ came about, we are told both in the Acts and in Paul, after his death and resurrection. In short, Jesus was not yet the object of a religious cult in the primitive church; it was not to him, but to God, the Father, that prayers were directed by the apostles released from prison, when Peter, John and the rest of the community 'lifted their voices together to God and said, Sovereign Lord, who didst make the heaven and the earth' (Acts 4:24). Similarly, Paul and Silas, imprisoned in Philippi, addressed their hymns to God (16:25), and not to 'Christ as God', as the Bithynian Christians did half a century later, according to the testimony of Pliny the Younger (cf. above, p. 53).

From the very first, the religion of Peter and his colleagues was basically common Judaism, which they continued to observe and to which they stayed firmly attached, and in which the Temple of Jerusalem still occupied the centre point.

According to the evidence contained in the Acts the followers of Jesus still considered the Temple of Jerusalem their principal venue for preaching and prayer. They did not see themselves cut off from the rest of Jewry. They regularly taught in the Temple: 'Every day in the Temple . . . they did not cease . . . preaching Jesus as the Christ' (5:42; 5:20–21, 25). Like their fellow Jews, 'day by day . . . together' (2:47) they participated in the worship performed in the sanctuary. We encounter Peter and John 'going up to the Temple at the hour of prayer, the ninth hour' (3:1), i.e. at 3 p.m. when the afternoon sacrifice known as *tamid* was offered for the Jewish people every day. As I have noted (p. 61), even Paul, who in Gentile surroundings paid little attention to the ritual laws, subjected himself to ceremonial purification before entering the sanctuary to present his offerings (21:26; 24:18). The author of the Acts quotes him as saying that he has worshipped in Jerusalem (24:11) and that once while praying he had fallen into a trance in the Temple (22:17). The centre of Jewish worship remained the favourite locus of public prayer and cultic activity among the adherents of the Jesus movement at least until AD 58, the date of Paul's final visit to Jerusalem, and probably until the destruction of the sanctuary in AD 70.

This ultimate manifestation of loyalty to the people of Israel did not mean, however, that the fellowship of the disciples of Jesus failed to form a distinct and progressively more and more recognizable community within Jewry. At the beginning they were hardly distinguishable. During one of the early appearances of the apostles before the Sanhedrin, the book of Acts has the famous teacher Gamaliel allude to them simply as 'these men' – not as sectaries or heretics – and adopt the line typical of a cautious religious leader of letting them be, since most novelties prove to be no more than three-day wonders (5:38–9). Three decades later Palestinian Christianity was still perceived from outside as part of Judaism, but identifiable within it; it had become a 'sect', *hairesis* in Greek, a term without any pejorative nuance (like the 'sects' of the Pharisees, Sadducees and Essenes, following the terminology of Flavius Josephus). The lawyer Tertullus, hired by the high priest Ananias and the elders to lay charges against Paul before the Roman procurator Felix, referred to him as the 'ringleader of the sect of the Nazarenes' (24:5). Felix's successor, Festus, put both Paul and his accusers into the same bag: they all belonged to the Jewish 'superstition' (25:19). By the time Paul arrived in Rome in the early sixties, the local Jews had learned that 'this sect' was opposed all over the place (28:22), yet its members still counted as unruly insiders.

'Church' is the general designation of the Jesus brotherhood in the Acts. However, contrary to its modern usage which possesses a definite Christian connotation, the Greek *ekklesia* had no such denominational meaning. In Stephen's speech the term refers to the '*congregation* [of the Jews] in the wilderness' (7:38).

The first specific title chosen by the Christian community was that of 'the Way' (9:2; 19:9, 23; 22:4; 24:14, 22). This is the shortened version of 'the Way of the Lord', probably of God rather than Jesus, as implied in the statement that the learned Alexandrian Jew Apollos was 'instructed in the Way of the Lord' (18:24–5). Regarding the meaning of the phrase, the passages in the Acts do not suggest a duality, a way of light opposed to a way of darkness; they always speak simply of 'the Way'. The idiom recalls the Community Rule of Qumran. The Dead Sea sectaries abandoned the wicked urban civilization to prepare in the wilderness the Way of Him, i.e. God (1QS 8:14). In brief, they were the community of 'those who had chosen the Way' (1QS 9:18). Part of the document is entitled 'The rules of the Way for the Master' (9:21) and the faithful members are called 'the perfect of the Way' and walk in 'the perfection of the Way' (4:22; 8:10, 21; 9:5).

The presence of the church is fully attested only in Jerusalem, though communities in Lydda, Joppa, Ptolemais and Caesarea are also mentioned incidentally (9:32; 10:23; 21:7, 16) and Paul refers to the churches of Christ in Judaea (Gal. 1:22). Nevertheless it is quite astonishing, bearing in mind that according to the Synoptics almost the whole public career of Jesus had a Galilean setting, that the Acts alludes to no Christian group activity in Galilee.

This Jerusalem church was led by the college of the apostles of Jesus, but within the group three leaders enjoyed particular influence: Peter, John and James. Paul referred to them as 'three pillars' (Gal. 2:9). In the first ten chapters of the Acts Peter is the dominating figure, but by the time Paul appears on the horizon, Peter, still the leader, is closely shadowed by James (Gal. 1:18–19). Thereafter James progressively takes over the leadership. In the mixed Jewish-Gentile church in Antioch, Peter, at first a liberal eating with Gentile Christians, feels obliged to backtrack when envoys arrive from Jerusalem, and to follow James's rigorous separation from non-Jews at table, thus infuriating Paul (Gal. 2:11–12). And if the account of the Acts can be trusted, at the great debate in Jerusalem concerning the treatment of Gentiles wishing to join the church, although Peter makes the first speech, the presidential decision is left to James: 'My judgement is that we should not trouble those of the Gentiles who turn to God' (Acts 15:19). On the occasion of Paul's last visit to Jerusalem, Peter is no longer mentioned, and Paul pays his respects to James alone (21:18).

This James, 'the brother of the Lord' (Gal. 1:19), probably owed his importance in the Jerusalem church to his close kinship to Jesus. As I have mentioned earlier, the brothers of the Lord are explicitly named by the author of the Acts as forming part of the initial nucleus of the movement (1:14). Jude, another brother said to be the author of one of the New Testament letters, also wielded some influence in Palestinian Christianity. If one can give some credence to the church historian of the fourth century AD, Eusebius of Caesarea, quoting the second-century Hegesippus as his source, the great-nephews of Jesus (the grandsons of Jude) still played a sufficiently important role in the church around the end of the first century to be placed on the emperor Domitian's list of political suspects; this on the grounds that they were the descendants – even though impoverished descendants – of King David (*Ecclesiastical History* 3:20–21). With the decline of the Jewish-Christian movement, the influence of the kin of Jesus declined and their names vanished from the records.

Two brief passages in the Acts of the Apostles sketch the primitive church. The first, shorter, passage describes this community as made up of Jews who, under the impact of Peter's speech on the Feast of Pentecost, joined the original nucleus of 120 members (1:15). These were the apostles and disciples of Jesus together with his closest relations: his mother, of whom this is the last mention in New Testament history, and his brothers (1:14). 'And they devoted themselves to the apostles' teaching and fellowship, to the breaking of the bread and prayers. And fear came upon every soul; and many wonders were done through the apostles. And all who believed were together and had all things in common; and they sold their possessions and goods and distributed them to all, as any had need. And day by day, attending the Temple together and breaking bread in their homes, they partook of food with glad and generous hearts, praising God and having favour with all the people. And the Lord added to their number day by day those who were saved' (2:42–7).

How large was this primitive community in the first weeks or months of its existence? The figure recorded in Acts 2:41, 'about three thousand', needs to be taken with a pinch of salt. Jewish story-tellers, be they biblical writers or Josephus, tend to exaggerate numbers. The membership of the religious parties of the Pharisees and the Essenes quoted by Josephus and Philo amounted to 6,000 and 4,000 respectively at the beginning of the first century AD, by which time they had had at least a century and a half of history behind them. The embryonic church is more likely to have counted its adherents in hundreds rather than in thousands.

As far as their congregational life is concerned, members of the Jerusalem church received instruction in common, prayed in common and broke bread in common (2:42). This joint 'breaking of the bread' designates the communal meals out of which the eucharist was to develop (reported in greater detail in the chapter on Paul, pp. 97–9). They also held 'all things in common', selling all 'their possessions and goods' and using the money to cater for the needs of the entire community.

How this redistribution of wealth came about is explained in the longer second sketch of the primitive church (4:34 to 5:11). The better-off members of the church disposed of their fields and houses and handed over the proceeds to the apostle who administered the common purse. Apparently the members were not compelled to divest themselves of their possessions; the anecdote of Ananias and Sapphira suggests that the obligation was moral rather than legal. The couple in question are said to have turned a piece of property into cash and pretended to 'lay [the whole money] at the apostles' feet', but in fact they kept part of it for themselves. The lie cost them their lives as both were punished by sudden death for 'tempting the holy Spirit'. It would seem that even without being under a strict obligation, the associates of the brotherhood were under heavy moral pressure to follow the example of more generous members. Be this as it may, the general impression given by the Jesus fellowship was that generally speaking religious communism was the order of the day among them.

Such a renunciation of private property was quite unusual. In inter-testamental Jewish society it is attested only among the Essenes described by Philo, Josephus and Pliny the Elder, and in the ascetic unmarried branch of the Qumran-Essene sect represented by the Community Rule in the Dead Sea Scrolls. The less extreme married members of the Essene movement did not reject private property, but insisted on a compulsory monthly contribution to a charitable fund, handled by the guardian and the judges, from which the poor, the sick and the oppressed were supported. It is possible, even likely, that the Jerusalem church leaders were influenced by the example of the Essene practice when they introduced the principle of the common kitty. However, to speak of a direct dependence on, let alone an identity with, Essenism would be quite unjustifiable, for two reasons. First, common ownership was obligatory in the strict Essene regime and not just optional. Secondly, it was not only adhered to in stages during the years of Essene initiation but also contained a definite ritualistic element (the possessions of a non-member were unclean), an element lacking in the system adopted by the Jerusalem church. The adherence of the Jesus movement to religious communism is rather attributable to the intense eschatological fervour pervading the community. When the arrival of the reign of God was believed to be imminent, material possessions not only became less appealing but constituted a hindrance for those who intended to labour with a whole heart for the kingdom of heaven. In fact, the regime adopted by the Jerusalem church was itself a compromise if we compare it with Jesus' extreme counsel to a wealthy man not just to share but give away his possessions and rely entirely on God and the charity of his fellow human beings (Mark 10:21; Matt. 19:21; Luke 18:22).

## The Kingdom of God and charisma

The expectation of God's Kingdom, essential to the religion of Jesus and the theology of Paul, but almost totally ignored in John, still occupies a central position in the early Christianity of the Acts of the Apostles. In fact the message which the risen Jesus is said to have delivered during the forty days between Easter and the Ascension is pointedly summarized as the doctrine of 'the Kingdom of God' (1:3). The vividness and urgency of the expectation are demonstrated by the fact that, according to the Acts, the final question Jesus had to answer immediately before he rose into the air to disappear from sight behind a cloud was whether the time had come for the establishment of the promised Kingdom (1:6). Throughout the Acts, the proclamation of the good news is shown as identical with the preaching of the Kingdom of God, by Philip in Samaria, Paul and Barnabas in Antioch, or by Paul alone in Ephesus, Miletus and Rome (8:12; 14:22; 19:8; 20:25; 28:23, 31). The gospel of Jesus was the gospel of the Kingdom; the ultimate hope of the initiates of the Jesus movement was, after 'many tribulations', to 'enter the Kingdom of God' (14:22). The idea of the second coming of Christ is less prominent in the Jerusalem church of the Acts than in the letters of Paul, perhaps because the completion of Acts follows the Pauline letters by some thirty or forty years, when the Parousia expectation was already on the wane. It is not completely absent, however, as is clear from Peter's speech in the Temple alluding to the return of Christ from heaven: 'Repent, therefore . . . that times of refreshing may come from the presence of the Lord, and that he may send the Christ appointed for you, Jesus, whom heaven must receive until the time for establishing all that God spoke by the mouth of the holy prophets' (3:19–21). Likewise, it is the same Jesus who is proclaimed by Peter to the Roman centurion Cornelius as the one ordained by God to come as the future judge of the living and the dead, the final arbiter of the whole human race (10:42).

A lively eschatological outlook cannot maintain itself in the context of ordinary routine existence. The primitive Jesus movement was indeed steeped in charisma, especially – though by no means exclusively – in its original Palestinian setting. Jesus, as we shall see, was primarily portrayed in the Synoptic Gospels as a divinely empowered healer-exorcist; his Jewish disciples mirrored their master and continued in his footsteps as healers and exorcists. The heavenly gift which Jesus possessed was passed on, according to the testimony of the author of Acts, to the spiritual leaders of the church. In Jerusalem, in scenes reminiscent of those in Galilean villages during the lifetime of Jesus, people 'carried out the sick into the streets, and laid them on beds and pallets, that as Peter came by at least his shadow might fall on some of them' (5:15). Even from the neighbouring towns the sick and the possessed of unclean spirits were brought to Peter to be healed (5:16). A number of individual beneficiaries are listed: a lame beggar cured by Peter and John in the Temple (3:2–10); a man called Aeneas, bedridden with paralysis for eight years restored to mobility by Peter in Lydda (Lod) (9:33–4), and a woman disciple called Tabitha ('Gazelle') who was thought to be dead was revived by the same Peter in Joppa or Jaffa (9:36–41). The deacon Philip is also credited with the healing of many lame and paralysed people and with expelling many demons in Samaria, where in blatant disregard of the command of Jesus (Matt. 10.5) he successfully preached the gospel (8:7).

The author of Acts pictured the same charismatic aura even outside the Holy Land. Paul is portrayed as wholly surrounded by it. This clashes with the image in Paul's letters, where faith, hope and especially love appear as superior gifts, and Paul's own charismatic behaviour is restricted to private *glossolalia* or ecstatic prayer: 'I thank God that I speak in tongues more than you all; nevertheless in church I would rather speak five words with my mind, in order to instruct others, than ten thousand words in a tongue' (1 Cor. 14:18–19).

In the Acts, Paul joined the Christian community on account of a vision of Jesus; he was charismatically healed from blindness (9:17), and claimed further visions and revelations in Arabia (2 Cor. 12:1–4). Through his first supernatural act he inflicted temporary blindness on Bar-Jesus or Elymas, a Cypriot magician (13:11), but his subsequent charismatic interventions are presented as positive. He made a cripple walk in Lystra (14:8–10), exorcized evil spirits from a slave girl in

Philippi (16:16–18) and in Troas restored to life the young Eutychus who, sitting in a third floor window, had dozed off during Paul's long sermon and had fallen to his death, or almost (20:9–12). Even without Paul's actual presence, a mere touch of his handkerchief or apron is said to have cured many sick people and freed some Ephesians from demonic possession (19:12). After his shipwreck he escaped unharmed when a viper fastened on his arm, and he healed the father of a Maltese chief from fever and dysentery through the laying-on of his hands (28:3–5, 8–9). Throughout his whole account the author of Acts stresses the charismatic nature of primitive Christianity, and since Paul was his champion, he portrays him as the greatest charismatic of them all.

Christ was believed to be the moving spirit behind all these healing and exorcistic miracles. Peter, Philip, Ananias, Paul and their disciples thought of themselves as instruments or channels through which the Lord acted from his heavenly glory. The cures were effected 'in the name of Jesus Christ of Nazareth' (3:6), 'through the name of thy holy servant Jesus' (4:30), or as a result of the proclamation of Christ (8:5), and the cripple Aeneas was told that figuratively speaking he was healed by Jesus Christ himself (9:34). To show that the miracles were produced not by the recitation of a magical incantation but by Christ's spiritual power granted to believing Christians, the author of Acts cites the case of seven itinerant Jewish exorcists, sons of the otherwise unknown 'high priest Sceva'. They apparently tried to add the Jesus formula to their conjuring repertoire by addressing a demon, 'I adjure you in the name of Jesus whom Paul preaches'. Needless to say, their attempt ended in failure. The possessed man is said to have gone berserk and put them to flight, and the evil spirit mocked them with the words, 'Jesus I know, and Paul I know, but who are you?' (19:13–14).

Throughout his work, the writer of the Acts recounts the many 'signs' enacted by the apostles and disciples (2:43; 4:16; 5:12; 6:8; 8:6–7; 8:13, etc.). Moreover, since the performers of the wonders in Jerusalem were not persons expert in the art of healing, or professional magicians, but 'uneducated and common men' (4:13), their powers were thought to come from above. Indeed, in addition to miraculous healings and mastery over evil spirits, many other phenomena were associated with the leaders of the Jesus movement. They included supernatural visits by angels (5:19; 10:3; 12:7; 16:9; 27:23), visions of Jesus (7:56; 9:4–5), and the experience of trance while praying (10:10–11; 22:17). A number of Christian prophets, male and female, are mentioned, among them four unmarried daughters of the evangelist Philip in Caesarea (21:9) and a whole group which travelled from Jerusalem to Antioch (13:1). One of them, by the name of Agabus, predicted a great famine which actually happened during the reign of the emperor Claudius, and announced the arrest and Roman captivity of Paul (11:27; 21:10–11). The author of Acts sees and makes his readers see spiritual manifestations everywhere.

Ecstatic experience and behaviour are also reported in groups previously unconnected with the Jesus movement, and are presented as manifestations of the sudden descent of the holy Spirit. They are modelled on examples of primitive prophecy in the Old Testament, such as the scene of Eldad and Medad and the rest of the elders chosen by Moses (Num. 11:25–6) and the frenzied agitation of the newly appointed Saul as first king of Israel when he met a 'band of prophets' and 'the spirit of God came mightily upon him, and he prophesied among them' (1 Sam. 10:10).

Perhaps the most spectacular charismatic event reported in the Acts concerns the *glossolalia* ('speaking in tongues') first performed by the disciples of Jesus in Jerusalem on the feast of Pentecost, which marked the birth of the church as a social body. The original company of 120 persons (1:15), or perhaps just the reconstituted groups of twelve apostles (1:26 to 2:1), were 'filled with the holy Spirit'. The sound of the roaring of wind and the appearance of light phenomena, i.e. flames of fire, attached to the event are customary features in the description of supernatural occurrences in Jewish literature. The recipients of the *glossolalia* considered this divine gift as a heavenly sign confirming them as witnesses and preachers of the gospel. It was also the tangible fulfilment in their eyes of the promise made by Jesus that before many days they would be baptized with the holy Spirit (1:5).

The *glossolalia* envisaged here is different from the ecstatic prayer of meaningless noises referred to by Paul among the spiritual gifts in the church of Corinth (cf. above, pp. 99–100). In fact, the speech uttered 'in other tongues' under the influence of the holy Spirit by the Galilean apostles could apparently be understood by many in the assembled Jewish crowd recruited 'from every nation under heaven' (2:5). Others, less attuned to the paranormal, thought that the babble was that of drunken men. Their sarcastic comment was rebutted by Peter on the grounds that at nine o'clock in the morning nobody could yet be inebriated (2:13, 15)!

What we have to ask is whether this supposed *glossolalia* affected the speakers or the listeners. Were the ecstatic apostles talking in *other* tongues or did they use their day-to-day vernacular, yet the audience perceived the message in their own diverse languages? Only an audio-cassette recording could decide this question. Nevertheless an anecdote surviving in rabbinic literature may put the story into a different perspective.

In the biblical account of the selection of seventy elders to assist Moses in the government of Israel in the wilderness (Num. 11:24–30), two of them, Eldad and Medad, are singled out as having been seized by the spirit of God to prophesy in the camp. The Palestinian Aramaic commentaries on this passage convey the content of their ecstatic utterances. One of these (Targum Ps.-Jonathan) includes the following short statement: **Kiris etimos lehon besha'at aniki** signifying 'The Lord is present to them in the hour of distress.' In this Aramaic document the three words printed in bold characters are in Greek, the other two in Aramaic. In other words, Pseudo-Jonathan may provide us with a bilingual prophetic *glossolalia*!

Reverting to the story of the apostles at Pentecost, let us first assume that in their frenzy they are represented as speaking in an irregularly mixed jargon consisting of chunks of Aramaic and chunks of Greek. How would this have affected the assembly of 'Parthians, and Medes and Elamites and residents of Mesopotamia, Judaea and Cappadocia, Pontus and Asia, Phrygia and Pamphilia, Egypt and parts of Libya belonging to Cyrene and visitors from Rome, both Jews and proselytes, Cretans and Arabians [i.e. Aramaic-speaking Nabataeans]' (2:9–11). At first sight the bilingual parallel from the Palestinian Targum appears to be irrelevant against the list of some fifteen nationalities. Yet when one scrutinizes the register, one realizes that all the Jews in question were probably sufficiently familiar with either of the two main Jewish tongues of the period, Aramaic and Greek, to understand the gist of the message in their 'own native language' (2:8).[5]

Such a charismatic phenomenon was later recognized by the primitive church as the outward proof of the inward transformation of new recruits to the faith. A spontaneous happening on the first occasions (2:4; 10:44), the advent of the Spirit was afterwards promoted and induced, when necessary, by the laying-on of hands. Peter and John did so to Samaritan converts (8:14–17), and Paul to twelve disciples of Appolos in Ephesus (19:1–7) who had received the baptism of John but had never heard of the baptism of Jesus or of the holy Spirit. The primitive church was in fact soon able to transform ecstatic enthusiasm, the Spirit 'falling on' believers, into a formalized rite of initiation into Christianity, ecclesiastical liturgy taking the place of the pouring out of the Spirit.

# THE CHRISTIANITY
# OF THE PRIMITIVE CHURCH

The best way to understand the nature of the primitive church and the place that Jesus occupied in it is by trying to determine how outsiders were able to attach themselves to the original company of disciples of Jesus. All these disciples were Jews, considered themselves Jews, behaved as Jews, and whole-heartedly adhered to the religion professed by other Jews. The issue that was sharply to divide the community, the admissibility of Gentiles into their ranks, did not arise straight away. In fact, despite the purported initiative of Peter to bring a Roman centurion and his household into the group of the Jesus followers – an event of questionable historicity – a favourable policy decision concerning the entry of non-Jews into the church was not taken until the initial success of Paul's mission among Gentiles in Syria and Asia Minor made it unavoidable.

5. It is not possible to determine to which class of *glossolalia* the 'speaking in tongues' performed by Gentiles seized by the holy Spirit in the house of Cornelius in Caesarea (10:46) and those in Ephesus (19:6) actually belong. The first description suggests charismatic prayer ('they heard them speaking in tongues and extolling God'), but the second, where prophesying is also mentioned, may refer to meaningful utterances.

Christianity began as a Jewish revivalist movement; it was first proclaimed only to 'Hebrews and Hellenists' (6:1), i.e. Semitic and Greek-speaking Jews, and later to Samaritan Jews in Palestine. Even in the Diaspora, in Phoenicia and Cyprus the gospel was strictly confined to Jews (11:19-20) before the mission of Antioch and the rise of Paul. Jews in Jerusalem, who listened to the apostles' appeal to save themselves 'from this crooked generation' (2:40), were instructed to turn away from wickedness and purify themselves. In other words, they were urged to undergo a spiritual conversion according to the pattern set by John the Baptist, but with a difference: they had to repent and be baptized for the forgiveness of sins ... '*in the name of Jesus Christ*' (2:38). These words of instruction uttered by Peter on the day of Pentecost seem to represent a standard primitive Christian exhortation. Belief and obedience were immediately followed by baptism and, as we have seen, accompanied either at once or later by signs of ecstasy, or in the apostolic jargon, the reception of the holy Spirit (2:38; 8:5-6, 14-17).

It would seem that in the case of Jews and even of Samaritans, acceptance of the proclamation (however brief) of the gospel was enough for baptism to ensue. Paul, having seen 'the Righteous One' and confessed his faith in Jesus, was commanded by Ananias in Damascus: 'Rise and be baptized and wash away your sins, calling on his [Christ's] name' (22:16). The same on-the-spot admission into the church is recorded in the case of the Ethiopian proselyte who pleaded for the preliminaries to be cut short: 'So here is water! What is to prevent my being baptized? And he commanded the chariot to stop, and they both went down into the water, Philip and the eunuch, and he baptized him' (8:36-8).

Such an expeditious admission into the church presupposed, not a real change of religion, the leaving of one faith and the embracing of another, but merely a step, a momentous step, within the same Judaism along what was believed to be a providentially preordained path. The real problem arose when the first non-Jews started knocking on the door of the church.

Disregarding the Ethiopian proselyte, already familiar with Judaism (he had gone to Jerusalem to worship and was reading the Book of Isaiah), the first alleged case of a non-Jew seeking entry is that of

Cornelius, the Roman army officer of the Italian Cohort stationed in Caesarea. The story as it is told can best be understood as having a 'political' bias. Bearing in mind the conflict between Peter and Paul resulting from their different attitudes to Gentiles in the church (cf. pp. 65–6), it was in the interest of Peter's supporters to attribute the innovation to their leader.

The issue was unforeseen and the solution proposed revolutionary. No one in the Jerusalem church seemed to be ready and willing to receive Gentiles. Nor were they aware that Christ had ordered the gospel to be preached to all the nations; rather the contrary. So the desire of Cornelius, prompted by a supernatural premonition, to join the church also faced Peter and his colleagues *qua* Jews with a terrible dilemma: could they permit a Gentile to become a member of a Jewish brotherhood without the candidate first fully embracing Judaism? And since the most important expression of church membership was 'the breaking of the bread' at a common meal, how could a pagan be accepted as one of their table-fellows? Could they, *Jewish* Christians, enter the house and share the food, presumed to be unclean, of a non-Jew?

The author of the Acts offers a twofold supernatural solution. The first is a heavenly vision enjoining the flabbergasted Peter to discard Jewish dietary law. His protest that he has never eaten 'anything that is common' is countered by a voice from on high, 'What God has cleansed, you must not call common' (10:14–15). This 'Pauline' view scarcely fits the outlook of the Judaeo-Christian members of the Jerusalem church or, for that matter, the deep-seated attitude of Peter, who – true to his character – was a *hesitant* Judaizer. His claim that 'neither our fathers nor we have been able to bear' the yoke of the Law sounds hollow when judged against his volte-face in Antioch which was fairly castigated by Paul.[6] However, the decisive proof of the acceptability of Gentiles came, we are told, from heaven when the holy Spirit 'fell' on Cornelius and his household and they burst out in *glossolalia*. Nonplussed, Peter exclaimed: 'Can anyone forbid water for baptizing

6. Paul in turn was equally inconsistent. For despite all his tirades against circumcision, he circumcised his favourite disciple, Timothy, son of a Jewish mother and a Greek father, on account of the Jews who lived in the area of their joint preaching tour (Acts 16:3).

these people who have received the holy Spirit just as we have?' (10:47).

The edict of tolerance issued by James, the brother of the Lord, at the so-called 'Jerusalem council' was the second solution, allowing Gentiles into the church without subjecting them to the whole Mosaic Law including circumcision. Against the conviction of the extreme Judaizers of Pharisaic affiliation, who considered circumcision and Torah observance as *sine qua non* even in the Jesus movement (15:1), the 'legal' obligations of the Gentile Christians were reduced to the so-called Noachic commandments: abstention from the pollution of idols (or from meat deriving from an animal offered as sacrifice to a pagan god), from unchastity, from what is strangled and from blood (15:20, 29). So thereafter officially the compromise prevailed, but all the evidence suggests that it was resented by the 'circumcision party' of the Judaizers in whose eyes Peter was a turncoat (11:2–3) and Paul a traitor, teaching all Diaspora Jews to abandon the Law of Moses and advising them against the circumcision of their children (21:21). It would seem that for as long as Law-observing Jewish Christianity endured, there was friction between the Palestinian and the Gentile church which ended in a split, and the progressive eclipse of the original form of the Jesus movement coincided with the triumphant rise of Gentile Christianity.

To sum up, how reliable is the picture of the early years of Christianity offered by the Acts of the Apostles? Admittedly it contains many editorial manipulations in seeking to harmonize the concepts of its author with the later outlook of the church. To these harmonizing and correcting efforts belong, for instance, the presentation of Peter as a champion of the Gentiles, the portrayal of Paul as a Palestinian charismatic, and the blaming of the whole Jewish nation for the death of Jesus.[7] But such revisions apart, which the perspicacious and

---

7. This oft-repeated accusation in the Acts makes no sense. Neither the Jewish pilgrims addressed by Peter at Pentecost (2:23) nor the crowd which accidentally witnessed the healing of a lame man in the Temple (3:14) were likely to be identical with the small group of the henchmen of the high priests who screamed, 'Crucify him' in the courtyard of Pilate's fortress. Besides, such an indiscriminate accusation would have alienated the people whom the apostles attempted to attract, persuade and convert. The charge would have been more appropriate if directed towards the chief priests and the council (4:10; 5:30). Yet even in that case Peter cited ignorance as a mitigating circumstance

receptive reader can easily detect, the Acts offers a genuine insight into the life, thinking and aspirations of the first generation of Christians. Its canvas stands between on the one hand the Christianity of Paul and John and on the other the picture of the hopes, aims and message of Jesus of Nazareth transmitted by the Synoptic Gospels. It may be stated in anticipation that it is closer to Jesus than to the elaborate theology of Paul and John.

The first unquestionable fact that appears from the Acts is that the companions of Jesus, and more generally the emerging adherents of Christianity in Palestine, did not consider themselves a separate religious entity, and at least during the infancy and childhood stages of the Jesus movement they still saw themselves as an integral part of the main body of Jewish society. Not only did they conform to the ordinary customs of the Jews (for example, the dietary laws), but they also practised the Jewish religion and prayed and worshipped as Jews. Their belief in Christ as master and Lord simply added a special, though fundamentally important, colouring to their common Judaism. Apart from the gut reaction of nausea attributed to the Jew Peter at the idea of eating non-kosher food or mixing socially with Gentiles, the most revealing feature in the behaviour of the members of the primitive church was their continued and unquestioning attachment to the Temple when they were in Jerusalem. This is all the more significant because after the destruction of the city in AD 70 the demolished sanctuary came to symbolize in the church the divine rejection of the Jews and their replacement by the Christians as the chosen people of God. Apart from the diatribe of the Hellenist Stephen against cultic worship, elements of an anti-Temple ideology are completely absent from the outlook of the apostolic group. Now if the historical Jesus had adopted a basically hostile attitude to Judaism and its institutions, this instinctive resumption of the ancestral religion by his closest disciples would have been quite incomprehensible. If the image of the primitive church in the Acts of the Apostles contains a grain of truth, one can assert with confidence that it is incompatible

---

(4:17). This leads one to assume that the idea of the charge of a wholesale Jewish culpability for the execution of Jesus penetrated these accounts after the failure of the apostles' mission to their co-religionists.

with the notion that Jesus was the founder of a new religion divorced from Judaism.

The only particular novelty in the primitive church of the Acts is the extraordinary spiritual exuberance of its members, but such external signs of ecstasy go hand in hand with the natural enthusiasm of a newly-born movement. The power that possession by the holy Spirit, dispatched by the glorified Jesus from heaven, conferred on believers was seen by them as proof of the risen Christ's continuing activity on earth.

We have seen that for the primitive church Jesus was the Christ, but his 'messianic' character conceived by the Acts is something quite special. This Jesus is devoid of kingly traits and there is nowhere the slightest suggestion that he played a political role.[8] The elevation of Jesus to a superhuman status does not precede (as in John), but follows his earthly career. While alive and among his disciples, he is portrayed as a holy Servant of God and God's final prophetic spokesman who is engaged on the establishment in the Jewish world of the awaited Kingdom of heaven.

The testimony of the Acts, conveying the impressions, beliefs and convictions of people who knew and heard Jesus, is of vital significance in the search for the historical figure hidden in the New Testament. It may be summarized in a blunt statement: the Acts of the Apostles contains nothing that could possibly be interpreted as pointing to a divine Jesus. It contains no prefiguration, not even a shadowy foretaste of Paul's Christ/Son of God, let alone John's eternal *Logos*. The contrast with John is complete and with Paul is substantial and the main cause of the difference is that the Acts, especially its pre-Pauline chapters, reflects the message addressed to the Jewish contemporaries of Jesus while Paul and John spoke to Gentile Christians.

Far from considering Jesus as God or a temporary expatriate from heaven, Peter qualifies him in the first public christological statement of the Acts as a Jewish prophet: Jesus of Nazareth, 'a man attested to you by God with mighty works and wonders and signs' (2:22; cf. 13:38). Our remaining task is to discover whether, and if so how, this concept

8. Only the Jewish critics of Paul in Thessalonica accused his followers of disloyalty to Rome by asserting that their Messiah was a rival of Caesar (17:7).

tallies with the evidence of the Synoptic Gospels and how the Jesus portrait in the Acts of the Apostles can be used to identify later Christian theological glossing in the biographical sketches produced by Luke, Matthew and Mark in their lives of Jesus.

# 6

# The Jesus of the Synoptic Gospels: charismatic healer and teacher and eschatological enthusiast

Unlike the theological pictures of Christ revealed in John and Paul and of the recently glorified and no longer physically present Master disclosed in the Acts of the Apostles, the portrait of Jesus in the Synoptic Gospels takes the form of a biographical sketch. Admittedly Mark, Matthew and Luke were not professional historians in search of critical objectivity; nevertheless they acted as narrators of the life, ideas, activities, teaching and death of a holy man of flesh and blood who lived a few decades before they sat down to record traditions forming around him. Finally, and succinctly, the evangelists testified to their belief in the resurrection of Jesus. Yet instead of conceding that the Synoptic evangelists were popular story-tellers, a large number of New Testament experts prefer to see them primarily as conveyers of a doctrinal message disguised as history. These authors are still under the influence of the famous policy statement of the great German scholar Rudolf Bultmann (1884–1976) who in 1926 wrote, 'We can know almost nothing about the life and personality of Jesus since the early Christian sources' – i.e. the Gospels – 'show no interest in either' (*Jesus and the Word*, 14).

This view is inspired, I fear, more by a learned Christian believer's disinclination to face up to the real Jesus than by the nature of the Gospel evidence itself. If the evangelists had intended to report, as Bultmann and his followers claim, not the life, ideas and aspirations of Jesus, but the doctrinal message corresponding to the spiritual and organizational needs of the primitive church, they would have been better advised to adopt the more suitable literary form of letters, tracts or sermons than to write a fake biography.

## THE LITERARY SOURCES

Starting therefore from the working theory that it is possible to approach the Jesus of history with the help of the first three Gospels, let us first glance at our sources. These Gospels have been attributed, in traditional order, to Matthew, Mark and Luke. However, the titles indicating authorship – the Gospel according to Mark, etc. – do not belong to the original compositions but have been added to them later by the church. The oldest reference to Matthew and Mark as authors of the first two Gospels comes from the fourth-century *Church History* by Eusebius of Caesarea (iii. 39, 16), who in fact cites Papias, the second-century bishop of Hierapolis. According to Papias, 'Matthew compiled the Sayings (*Logia*) in the Hebrew dialect' – the phrase normally means in Aramaic – 'and everyone translated them as well as he could.' Whether these *Logia* allude to our Gospel of Matthew, which contains more than just 'Sayings', and whether this Matthew was one of the apostles of Jesus, is highly questionable; none the less Papias supplies an early association of someone named Matthew with the first Gospel or parts of it.

The same Papias presents Mark as 'Peter's interpreter' who 'wrote down carefully, but not in order, all that he remembered of the Lord's sayings and doings'. This Mark may have been the John Mark mentioned in the Acts of the Apostles, who first accompanied, then abandoned, and later once more rejoined Paul (Acts 12:25; 13:5, 13; Philem. 24; 2 Tim. 4:11). On the other hand, the pseudonymous author of 1 Peter (cf. p. 110) alludes to an associate of his whom he calls 'my son Mark' (1 Pet. 5:13). Papias explicitly states that Mark did not hear or follow Jesus and consequently was not an eye-witness of the Gospel events, but was the mouthpiece of Peter.

As for the third Gospel, the earliest ascription to Luke, who as we have seen was possibly one of Paul's companions, is found in the late second-century list of New Testament writings known as the Muratorian canon, already mentioned in connection with the authorship of the Acts of the Apostles. In short, it cannot be taken for granted that any of the Synoptic evangelists was a close associate of Jesus, but all three belonged to the apostolic age.

The first three Gospels are named *Synoptic* because in general they reflect the same viewpoint and follow essentially the same story line; in consequence the three of them can be set out in parallel columns in a Gospel *synopsis*. The interrelationship of Mark to Matthew and Luke, and of Luke to Matthew, the so-called Synoptic problem, has been the subject of continuous debate for over two centuries without producing a wholly satisfactory and generally agreed result. For our purposes it is unnecessary to detail the pros and cons of the many theories advanced so far. I think it would be more useful to point out some facts and outline the most widely supported hypothesis.

Though roughly identical in structure, the three Gospels differ considerably in length. Mark is the shortest, eighteen pages in English translation in the Revised Standard Version, compared with the twenty-nine pages of Matthew and thirty-one pages of Luke. Matthew is more than 60 per cent and Luke more than 70 per cent longer than Mark. Most of the substance of Mark can be found in the other two Gospels, and most of the supplementary material in Matthew and Luke is roughly the same, but it does not appear in the same order. The bulk of the additional material common to Luke and Matthew is doctrinal in nature; in other words, they represent more fully the teaching attributed to Jesus which is included only sparingly in Mark.

These easily observable data have led Gospel experts to conjecture that Mark is an independent composition and that Matthew and Luke, apart from some elements peculiar to each, depend on Mark into which they insert the contents, variously arranged, of another compilation consisting of sayings and some stories. This is the so-called 'two-source theory': the first source is Mark and the other should be called S for Source, but since most of the pioneering literature was written in German, it is known in every language as Q (from *Quelle*, the German word for source). So the conjectural explanation of the Synoptic problem is that both Matthew and Luke, sitting at their desks, had in front of them the Gospel of Mark on the one hand and Q on the other, and wrote each in his own way an enlarged edition of Mark with here and there bits of Q, plus their own special traditions, interspersed in it. Even if we shut our eyes to the nineteenth-century concept of a scholar working in his study with open books before him, the main difficulty with this theory arises from the totally hypothetical character of Q. Despite all the speculative efforts of generations of scholars, and lately of the Q-Seminar in the United States, the fact remains that Q is nowhere attested in an independent written form; there are no Q manuscripts, no Q papyrus fragments, no quotations from Q cited in the books of the church fathers. We come closest to it in Papias's vague hint at Jesus' Aramaic *Logia* compiled by Matthew and in the Coptic sayings known as the Gospel of Thomas, the Greek original of which dates to the second half of the second century AD. However, neither would account for the stories in Q. Moreover, in my opinion most of the Gospel of Thomas is plainly secondary to the Greek New Testament. Strictly speaking, the correspondences between Matthew and Luke could be accounted for by either of them using and re-editing the other, and completing the revision with some additional traditions orally handed down in their respective communities.

From the point of view of our quest for the faces of Jesus in the Gospels, the precise solution of the literary conundrum is of little importance. So instead of wasting more time on it, I will start from the assumption that the general scholarly dating of the Synoptic Gospels is acceptable. Mark will be taken as originating shortly after the destruction of Jerusalem in AD 70; Matthew and Luke follow somewhat later, say between AD 80 and 100. Church tradition holds, without any solid evidence, that Mark was written in Rome. The derivation of Matthew from Palestine or Syria, and Luke from outside Palestine, is mere guesswork.

Of greater interest is the progressively widening chronological framework of the Gospels. Mark's is the most compact. He begins his narrative with the public appearance of John the Baptist and, if we discard the so-called longer ending (Mark 16:9–20) which is lacking in the oldest manuscripts, he concludes it with the disconcerting picture of three terrified women fleeing from an empty tomb. Matthew prefaces Mark with the genealogy and the story of the birth and early childhood of Jesus, and supplements it with an account of the resurrection of Jesus and his apparition to his disciples. Luke stretches the story further in both directions. The account of the birth of Jesus is preceded by that of John the Baptist and the childhood section is followed by an anecdote about Jesus as a twelve-year-old youth. At the other end, we find a canvas, more detailed than in Matthew, of the resurrection and repeated apparitions of Christ, crowned by a statement concerning his ascension to heaven. To sum up: having adopted the central core of the Gospel of Mark, Matthew and Luke attached to it a profoundly theological prologue and a similar epilogue, thus giving a peculiar slant to the whole story.

## THE JESUS PORTRAIT
## IN THE SYNOPTIC TRADITION

Under this heading, and divided into three sections, I survey the material relating to Jesus in the Synoptic Gospels. The elements of the portrait embedded in stories will come first, followed by the image emerging from the perception of Jesus by his contemporaries and reflected in the titles he bears in these Gospels. Thirdly, an analysis of his main teachings will complete the picture and help to determine his personality, ideas and ideals. When appropriate, additional information garnered from the Fourth Gospel will also be utilized. The task confronting us requires a painstaking inquiry; however, since the Synoptic Gospels comprise the richest raw material in the New Testament for building up an image of the historical Jesus, we cannot afford to spare our efforts.

## The Jesus of the Synoptic stories

### THE CARPENTER FROM NAZARETH

The main Gospel story, corresponding in substance to that of Mark, supplies a very patchy and schematic picture of the life of Jesus. He was already an adult, according to Luke about thirty years of age (Luke 3:23), when we first meet him on his way to his baptism by John. Today a thirty-year-old man is considered young, in his prime, but in the first century AD he would have counted as mature, middle-aged, almost verging on old age. Among the Dead Sea sectaries this age qualified members for the most senior offices, including that of Guardian General, and it should also be remembered that only a few of the skeletons exhumed from the Qumran cemetery belonged to men who were over forty.

By the age of thirty practically all male Jews, apart from the celibate Essenes, had been married for years. According to rabbinic rules a Jewish man was expected to go under the wedding canopy aged eighteen years, or twenty in the married branch of the Qumran sectaries. Yet none of the Gospels implies that Jesus at any time had a wife or children, certainly not during his public life. Misogyny is not evoked as the reason for his celibacy, as in the case of the Essenes, according to Philo and Flavius Josephus. In fact Jesus is depicted by the evangelists as surrounded by women friends and by incidental admirers. The Gospels do not remark on the anomaly and I reserve my own comments for Chapter 7, dealing with the Jesus hidden beneath the Synoptics.

Again the main Gospel tells us precious little about the family background, education and secular profession of Jesus. He grew up in Galilee, in Nazareth, an insignificant locality not mentioned in Josephus, the Mishnah or the Talmud, and first alluded to in inscriptions centuries later. His father Joseph and mother Mary were well-known citizens of Nazareth (cf. pp. 15–16), where they appear to have brought up a large family – Jesus, his four brothers, Jacob or James, the later head of the Jerusalem church, Jude the presumed author of a New Testament letter, Joseph and Simon, as well as several unnamed sisters (Mark 6:3; Matt. 13:55–6). Nothing in the New Testament itself would suggest that these men and women were not Jesus' full brothers and sisters. Mary is nowhere called a virgin except in the 'infancy' stories which were later added to the main Gospel tradition. In fact, only with the development of the belief in the *perpetual* virginity of the mother of Jesus did the need arise to find an innocuous explanation for the embarrassing presence of brothers and sisters in the Gospels. Some of the more recent New Testament apocrypha, like *The History of Joseph the Carpenter*, which survives in Arabic and Coptic, ascribe the four boys and two girls to an earlier marriage of Joseph, and modern Christian interpreters propose to extend the meaning of brother and sister so as to include less immediate relations such as cousins. But it is hardly necessary to point out that in any context other than the New Testament it would occur to no one to query the ordinary plain meaning of the words.

According to Gospel tradition, the family of Jesus were Galilean artisans. His royal descent on the paternal side is a theological embellishment which will be considered later. His father Joseph was a carpenter (*tekton*) and Jesus himself is described as practising the same trade: 'Is not this the carpenter's son?' (Matt. 13:55) or 'Is not this the carpenter?' (Mark 6:3). In Jewish society of the period the combination of religious learning with manual work or handicraft was by no means unusual. Peter and a number of his colleagues were fishermen; St Paul was a weaver and tentmaker, and well-known rabbis were surnamed 'the cobbler' or 'the smith', and so on.

For centuries Christian tradition cherished the idea of Jesus as a humble artisan working with his father, but lately some scholars have been keen to raise his social status: from a jobbing carpenter he has been elevated to the position of a building contractor. The background for this change was the 'discovery', in connection with the recent archaeological excavations of Sepphoris, that this important Gentile-Jewish city lies only four miles away from Nazareth. So if the firm Joseph & Jesus was looking for business, there was plenty of work in the Greek quarters of the nearby regional capital of Galilee where, with other projects, a large amphitheatre was being constructed. The fertile mind of certain researchers does not stop at this point. They further assume that Jesus watched plays in the theatre at Sepphoris. For how else could one explain his repeated use of the term *hypokritai* ('hypocrites') which in Greek can denote, among other things, 'actors'? Yet even if we assume that Jesus actually uttered the passages containing the word in question and disregard the fact that the theory presupposes Jesus' Greek was good enough to enable him to enjoy plays, and that, contrary to the ethos of Judaism, he was a theatre-goer, we are still faced with the firm pronouncement of a leading etymological expert against the interpretation of the Gospel terms *hypokrites* and *hypokrisis* in the sense of 'actor' and 'acting'. We are reminded that the Greek words in question, which normally mean 'self-righteous' and 'self-righteousness', are nowhere accompanied in the Gospels by association with the stage, drama, tragedy, dialogue, the watching public, etc., and that above all the concepts of actor and acting had no foothold in ancient Jewish culture.[1] All in all it is advisable to stick to tradition and accept that before his joining John the Baptist, Jesus of Nazareth was an unmarried, thirty-ish, small-town *tekton*, carpenter or builder.

Although the first-century apologists of Judaism, Philo and Josephus, enthused about the early religious instruction of Jewish boys – taught 'from their swaddling-clothes' by parents and teachers (Philo, *Legatio*, 115), and instructed in the laws from their 'earliest consciousness', having them 'as it were engraved on [their] souls' (Josephus, *Contra Apionem* ii. 178) – the common Gospel tradition remains silent on Jesus' education. Luke's legend concerning the twelve-year-old Jesus' extraordinary knowledge will be discussed later. The substance of this silence coincides, however, with an explicitly stated denial of formal training included in the Fourth Gospel: 'How is it that this man has learning, when he has never studied?' (John 7:15; cf. Mark 6:2; Matt. 13:54).

## JESUS THE TEACHER

How then did this apparently untaught and unqualified man metamorphose locally and regionally, and later perhaps nationally, into a renowned and profoundly influential teacher? We have mentioned earlier (see pp. 14–15), that the turning-point in the life of Jesus was unquestionably his meeting with John the Baptizer or Baptist, that extraordinary prophetic and eschatological figure who in the fifteenth year of the emperor Tiberius (AD 28/29) launched a crusade of repentance in Judaea (Luke 3:1). John, an ascetic from the desert, wearing rough clothes and living on a diet of locusts and wild honey (Mark 1:6), was the herald of the impending arrival of the Kingdom of God. According to his preaching, entry into the Kingdom required retreat to the wilderness without the creature comforts of ordinary life, a

1. James Barr, 'The Hebrew/Aramaic Background of "Hypocrisy" in the Gospels', in *A Tribute to Geza Vermes* (ed. P. R. Davies and R. T. White (Sheffield, 1990), 307–26, esp. 320. Some years ago I pointed out that in Talmudic Aramaic, the words 'carpenter' or 'son of a carpenter' (*naggar* or *bar naggar*) can also denote a scholar or a learned man. On reflection, I now consider that the probability of this surmise is extremely limited.

turning back from the ways of wickedness, and a simultaneous turning towards God. It is possible that he also announced the coming of a Messiah – 'After me comes he who is mightier than I' (Mark 1:7–8) – but this reference may be a later interpolation into John's message. The followers of Jesus no doubt felt the need to prove the higher status of their master because by seeking to be baptized by John, Jesus first tacitly recognized him as his superior.

It is implied in the Synoptics, without being stated in as many words, that Jesus remained in the company of John in the wilderness and did not start his own preaching mission until the imprisonment of the Baptist by Herod Antipas. In Galilee, the initial proclamation of Jesus echoed that of John: 'The time is fulfilled, and the Kingdom of God is at hand; repent and believe in the gospel', that is, in the good news of salvation (Mark 1:15; cf. Matt. 3:2).

The Gospels do not mention any further direct contact between the two preachers and suggest that John continued to entertain doubts about the religious role of Jesus. To dissipate these doubts, the Baptist is reported to have dispatched two of his disciples from the fortress of Machaerus, east of the Dead Sea, where he was imprisoned to face Jesus with the question, 'Are you he who is to come, or shall we look for another?' (Matt. 11:3). Jesus' reply is evasive, yet unmistakable because of its allusions to the prophet Isaiah (29:18; 35:5–6; 61:1): 'Go and tell John what you hear and see: the blind receive their sight and the lame walk, lepers are cleansed and the dead are raised up, and the poor have good news preached to them' (Matt. 11:5). In everyday language he would have said, 'You should draw your own conclusions once you have observed what is happening around me.'

If John's appreciation of Jesus was mixed with hesitancy, Jesus' praise of John also had a sting in the tail: 'Truly I say to you, among those born of women there has risen no one greater than John the Baptist; *yet he who is the least in the Kingdom of heaven is greater than he*' (Matt. 11:11). Whether this is understood as referring to the glory of the future elect contrasted with John's distinction on earth, or 'the least' is taken in the Hebrew/Aramaic sense of the term as the youngest one, the most recent one in a series, i.e. that Jesus is God's last and greatest messenger, John unsurprisingly comes out the worst in the comparison. Be this as it may, we must conclude that in the eyes of the writers of the Gospels, notwithstanding the initial appearances, Jesus stood out as the more eminent of the two preachers of repentance. However, outsiders like Herod Antipas placed both in the same category as is apparent from the exclamation attributed to him on hearing about the activities of Jesus: 'John whom I beheaded has been raised' (Mark 6:16). Similarly, non-committed Galilean contemporaries of Jesus thought that he was 'John the Baptist . . . Elijah . . . [or] one of the prophets' (Mark 8:28).

Ignoring for the moment the Jesus picture encapsulated in the doctrinal sections of the Synoptic tradition, let us try to determine the type of preacher Jesus was by eliminating those teaching classes to which he definitely did *not* belong.

Jesus did not proclaim – nor did John, for that matter – mysteries reserved for an esoteric group of initiates. It is true that he addressed exclusively the Jewish world, convinced as he was of being sent only to the lost sheep of the house of Israel (Matt. 15:24). Nevertheless, he addressed the Jewish world at large, unlike, for example, the Guardian or Master of the Dead Sea Community who was to 'conceal the teaching of the Law from men of injustice' (1QS 9:17). This open approach did not prevent him from occasionally granting supplementary explanation to his closer associates.

The Gospel passages which insist on Jesus and his disciples being sent exclusively to the Jews (cf. Mark 7:27; Matt. 10:6), with deliberately disparaging remarks about Gentiles called 'dogs' and 'swine' (Mark 7:27; Matt. 15:26; cf. Matt. 7:6), flatly contradict other sayings attributed to Jesus which envisage a universal mission of the apostles to all the peoples. In the so-called eschatological discourse Jesus declares that the gospel must be preached 'throughout the whole world, as a testimony to all the nations' (Matt. 24:14). The same theme is echoed in the saying reported by the two disciples on the road to Emmaus, namely that 'repentance and forgiveness should be preached in his name to all nations' (Luke 24:47). And above all, we have the solemn conclusion of Matthew: 'Go therefore and make disciples of all nations' (Matt. 28:19). The dilemma of Jewish versus universal mission is easy to resolve. If Jesus had made plain to his apostles that his message was meant for the whole world and not for the Jews alone, it would be impossible to explain why according to the Acts of the Apostles the primitive church, and Paul in particular, encountered so much well-nigh insurmountable difficulty apropos the admission of Gentiles into the Christian community. The only possible logical conclusion is that in order to legitimize the growing presence of non-Jews in the church, fictitious sayings were inserted into the Synoptics in which Jesus himself orders the promulgation of the gospel far beyond the confines of the Jewish world. The study of Mark confirms this understanding. The genuine core of this Gospel contains no mention of any dispatch of Jesus' disciples among the Gentiles – Mark 13:10 and 14:9 are surely inauthentic – but that event makes its appearance in the patently late longer ending where the apostles are enjoined, 'Go into the world and preach the gospel to the whole creation' (Mark 16:15).

Neither Jesus nor John was a teacher permanently resident in one locality. Jesus is definitely an itinerant preacher, visiting towns, villages and hamlets around the Lake of Galilee and occasionally venturing just across the border to Caesarea Philippi in the Golan, to the district of Tyre and Sidon in Phoenicia (Lebanon), or to the territory of the Decapolis in Transjordan.

As a preacher, Jesus did not adopt the traditional style of teaching in the form of Bible interpretation. Of course, the Synoptic Gospels ascribe to him a limited amount of instruction linked to scriptural exegesis; but this is often of the *pesher* type which, as we have seen in the Acts of the Apostles, is more natural in the setting of the primitive church than on the lips of Jesus. It represents, especially in Matthew, later Judaeo-Christian disputation with the Pharisees. The venue of Jesus' preaching varies: he taught in synagogues, streets and squares, in plains and on hillsides, and once even addressed from a boat an audience standing on the lake shore.

His teaching had always an informal air, and was often expressed in short proverbial sayings or in colourful similes and poetic parables. Joseph Klausner, who was the first and so far also the last modern Jewish scholar to publish a book on Jesus in Hebrew in 1922, hailed him as a truly outstanding teacher of morality and a master in the art of the parable, whose remarkable talent in these fields he considered unmatched anywhere in Jewish literature (*Jesus of Nazareth*, 414). The main topic of Jesus was the Kingdom of God, or Kingdom of heaven, and its moral requirements. The importance of the subject is disclosed by the sheer frequency of the expression, used about eighty times in the Synoptics. And since the Kingdom was a reality both momentous and impending, the message of Jesus was made distinctive by its essentially eschatological colouring and also by his own particular mode of delivery.

From the beginning Jesus' audience was stunned by his manner of preaching: 'He taught them as one who had authority, and not as the scribes' (Mark 1:22; Luke 4:32). This statement has frequently been misinterpreted by New Testament scholars. They have often contrasted the prophetic authority of Jesus with the teaching style of the rabbis who liked to hand down their doctrine in the name of the master from whom they had learned it, that is to say in the form of a chain of tradition which they traced back to Moses. But if the Gospel passage is read attentively and in full, it is almost impossible to miss the point. The evangelists indicate that the authority of Jesus' instruction arose from the cures and exorcisms that preceded or followed his preaching. What else can the exclamations of the astounded onlookers mean? 'What is this? A new kind of teaching with authority. When he commands, even the unclean spirits obey him!' (Mark 1:27; Luke 4:36). Consequently Jesus the teacher must be considered side by side with Jesus the healer and the exorcist.

## JESUS THE HEALER AND EXORCIST

Healing and exorcism are not always easily distinguishable in the Synoptic accounts since the expulsion of an evil spirit normally amounts to curing the possessed person. A fuller examination of ancient Jewish ideas relating to these subjects and to their historical and religious-social context will follow later. At this point it is enough to signal a formal differentiating factor: exorcism is always performed by a verbal command, whereas healing quite often entails some kind of a ceremony in the course of which the sick person comes into physical contact with the healer.

In several cases the Synoptic Gospels credit Jesus with mass healings. In Capernaum 'they brought to him all who were sick ... and he healed many who were sick with various diseases' (Mark 1:32, 34). From the shore of the Lake of Galilee he escaped in a boat, for after having healed many, 'all who had diseases pressed upon him to touch him' (Mark 3:10; Matt. 12:15; Luke 6:17–19). His reputation was such that as soon as it was heard that Jesus was approaching, people immediately brought to him all those afflicted with illness (Mark 6:53–5; Matt. 14:34–5). The same scenario is said to have been repeated all over Galilee. 'Wherever he came, in villages, cities or country, they laid the sick on the market places, and besought him that they might touch even the fringe of his garment; and as many as touched it were made well' (Mark 6:56; Matt. 14:36). In the Acts, the apostles Peter and Paul are shown in a similar role (cf. pp. 136–7), but the accounts also call to mind the modern spectacle of crowds flocking to famous faith healers, or for that matter visiting Hasidic rabbis (*Wunderrebbe*) renowned for their miraculous healing powers.

Faith on the part of the sick is an essential element in the healing process. It is always presumed and several times expressly stated, as in the cases of the blind Bartimaeus ('Your faith has made you well', Mark 10:52; Luke 18:42), the woman cured of a flow of blood ('Daughter, your faith has made you well', Mark 5:34; Matt. 9:22; Luke 8:48), and the centurion from Capernaum whose limitless trust in the healing power of Jesus obtained the instant cure of his servant (Matt. 8:13; Luke 7:9). On a sabbath day in a synagogue Jesus is described as restoring strength to the paralysed hand of a man by command alone, i.e. without any healing action, to avoid offending over-sensitive Jews who might have (wrongly) cavilled that the imposition of hands amounted to 'work' (Mark 3:5). Nevertheless, in many of the stories either the diseased person touches the healer, or even more often the healer lays his hands on the sick or performs some other therapeutic action involving bodily contact.

The former process is well illustrated by the woman suffering from haemorrhage, who was convinced that contact even with the garment of Jesus would restore her health (Mark 5:25–8; Matt. 9:20–21; Luke 8:43–4). According to the evangelists, Jesus in the middle of a madding crowd was aware of having come into contact with a particular individual: 'Someone touched me; for I perceive that power has gone forth from me' (Luke 8:46; Mark 5:30).

More commonly, however, it was the healer who took the initiative. Jesus lifted up the sick mother-in-law of Simon Peter by his hands

(Mark 1:31); he touched the body of a leper (Mark 1:41; Matt. 8:3; Luke 5:13) and the eyes of a blind man (Matt. 9:29); he laid his hands on sick people in Nazareth (Mark 6:5; Matt. 13:58) and on a crippled woman to straighten her (Luke 13:13).

The Gospels also include two accounts of healing ceremonies performed by Jesus in private. Somewhere east of the Jordan in the region of the Decapolis, he is said to have taken a deaf-mute aside from the crowd and putting his fingers into the man's ears he spat and touched his tongue; and looking up to heaven, he sighed, and told him in Aramaic, 'Ephphatha', or 'Be opened!' (Mark 7:33–4). Again at Bethsaida, on the northern shore of the Lake of Galilee, he led a blind man out of a village and 'spat on his eyes and laid his hands upon him' (Mark 8:22–3; cf. pp. 11–12). Since a number of healings took place at sabbath gatherings in various Galilean synagogues, the question of the lawfulness of curing the sick on the day of rest is raised repeatedly. I will return to it when discussing the Gospel picture of Jesus' relation to the Mosaic Law (see p. 195).

Jesus, the famous popular healer, is also a much sought-after exorcist, according to the Synoptic Gospels. Let us first glance briefly at the phenomenon of exorcism as outlined by the evangelists. It goes without saying that in intertestamental Judaism expelling demons was common practice and was performed by people from various strata in Palestinian society. The Gospels mention exorcists of Pharisee affiliation (Matt. 12:27; cf. Luke 11:19), and in our survey of the Acts of the Apostles we came across a group of itinerant priestly exorcists, the seven sons of the high priest Sceva (cf. p. 137).

In his Galilean career, exorcism seems to have been one of the chief occupations of Jesus. In Capernaum the inhabitants flocked to him with people who were ill or possessed by evil spirits, 'and he healed many who were sick with various diseases, and cast out many demons' (Mark 1:32, 34; Matt. 8:16; cf. Luke 4:41). He is pictured as continually criss-crossing Galilee, 'preaching in their synagogues and casting out demons' (Mark 1:39). Luke even attributes a saying to Jesus in which he defines his current and future mission essentially as that of an exorcist and healer: 'Behold I cast out demons and perform cures today and tomorrow, and on the third day I finish my course' (Luke 13:32).

Besides such general allusions, we find in the Synoptic Gospels particular exorcisms credited to Jesus. Apart from cases of demonic possession linked to physical or psychosomatic infirmities (dumbness, or blindness and dumbness combined, Matt. 9:32–3; Luke 11:14; Matt. 12:22), most of the Gospel examples belong to the category of mental or nervous illness. There was the screaming and convulsed man with an unclean spirit whom Jesus met in the synagogue at Capernaum (Mark 1:26; Luke 4:35), and the Gergesene demoniac 'with an unclean spirit', who lived among the tombs, could not be held even with a chain and was continuously shrieking and wounding himself with a stone (Mark 5:1–5; Luke 8:26–7). Less explicit, yet still fairly clear, is the description of the daughter of the Greek woman from the region of Tyre and Sidon who was severely possessed by a demon before it was exorcized by Jesus, but lay quietly on her bed afterwards (Mark 7:24–30; Matt. 15:21–8). Finally all three Synoptics contain a vivid picture of a young epileptic deaf-mute facing Jesus. 'When the spirit saw him [Jesus], he immediately convulsed the boy, and he fell on the ground and rolled about, foaming at the mouth' (Mark 9:17–18, 20; cf. Matt. 17:14–21; Luke 9:37–43). The father explained that the demon had often cast the child into fire and water; when Jesus ordered it to go, the boy suffered seizures and became rigid like a corpse, so that the bystanders thought he was dead before Jesus wakened him (Mark 9:22–8).

Among both Jews and non-Jews the expulsion of evil spirits was usually performed by means of an incantation. No such 'liturgy' is attested in connection with Jesus in the Synoptics. As for the Jesus of John, he has nothing to do with exorcism (cf. p. 11). Among the four anecdotes on the subject recounted by the Synoptists, in the case of the daughter of the Syro-Phoenician woman the expulsion of the demon achieved from a distance is simply declared to be a *fait accompli* (Mark 7:29; cf. Matt. 15:28). Elsewhere Jesus is portrayed as ordering the devil out of the possessed person: 'Be silent, and come out of him!' (Mark 1:25; Luke 4:35), or 'Come out of the man, you unclean spirit!' (Mark 5:8; Luke 8:29). Or with greater solemnity, 'You deaf and dumb spirit, I command you, come out of him, and never enter him again!' (Mark 9:25). The final clause implies that in some cases, like one detailed in a later Gospel incident, the return of the expelled demon was foreseen: 'When the unclean spirit has gone out of a man, he passes through waterless places seeking rest, but he finds none. Then he says, "I will return to my house from which I came." . . . Then he goes and brings with him seven other spirits more evil than himself, and they enter and dwell there, and the last state of that man becomes worse than the first' (Matt. 12:43–5; Luke 11:24–6). To put it in contemporary jargon, some of the exorcisms produced a temporary remission and could be followed by a serious relapse.

Not only Jesus but also his disciples devoted themselves to the practice of exorcism and healing. On their first independent mission the apostles were granted by Jesus 'authority over the unclean spirits' (Mark 6:7; Matt. 10:8). Another group, the seventy-two disciples, proudly reported on their return, 'Even the demons are subject to us in your name' (Luke 10:17). What is more, an outsider to the fellowship of Jesus is said to have expelled demons in his name (Mark 9:38), and rabbinic literature alludes to a certain Judaeo-Christian by the name of Jacob of Kefar Sama who claimed to heal 'in the name of Jesus' (tHullin 2:22–4). In short, a charismatic atmosphere surrounded the whole Jesus movement.

Other 'miracle' stories may be treated as a brief appendix to healing and exorcism. The raising of the dead as depicted in the Synoptics is an extension of healing. The epileptic boy in Mark 9:26 (cf. p. 161) and Eutychus in Acts 20:9–10 (cf. p. 137), whom the onlookers believed to be dead, were probably only comatose; they were revived, the first by Jesus and the second by Paul. The story of the awakening of the daughter of Jairus occurred shortly after neighbours had declared her gone; according to Jesus she was only asleep (Mark 5:39; Matt. 9:24; Luke 8:53). Even the young man from Nain must have been pronounced dead no more than a few hours earlier, since according to Jewish custom the funeral takes place soon after the person has expired. When Jesus touched the bier, the 'deceased' got up (Luke 7:14). The only person definitely described as dead who is said to have been reawakened by Jesus was Lazarus, already buried for four days. 'Lord, it already stinks,' Martha, the deceased's sister, apparently warned Jesus. But this story is unknown to the Synoptics and is one of John's special features (John 11:39).

Only a few other miracle accounts remain. The stilling of the storm on the lake (Mark 4:39–41; Matt. 8:26–7; Luke 8:24–5) belongs to the class of weather miracles known from the Bible and rabbinic literature. The feeding of a crowd with a disproportionately small quantity of food (Mark 6:35–44; Matt. 14:15–21; Luke 9:12–17) also has a scriptural antecedent (2 Kings 4:42–4). Some stories seem to be patently legendary, such as Jesus taken for a ghost and walking on the lake by night (Mark 6:49; Matt. 14:26), and the miraculously large catch of fish (Luke 5:6). One obviously midrashic-legendary story outshines them all. I refer to the lucky discovery of a shekel coin in the mouth of a fish caught by Peter on Jesus' instruction and providing just the right amount of money to pay the Temple tax, one half-shekel each, for both master and pupil (Matt. 17:24–7).

However, the fame of Jesus was not based only on his healing and casting out demons. He was also the renowned physician of the spiritually sick, those whom 'decent' Jews despised and relegated to pariah status. They were symbolized by the 'publicans and sinners', the tax-collectors and prostitutes. Just as he did not avoid contact with contagious disease, Jesus did not shun the company of social outcasts, thereby causing astonishment and even scandal in bourgeois circles. To their query about his participation in a meal given by a publican and attended by many of his colleagues, Jesus justified his presence by identifying them with those who are ill and need the help of a physician (Mark 2:17; Matt. 9:12; Luke 5:31). It is also specifically reported that he allowed a prostitute ('a woman of the city who was a sinner', Luke 7:37, 39, cf. Mark 14:3; Matt. 26:6–7) to anoint him. This custom of accepting the companionship of the despised was sufficiently well established and of common knowledge to endow Jesus with the contemptuous nickname 'friend of tax-collectors and sinners' (Matt. 11:19; Luke 7:34). If his vocation as a healer and exorcist was for the sick and the possessed, he also saw himself primarily as one sent to assist those in the greatest spiritual need: 'I came not to call the righteous, but sinners' (Mark 2:17; Matt. 9:13; Luke 5:32). And again the overriding concern of both Jesus and his disciples was for the miserable and the helpless: 'I was sent only to the lost sheep of the house of Israel' (Matt. 15:24). 'Go to the lost sheep of the house of Israel' (Matt. 10:6).

## JESUS SEEN BY FRIENDS AND FOES

As we would expect in the case of an unconventional and influential person, we find in the Synoptics two very different attitudes towards Jesus depending on whether we consider the views of his admirers or his critics.

### FRIENDS

The twelve chosen apostles, the constant companions of Jesus, seem to have turned their backs on families, jobs and property in order to follow their itinerant master. They resembled to some extent the Therapeutae, or Egyptian Jewish ascetics akin to the Palestinian Essenes, who left behind their possessions, 'their brothers, their children, their wives, their parents, the wide circle of their kinfolk, and the groups of friends around them' in order to seek holiness (Philo, *Vita contemplativa* ii. 18). The first four apostles, Simon, surnamed Peter or Cephas (Rock), his brother Andrew and the two sons of Zebedee, James and John, were Galilean fishermen. According to John 1:44, Philip too came from Bethsaida, the fishing village of Peter and Andrew; so he may reasonably be presumed to have been a fisherman too. The background of the remaining eight remains obscure. If the apostle Matthew was identical with the tax-collector Matthew or Levi son of Alphaeus (Matt. 9:9; Mark 2:14; Luke 5:27), he may have belonged to a higher, but also highly unpopular, social stratum. Finally, should the tag 'Cananean' (*Qannai* in Hebrew/Aramaic) or 'Zealot' mean, not a particularly zealous and devout Jew, but a political revolutionary (a dagger-man or *Sicarius*), the anti-Roman faction of Galilee would also have had a representative in the immediate circle of Jesus. Some scholars also interpret the term Iscariot, the surname of Judas, as derived from *Sicarius*, but the grounds for this derivation are flimsy.

Another somewhat larger group, which included several women, formed Jesus' regular entourage. Originally the members of his family distanced themselves from him (cf. p. 15), but if the Acts of the Apostles can be trusted they re-established a link with his disciples following the death of Jesus and some time before the first Pentecost (Acts 1:14).

At that moment the number of the faithful is listed as 120 (Acts 1:15), but this is a symbolic figure (twelve represents the Israelite tribes and ten is the minimum quorum of a Jewish assembly). The real size of the circle was probably smaller; some of those who abandoned Jesus and fled when he was arrested (Mark 14:50; Matt. 26:56) may never have rejoined the company of the apostles.

According to the Gospels, Jesus was often surrounded by large Galilean crowds, thanks to his reputation as a charismatic healer (Mark 3:7; 5:21; Matt. 4:25; Luke 6:19, etc.). The evangelists give the impression that he was extraordinarily successful. Soon after the start of his ministry, he 'could no longer openly enter a town, but was out in the country' (Mark 1:45). Although his fame reached as far as Tyre and Sidon, Transjordan, and possibly even further (Mark 3:7–8; Matt. 4:25; Luke 6:17), he was not extended a warm welcome beyond the borders of Galilee. The inhabitants of the place variously designated as Gergesa, Gerasa or Gadara politely urged him to keep away from their neighbourhood. No doubt they resented the loss of their swine, which like lemmings jumped into the lake and perished, after – as people thought – Jesus permitted exorcized demons to enter the local herd of pigs (Mark 5:11–17; cf. Matt. 8:30–34; Luke 8:32–7). The site of the episode is more likely to have been Gergesa, close to the eastern shore of the lake. Manuscript variants identify the town as Gadara or Gerasa (Jerash). But if the swine had taken off from either of those places they would have been required to fly rather than jump, if they were to land in the Sea of Galilee. No multitudes greeted Jesus when he ventured to visit the district of Tyre and Sidon in Syro-Phoenicia (Mark 7:24; Matt. 15:21) or Caesarea Philippi (Mark 8:27; Matt. 16:13) in the region of Panaias-Ituraea. In Samaria, Jesus as a Jew was positively cold-shouldered: 'He sent messengers ahead of him . . . to make ready for him, but the people [of a Samaritan village] would not receive him, because his face was set towards Jerusalem' (Luke 9:52). Unsurprisingly, Jesus enjoined his disciples to avoid Samaria (Matt. 10:5), but his command seems to have been forgotten in later years.

The Synoptic evangelists supply few details of Jesus' reception in Judaea, but since they, unlike John, make him travel only once to Jerusalem, this is perhaps to be expected. We are told in passing that on his way to the capital, as a healer he attracted a crowd in Jericho (Mark 10:46; Matt. 20:29; Luke 18:36). In Jerusalem, too, he had a large audience (Mark 11:18; 12:37), but this was normal because he was teaching at the Temple, where in the days leading up to Passover multitudes would gather. The only episode involving 'crowds of people' in Jerusalem outside the Temple is the so-called triumphal entry of Jesus to the city, when 'many' or 'most of the crowd' spread their garments on the road (Mark 11:8; Matt. 21:8). However, according to Luke Jesus was surrounded not by a throng of Jewish people attracted by his fame, but by the disciples who had accompanied him from Galilee (Luke 19:37). There is no evidence in the Synoptics of an enthusiastic welcome offered to Jesus outside his northern homeland.

## FOES

Curiously, hostility to Jesus came at first from the least expected quarter, namely his family and his neighbours. They were no doubt motivated by a feeling of awkwardness and petty jealousy at the sight of the sudden transformation of the local carpenter into a celebrated exorcist. Mark goes so far as to assert that his relations wanted to restrain him, as they thought that he had gone crazy (Mark 3:21). Similarly, the reason why his mother and brothers summoned him from the midst of his disciples was probably to stop the nonsense in which he had got himself involved. This would explain the sharp rejoinder in which he redefined his family: 'Who are my mother and my brothers? ... Whoever does the will of God is my brother and sister and mother' (Mark 3:31–5; Matt. 12:46–50; Luke 8:19–21).

As for the people of Nazareth, the brief Gospel accounts reveal among them a feeling of local patriotism mixed with the inferiority complex of small-minded people. In present-day language their reaction could be translated as 'Who does this fellow think he is?' This in fact is the sentiment which underlies their questions: 'Is not this the carpenter (or: the carpenter's son)?' (Mark 6:3; Matt. 13:55; Luke 4:22). The chauvinism of the Nazareth people is expressed in their complaints when Jesus performs wonders in Capernaum and not in his own town (Luke 4:23). Their *petit bourgeois* outrage and the family's embarrassment are countered by Jesus' stoical comment, 'A prophet is not without honour, except in his own country, and among his own kin, and in his own house' (Mark 6:4; Matt. 13:57). Yet even if his neighbours were genuinely scandalized (Mark 6:3; Matt. 13:57) and grudging, their jealous feelings cannot possibly account for their turning into an enraged lynch mob ready to push Jesus to his death from the local hilltop (Luke 4:29).

The Synoptic records of the conflict between Jesus and the doctrinal and religious authorities of Palestinian Jewry are easy to reproduce, but rather difficult to assess. The evangelists would like us to think that the official teachers, Pharisees, scribes and lawyers, as well as the Temple authorities and their allies, the aristocratic Sadducees and the supporters of the Galilean ruler Herod Antipas (the Herodians), all sought to bring down Jesus. Closer analysis of the Gospels, even without a comparison using evidence supplied by sources from outside the New Testament, tends to blur the picture. For instance, the Galilean opponents of Jesus are called Pharisees and Herodians in Mark (3:6), just Pharisees in Matthew (12:14) and scribes and Pharisees in Luke (6:7). Were these all the same? There is, too, a general tendency to consider 'Pharisees', 'scribes' and 'lawyers' as representing the same class. However, it should be remembered that Mark and Luke explicitly speak of 'the scribes of the Pharisees', thereby implicitly admitting that other scribes may have belonged to other parties or were without any party affiliation. And if by anticipation we bear in mind that any substantial presence of the Pharisees in Galilee in the early first century AD is at best unproven and in general highly improbable, and that the blame for handing Jesus over to the secular arm of Rome is placed by the Synoptists on the shoulders of the chief priests and their allies with no explicit mention of the Pharisees (Mark 11:27; Matt. 21:23; Luke 20:1; Mark 15:1; Matt. 27:1; Luke 22:66), we must conclude that in all likelihood Jesus only came into serious conflict with the Temple authorities in charge of law and order in Jerusalem at the very end of his public career. None the less, I would not wish to deny the possibility that in understanding and interpreting the Law in his own peculiar way Jesus incurred the muttered disapproval of conservative Galilean scribes and synagogue presidents. The aim of this argument is to emphasize that the collision which resulted in the actual death of

Jesus was not with the Jews in general, but with the Jerusalem-centred religious-political leadership.

As the issue of Torah observance will be discussed later, I will restrict myself to two examples to illustrate doctrinal discussions. In a debate which is probably more fictional than real, and corresponds to controversies between primitive Christianity and the Sadducees, Jesus disagreed with the Sadducean denial of the doctrine of bodily resurrection (Mark 12:18–27; Matt. 22:23–33; Luke 20:27–40) and sided with the Pharisees who believed in it. Similarly, on the point of the great commandment regarding the love of God and love of the neighbour (Mark 12:28–34; Matt. 22:34–40; Luke 10:25–8), as on Jewish ethics in general, he is voicing Pharisee opinion. Indeed, it is very likely that the anti-Pharisee diatribes put into the mouth of Jesus in chapter 23 of Matthew did not originate with him, but are echoes of controversy between the early Jerusalem church and the Pharisee teachers in the second half of the first century AD. Even there the Pharisees are criticized for not following their own correct teaching: they sit on Moses' seat (that of the president of the synagogue) and teach the truth; practise and observe whatever they tell you, but not what they do (Matt. 23:2).

## The account of the death and resurrection of Jesus

### THE PASSION STORY

The downfall of Jesus is presented as planned and executed essentially in Jerusalem. The crucial intervention by the chief priest and his circle was triggered by the disturbance caused by Jesus in the merchants' quarter in the Temple where the indignant Galilean holy man overturned the tables of the money-changers (who provided the right kind of currency in silver coins struck in Tyre for gifts to the sanctuary), and the stalls of the merchants selling approved sacrificial animals to worshippers (Mark 11:18; Luke 19:47; Mark 14:1; Matt. 26:3; Luke 22:2). Again we are told that it was to the chief priests that Judas betrayed Jesus (Mark 14:10; Matt. 26:14–15; Luke 22:3–4) and that they were the party responsible for his arrest, interrogation, and his delivery to Pilate (Mark 15:1; Matt. 26:47–27:2; Luke 22:54–23:1).

The real reason for the execution of Jesus will be examined in

Chapter 7. Here we need only say that he was the innocent victim of a hasty procedure which fell short of a formal trial either before the Jewish council or at the tribunal of the Roman prefect of Judaea. The Synoptic Gospels give a highly confusing account of events. Arrested after the Passover supper in the evening of 14 Nisan, Jesus is said by Mark and Matthew to have been brought before the high priest and the Sanhedrin at night on a charge of blasphemy for calling himself the Messiah, son of God (Mark 14:43–64; Matt. 26:47–66). Luke alludes to Jesus appearing before the council on the morning of Passover day (Luke 22:66). John brings forward the proceedings by twenty-four hours (cf. above pp. 20–21), eliminating the Passover supper, but avoiding the problem of placing the condemnation and crucifixion of Jesus on the feast-day.

Practically every detail of the Synoptic account conflicts both procedurally and substantively with any known Jewish law. No court hearing was legal at night, let alone on the feast of Passover, nor did the words attributed to Jesus amount to blasphemy. Next, without any further explanation the supreme Jewish authorities dispatched Jesus, already found guilty as a blasphemer, to appear before Pilate on the previously unmentioned charge of political agitation, or that of being a royal pretender. Once again there was only a summary hearing and not a proper Roman trial. It ended with Pontius Pilate pronouncing the death sentence on Jesus, who was to be executed on the Roman cross (Mark 15:1–37; Matt. 27:11–50; Luke 23:2–46).

The Synoptics tell us that after the arrest of Jesus all his disciples abandoned him and ran away (Mark 14:50; Matt. 26:56) except Peter, who followed him to the high priest's palace. However, even he denied Jesus when challenged by a maid in the courtyard to admit he was one of his associates: 'He began to invoke a curse on himself and swear, "I do not know this man of whom you speak"' (Mark 14:66–71; Matt. 26:69–74; Luke 22:54–60). Only a group of Galilean women stayed with Jesus to the end, watching him die 'from afar' (Mark 15:40–41; Matt. 27:55–6). It was left to the previously unmentioned Joseph of Arimathea to place, in great haste and before sunset, the body of Jesus in a rock tomb, discreetly watched by Mary Magdalen and the other women (Mark 15:43–7; Matt. 27:57–61; Luke 23:50–53). On the third day, in the early hours of Sunday, the same two or three women (in Mark's account a third one is called Salome) set out with spices and ointments to complete the burial rites of their lost master. With their experience at the tomb opens the Synoptic report on the afterlife of Jesus.

## THE RESURRECTION NARRATIVES

The topic of the resurrection of Jesus was of paramount importance in the thinking and belief of his followers, as its treatment in the Acts of the Apostles, the letters of Paul and the Fourth Gospel makes clear. Together with the redeeming death of Christ, it is the foundation and cornerstone of the theological edifice of Christianity. Yet it remains a puzzle, confusing even to those who find the notion of actual reunification of a dead body with a soul still rationally acceptable today. The handling of the story by the Synoptists therefore deserves particularly close scrutiny.

To grasp the true import of the problem, we must bear in mind that the idea of resurrection is not a theme that is frequently discussed in the Old Testament. Death and the shadowy semi-existence in the underworld were seen there as ineluctable parts of the destiny of man. Jewish tradition was more familiar with the notion of escaping Sheol, the biblical Hades, than with bodily resurrection. Thus the antediluvian patriarch Enoch is said to have moved from earth to Paradise, and the prophet Elisha witnesses the transfer to the celestial region of his master, the prophet Elijah, on a chariot of fire in the midst of a whirlwind (Gen. 5:24; 2 Kings 2:11). Intertestamental literature includes works on the ascension to heaven of Moses and of Isaiah.

The raising of the dead is occasionally intimated in the Old Testament. The same prophets Elijah and Elisha anticipated Jesus in reviving children; Elisha apparently achieved it by means of a kiss of life (1 Kings 17:19–22; 2 Kings 4:34–6). But since the resuscitation happened almost immediately after they were presumed to be dead no one paid much attention to its beneficiaries and we are not told what happened to the two boys in later life. The New Testament writers felt no need to report on the restored lives of the daughter of Jairus, the young man from Nain, or Eutychus, the accidental victim of Paul's over-long after-dinner speech in Troas. Nobody seems to question either what happened to the many risen saints who, according to Matthew, were seen by numerous witnesses wandering about in the holy city following the earthquake that shook Jerusalem at the moment of Jesus' death (Matt. 27:52–3). Did they repair to their tombs or did they live ever after? The truth is that Jews in the age of Jesus were unaccustomed to handling the problem of a 'historical' resurrection. The universal rising of the dead before the final judgement was quite a different matter and occupied a well-established slot in Jewish eschatological thinking from chapter 12 of the Book of Daniel onwards, though in the first instance resurrection was held to be the privilege of the righteous alone.

As far as Jesus is concerned, study of the Synoptics shows that the concept of resurrection did not play an important part in his vision of the hereafter; he preferred to speak about it more in terms of eternal life than of re-awakened dead bodies. We must also remember that neither the authors of the Old Testament nor post-biblical Jewish writers inferred that either the death or resurrection of Israel's Messiah was expected in any way. This means that Jesus and his disciples were not preconditioned by tradition or education to look forward to a risen Christ; so the first narrators of the Jesus story had no pattern to follow when they tried to explain what happened to their deceased and buried teacher.

What do we find, then, in the Gospels? It seems clear that the disciples did not entertain any hope of an impending resurrection, judging from their behaviour after Jesus' arrest – they all fled – and their original disbelief on Easter day. Neither did the women who set out for the tomb to anoint the body of Jesus. But this lack of expectation patently conflicts with the claim repeated no less than five times in the Synoptic Gospels that Jesus distinctly predicted not only his death, but also his resurrection on precisely the third day (Mark 8:31; 9:9, 31; 10:33–4; 14:28). This most significant prophecy of Jesus appears to have fallen on deaf ears or to have sunk straight into oblivion, with not a single apostle or disciple recalling it during the crucial hours between Friday and Sunday, or even later when the resurrection became the central topic of the preaching of the primitive church. Luke alone realized this internal contradiction and tried to overcome it by suggesting that the women were reminded of Jesus' prediction by the two men they had met in the empty tomb (Luke 24:7–8). If all his close companions had known exactly what was going to happen, despite their instinctive anxiety they would have comforted themselves with the thought that on the third day all would be well. As this manifestly was not the case, one is inclined to conclude that the announcements concerning the resurrection of Jesus are later editorial interpolations. They are often accompanied by clumsy explanations, namely that Peter was unwilling to believe the words of Jesus and began to rebuke him (Mark 8:32–3; Matt. 16:22–3), and that the apostles were dim-witted and could not comprehend what resurrection from the dead meant (Mark 9:10; 9:32; Matt. 17:23; Luke 18:34).

As we might expect, the earliest of the Gospels gives the least elaborate and polished account of the resurrection. According to Mark, as soon as the sabbath was over, i.e. Saturday after sunset, Mary Magdalen, another Mary and Salome purchased spices and early on Sunday morning before sunrise hastened to the tomb to complete the burial rites (Mark 16:1–2). Finding the stone rolled back, they entered and to their amazement they found seated there a white-robed youth from whom they learned that Jesus, who had risen and gone, had left for them an instruction to pass on to Peter and the apostles that they should meet him in Galilee (Mark 16:3–7). However, the women were so terrified that they ran away, intending to say nothing to anyone (Mark 16:8). In the oldest manuscripts Mark's Gospel stops abruptly at this point, with three women frightened out of their wits fleeing from the dark empty tomb.

The other Gospels endeavour to improve on this unsatisfactory ending. Even supposing that, when calm, Mary Magdalen and her two companions told the apostles what they had seen, the earliest evidence for the resurrection of Jesus would depend on hearsay, on the words of a *single* unknown young man – *unus testis nullus testis* – reported by three unreliable *female* witnesses. Luke increased the number of the women, but still let it be known that the apostles discounted their report as silly, an 'idle tale' (Luke 24:10–11). Finally Matthew (Matt. 28:2–3, 5) reinforced the primary source by substituting an angel as the herald of the resurrection for Mark's youth, while Luke wrote of two men, splendidly dressed (Luke 24:4). On second thoughts, Luke also identified the two men as angels (24:23).

The account as it related to the female witnesses also underwent various modifications. While Mark's women fled terrified and unwilling to speak, those of Luke calmly reported the story to the apostles (Luke 24:4, 6–8). Matthew represents a half-way house: his women, both frightened and joyful, ran to the disciples (Matt. 28:8). However, in the patriarchal society of intertestamental Judaism a woman's testimony could not be trusted. Hence Luke brought in male witnesses (Luke 24:24) and according to the Fourth Gospel Peter and another apostle went to check Mary Magdalen's account (John 20:3–8). No doubt still not satisfied with their record, the evangelists added to the list a series of apparitions of Jesus starting with two disciples travelling to Emmaus. They met a stranger on the road whom they later believed to be the risen Jesus (Luke 24:13–34).

Thereafter the story of the empty tomb was allowed to fade away and faith in the resurrected Jesus was supported by apparitions seen by an increasing number of disciples. Nevertheless even at this more advanced stage of the tradition the account of Matthew still contradicts that of Luke. According to Matthew, Jesus appeared some days later, and only once, to the eleven apostles on a Galilean mountain; most of them believed, but some doubted the reality of the manifestation (Matt. 28:16–17). Luke, on the other hand, having already stated that Simon Peter had seen the Lord, refers to a further visionary experience by all the apostles in Jerusalem. They first thought they were watching a ghost, but were reassured by Jesus that he was not bodiless. Luke knows nothing of a meeting with Jesus in Galilee and makes him ascend to heaven on Easter Sunday (Luke 24:50–51). But according to the beginning of the Acts of the Apostles, Jesus is allowed to spend another forty days on earth. The tradition transmitted by Paul ignores the empty tomb, and founds Christian faith in the resurrection of Jesus, not just on the word of Peter, James and all the apostles and on his own vision, but on the massive testimony of 500 brethren who experienced together, at an unspecified time and in an unnamed location, an apparition of the risen Christ (1 Cor. 15:5–7).

In short, Gospel tradition was manifestly trying to strengthen the reliability of the evidence from the 'idle talk' of panic-stricken women to what comes nearest to first-hand testimony, the attestation by trustworthy men, numbering from one to 500, of having seen Jesus alive.

As has been noted, doubts arose even in the circle of the closest intimates (Matt. 28:17), and the rumours of alternative explanations circulated in Jerusalem. One of these, apparently widespread among uninvolved Jews, is formally reported in Matthew, namely that the body of Jesus was stolen by his disciples (Matt. 28:13, 15). But if no one expected him (or the Messiah) to rise from the dead, why should anyone feign a resurrection?

Three further explanations are implicitly evinced in the Gospels. In John, Mary Magdalen wondered whether the body of Jesus was re-buried by someone in another place. Mistaking the resurrected Jesus for the 'gardener' in charge of the burial ground, she inquired of him, 'Sir, if you have carried him away, tell me where you have laid him, and I will take him away' (John 20:15).

The same Gospel of John tries to thwart another explanation, but it periodically resurfaces even nowadays, namely that Jesus did not really die on the cross and was revived later. To counter such gossip, the evangelist stresses that the Roman military executioners saw that Jesus had died before the other two men who had been crucified with him. However, just to make death absolutely certain, one of the soldiers sank his spear into Jesus' chest (John 19:33–4).

Finally, another sneaking suspicion had to be quelled. Did the women, by any chance, who were no doubt physically and mentally exhausted after two sleepless nights and who had dragged themselves – still in the dark – to anoint Jesus, enter the wrong tomb? The emphasis laid by all three Synoptists on the women's knowledge of the location of the grave was meant to refute the rumour about a possible mistaken identity of Jesus' burial place.

To summarize: no one can trace exactly the first stages of the spiritual conviction that led from despair followed by a belief mixed with doubt to the established doctrine of the resurrection of Jesus. In my opinion, the implicit evidence of the Acts of the Apostles may be of help. According to that chronicle the apostles attributed the continued efficacy of their charismatic healing and exorcistic activity to the power of the name of Jesus risen from the dead and enthroned in heaven. Put differently and looked at from an existential stance, the genuine Easter miracle can be seen in the metamorphosis of the apostles. In Paul Winter's apposite words, 'Crucified, dead and buried, [Jesus] yet rose in the hearts of his disciples who had loved him and felt he was near' (*On the Trial of Jesus*, 208).

## The titles of Jesus in the Synoptics

The titles, for example Messiah or son of God, given to Jesus in the Gospels represent a shorthand formulation of a religious judgement whereby sympathetic onlookers expressed their opinion about him. They furnish a very valuable complement to the Jesus portrait in the narrative accounts of Mark, Matthew and Luke. These titles have already been encountered in their theologically more advanced form in the Fourth Gospel and in Paul. Here in the Synoptics we find views which in essence are reasonably close to Jesus of Nazareth himself, and for this reason may be considered historical, at least in a broad sense.

As a rule, these titles do not come from the mouth of Jesus. Unlike the Christ of John, the Jesus of the Synoptic Gospels was not preoccupied with himself. His vision was focused on God and not on someone called Jesus. There is, however, one exception, the phrase 'son of Man'; so it is with this oddity that I shall begin.

## The 'son of Man' in the Synoptics

The meaning of 'son of Man' in the Synoptics has already been considered as a first step towards its interpretation in John, where it figures eleven times; Paul ignores it altogether and the odd occurrence of the phrase in the Acts and in the Book of Revelation is of no particular significance. Not wishing to repeat in detail the preliminaries dealt with earlier (cf. pp. 38–41), in summary the expression, literally 'the son of the man', renders in Greek the Aramaic *bar 'enasha* or *bar nasha*, the Aramaic words signifying either 'man' or 'the man', a noun, or 'someone', the indefinite pronoun. Used in combination with 'one like a son of man' from the apocalyptic vision of Daniel 7:13, the phrase has acquired a titular function referring to the figure of the messianic judge at the end of time. Linked to this in the Fourth Gospel is the idea of travel from heaven to earth and from earth to heaven, by virtue of which John's 'son of Man' is transformed into a heavenly being temporarily exiled on earth but longing to return to his real home (cf. p. 41).

In contrast, the bulk of the 'son of Man' instances in the Synoptics can best be interpreted in a non-titular sense. They may be categorized as Aramaic circumlocutions in which the speaker, always Jesus in the Synoptics, wishing to avoid a direct reference to himself, replaces 'I' by the equivocal and more modest 'son of Man'. Occasionally the context and/or the Synoptic parallels make absolutely plain that by 'son of Man' the speaker is meant. Take for example Jesus' words to a paralysed man, 'But that you may know that *the son of Man* has authority on earth to forgive sins . . . *I* say to you, Rise' (Mark 2:10), or his question to the apostles at Caesarea Philippi in Matthew's formulation, 'Who do men say that *the son of Man* is?' (Matt. 16:13) as against 'Who do men say that *I* am?' in the other Synoptics (Mark 8:27; Luke 9:18).

Jesus is often given as a topic his future suffering and death – a taboo, or his exaltation – a boastful subject in direct speech; hence the use of the circumlocution. We have on the one hand, 'How is it written of the son of Man, that he should suffer many things and be treated with contempt' (Mark 9:12; Matt. 17:12), and on the other, 'The son of Man has authority on earth to forgive sins' (Mark 2:10; Matt. 9:6; Luke 5:24). In one Gospel example, 'son of Man' combines the Aramaic notion of human beings as opposed to animals and the circumlocution is intended to conceal the destitute state of the speaker: 'Foxes have holes, and the birds of the air have nests, but the son of Man has nowhere to lay his head' (Matt. 8:20; Luke 9:58).

In the Synoptics, there are only two instances of 'son of Man' which explicitly allude to Daniel 7:13. The first, 'They will see the son of Man coming in clouds with great power and glory' (Mark 13:26; Matt. 24:30; Luke 21:27), is introductory to the scene of eschatological judgement, and the second, 'You will see the son of Man seated at the right hand of Power, and coming with the clouds of heaven' (Mark 14:62; Matt. 26:64; Luke 22:69), represents Jesus' answer to the high priest's question whether he was the Messiah. In short, the Synoptic 'son of Man' combined with Daniel 7:13 coalesces into an exegetical construct, often called an early church *midrash*, and *qua* title it has a definite messianic and eschatological significance. The same remark applies to the excerpts containing implicit references to Daniel 7 (Mark 8:38; Matt. 16:27; Luke 9:26, etc.).

## The Messiah or Christ

Let us turn to the genuine titles capable of shedding light on how Jesus was perceived by his Galilean and Judaean fellow countrymen. The foremost of these are Messiah or Christ, son of God, Lord, and Prophet. Before beginning a brief examination of these titles, I ought to warn the reader that their significance has developed during two millennia of Christianity. Our task is to determine, not how they are understood today, but what they meant to Jews in the first century AD.

## Messianism in Jewish sources outside the New Testament

In its basic meaning, the Hebrew/Aramaic *Mashiah/Meshiha* and the Greek *Christos* indicate someone anointed with oil. In the Hebrew Bible the rite of anointing occurs in ceremonies appointing an Israelite king like Saul (1 Sam. 10:1), a prophet like Elisha (1 Kings 19:16) or priests, for example Aaron and his sons (Exod. 28:41). 'The Anointed of the Lord', generally a royal title, is regularly given to David and his descendants, but once exceptionally to the Persian king, Cyrus (Isa. 45:1), the deliverer of the Jews from their Babylonian captivity.

In traditional parlance and expectation the phrase 'the Anointed King' acquired, after the dethronement of the Davidic rulers by the Babylonian emperor Nebuchadnezzar in 586 BC, the specific sense of *the* Messiah, the final Jewish monarch who would defeat all the foreign nations, subject them to Israel and his God, and thus inaugurate the Kingdom of heaven. Such a saviour figure was anxiously awaited in the intertestamental age, especially during periods of political agitation against the dominating foreign power, the Greeks in the Maccabaean period, and the Romans after the conquest of Palestine by Pompey in 63 BC, and even more so in the course of the years leading up to the two wars of the Jews against Rome in the first and second centuries AD.

Prayers are probably the best source to consult if one tries to discover what kind of deliverer ordinary people longed for. The Psalms of Solomon (17 and 18) of the first century BC, as well as most of the messianic texts among the Dead Sea Scrolls of a similar date, together with the famous synagogal prayer, the Eighteen Benedictions attributable in substance to the first century AD, all convey a colourful picture of the hoped-for royal Messiah. Here is the anointed ruler of the Psalms of Solomon (17:23–36), powerful, just and holy:

> Behold, O Lord, and raise up unto them their king, the son of David . . .
> And gird him with strength that he may shatter unrighteous rulers . . .
> And he shall gather together a holy people . . .
> He shall have the heathen nations to serve him under his yoke . . .
> And he shall be a righteous king taught by God . . .
> And there shall be no unrighteousness in his days in their midst,
> For all shall be holy and their king the Anointed [of] the Lord.

The prayer known as the Blessing of the Prince of the Congregation, the future military chief of the Qumran community, envisages a similar warlike figure endowed with features of godly wisdom:

> The Master shall bless the Prince of the Congregation . . .
> that he may establish the kingdom of his people for ever . . .
> May the Lord raise you up to everlasting heights and as a fortified
>     tower . . .
> [May you smite the peoples] with the might of your hand and ravage the
>     earth with your sceptre.
> May you bring death to the ungodly with the breath of your lips!
> [May he shed upon you the spirit of counsel] and everlasting might,
> the spirit of knowledge and the fear of God . . . (1QS$^b$ 5:20–25).

Admittedly, this prayer does not contain the actual term 'Messiah', but other Dead Sea passages come to our rescue and clarify the matter. They refer, for instance, to 'the Messiah of righteousness, the Branch of David' (4Q252 6 on Gen. 49:10), or describe as the 'Branch of David' the ultimate Prince of the Congregation who will defeat the Kittim-Romans (4Q285).

Finally, perhaps the most influential of all Jewish daily prayers, the Eighteen Benedictions, quoted here from its Palestinian recension, also witnesses the central hope in the coming of the anointed righteous king.

> Be gracious, O Lord, our God, according to thy great mercies
> to Israel thy people, and Jerusalem thy city,
> and Zion, the residence of thy glory,
> and to thy Temple and dwelling-place,
> and to the kingdom of the house of David, thy righteous Messiah.

Behind the central character of the eschatological anointed king, future conqueror of earthly empires and guardian of truth and justice in the Kingdom of God, stand in a less prominent position other figures produced by theological speculation in the priestly and mystical circles of intertestamental Judaism. With the rise of the Maccabaean-Hasmonean priestly family to the leadership of the Jewish nation in 152 BC moves towards the institution of priestly Messianism began. The Testament of Levi, a work dating back to the mid-second century BC but repeatedly revised, speaks in its chapter 18 of a 'new Priest' who will 'execute righteous judgement upon the earth'. His 'star shall arise in heaven as of a king' and will bring peace to all the earth.

The notion of the priestly anointed is firmly testified to in the Dead Sea community, which was awaiting a Messiah of Aaron and a kingly Messiah of Israel, a Priest and the Prince of the Congregation, or a priestly Interpreter of the Law and the Branch of David. This Messiah of Aaron is conceived of as the ultimate high priest presiding over the great battle liturgy during and after the final encounter between the forces of light and darkness described in the Qumran War Scroll. In another document, the Blessing of the High Priest, we read:

> May the Lord lift his countenance towards you . . .
> May He choose all of them that sit in your pries[tly college] . . .
> May he place upon your head [a diadem] . . . in [everlasting] glory . . .
> May he fight [at the head of] your thousands . . .
> May he lay the foundation of your peace for ever! ($1QS^b$ 3:1–21).

There are further messianic concepts, such as that of a messianic Prophet or a prophetic Messiah, in the Cave 1 manuscript of the

Qumran Community Rule in its reference to the coming of 'the Prophet and the Messiahs of Aaron and Israel' (1QS 9:11). We have some vague hints at a 'Messiah of the spirit', a heavenly or angelic Redeemer, in the Melchizedek document from Qumran (11Q13). The Fourth Book of Ezra and the Second Book of Baruch, two apocalyptic works of the late first century AD allude to a Messiah hidden in heaven and waiting to be revealed later. These non-royal figures are, however, of little assistance in a study of the Synoptics. And despite the crucifixion of Jesus, the same judgement applies to the representation of a slain Messiah of the tribe of Ephraim occasionally mentioned in rabbinic literature. This Messiah was expected to perish in the encounter with the final foe, Gog, whose army would subsequently be vanquished by the Messiah son of David. Since no text speaking of a slain Messiah predates the second Jewish revolt against Rome during the reign of Hadrian (AD 132–5), this picture is likely to have been modelled on the fallen leader of that rebellion, Simeon bar Kosiba, who was killed in the battle at Bethar in AD 135. Thus chronologically he is disqualified as a potential model of the Gospels' Messiah. This general sketch of Jewish Messianism should provide the historical context for a proper understanding of the relevant title of Jesus.

## The title 'Messiah' in the Synoptics

Of the two main usages of the title Messiah, the eschatological high priestly function is plainly not applicable to the Jesus of the Synoptics: he was not a hereditary Jewish priest. Not even the heavenly Pontiff of the Epistle to the Hebrews has any proper messianic connotation (cf. pp. 107–8). This leaves us with the image of the royal figure, the traditional anointed king of Israel. Clearly at some later stage clumsy attempts were made, especially by Matthew in his 'infancy' story, to create a Davidic pedigree for Jesus, but the main Synoptic tradition includes no support for it apart from the shout 'Hosanna to the son of David' at Jesus' entry to Jerusalem (Matt. 21:9; Mark 11:9–10; Luke 19:38), and the occasional call of 'Son of David', addressed to him by strangers. However, none of the latter appears in a context which has 'political' connotations; they are all linked to stories of healing by the 'son of David', that is to say the miracle-worker of the messianic age (Matt. 9:27; 12:23; 15:22; 20:30–31; Mark 10:47–8; Luke 18:38–9).

Neither did Peter issue a political manifesto when he answered Jesus' question 'Who do you [my disciples] say that I am?' with 'You are the Christ' (Mark 8:29; Matt. 16:16; Luke 9:20). The term 'Christ' is unspecified in Mark. Matthew's more detailed parallel, 'You are the Christ, *the son of the living God*', seems to confirm that the Synoptic Gospels have not royal Messianism in mind; neither is such a suggestion implicit in the Acts of the Apostles, when Jesus is simultaneously proclaimed 'Lord and Christ' (Acts 2:36; cf. p. pp. 119–20). Contrary to the claim of some contemporary New Testament interpreters, the general context of the portrait of Jesus in the Synoptics and in the rest of the New Testament shows that he was not a pretender to the throne of David, or a would-be leader of a revolt against Rome.

The accusation that Jesus sought to become king of the Jews or royal Messiah first surfaces in the Gospels on the day of his crucifixion, or more precisely at the moment of the transfer of his case from Jewish to Roman jurisdiction. Thereafter Pilate is always cited as referring to Jesus as the king of the Jews. The Roman charge or *titulus*, written on the cross, also read 'The King of the Jews' (Mark 15:26; Matt. 27:37). The explicit indictment of disloyalty to the emperor is probably Luke's creation: 'We found this man perverting our nation, and forbidding us to give tribute to Caesar, and saying that he himself is Christ the king' (Luke 23:2). Incidentally the charge is refuted by the only relevant reference to the payment of tax preserved in the Gospels, where Jesus is recorded as declaring, 'Render Caesar the things that are Caesar's' (Matt. 22:21). In fact, when under pressure from Pilate to substantiate their accusation, even in Luke's version the chief priests become rather vague: 'He stirs up the people, teaching throughout Judaea, from Galilee even to this place' (Luke 23:5). All in all, the whole political charge sounds hollow.

We must ask, therefore, did Jesus regard himself as *the* Messiah, the royal, Davidic Messiah? Or, to formulate the question more accurately, how do the Synoptic Gospels describe his reaction when he is called Messiah or is questioned about his messianic status? His response to being publicly proclaimed the Messiah oscillated between the unenthusiastic and the negative. Demon-possessed people, we are given to believe, and Satan himself in the legend of the Temptation (Matt. 4:3; Luke 4:3), were regularly silenced by Jesus when they called him the Messiah or son of God (Luke 4:41; Mark 1:34). More significantly, Peter's confession at Caesarea Philippi that Jesus was the Christ was also met, in what seems to be the original version of the story, with a strict order to keep silent (Mark 8:30; Matt. 16:20; Luke 9:21). This prohibition is not necessarily tantamount to a denial of messiahship, but the ensuing reference to the future suffering and death of Jesus was a tacit rejection of his role as the triumphant Christ, the only kind of Messiah ordinary Jews were expecting. In any case, this is how the outraged Peter understood it, provoking a firm reprimand from Jesus, 'Get behind me, Satan!' (Mark 8:33; Matt. 16:23).

The Gospel of Matthew inserts, between Peter's confession about Jesus being the Christ and the order issued by Jesus to leave the matter alone, the famous words of congratulation, 'Blessed are you, Simon Bar-Jona! For flesh and blood has not revealed this to you, but my Father who is in heaven', followed by the declaration that Peter would be the rock on which the church would be built (Matt. 16:17–18). Once again we are facing irreconcilable statements. It would seem, however, that in the circumstances it is more likely that the praise of Peter in Matthew represents a later attempt to alleviate the shocking impact of Jesus' unwillingness to confirm that he was the Messiah than the hypothesis that Mark and Luke omitted those significant words, especially if it is borne in mind that 'Jesus is the Christ' was the principal confessional formula of the primitive church.

When the evangelists refer to inquiries by the Jewish high priest and the Roman prefect regarding the messiahship of Jesus, with one exception the answer quoted is at best equivocal and more often seems to be negative. To 'Are you the Messiah (or: the king of the Jews)?', Jesus is said to have replied, 'You have said so' or 'You say that I am' (Matt. 26:64; 27:11; Luke 22:70–23:3; Mark 15:2). While it is not impossible to understand these words as a confirmation, the weight of probability favours an oblique denial: 'You have said so' followed by a tacit 'not I'. An English equivalent might be, 'I hear you' . . . but don't agree. The Gospel idiom is echoed in rabbinic literature with a phrase similar to 'You have said it'. As this was an answer to an insult

– 'Admit that the high priest's dog is more eminent than you' (tKelim I, 1:6) – it was bound to carry a negative sense.

There is, however, one exception to Jesus' evasiveness. To the high priest's inquiry about his messianic status, according to Mark he simply answered, 'I am' (Mark 14:62). This is an unparalleled case, which may be explained as a deliberate editorial attempt to eliminate equivocation. In any case, we cannot disregard those manuscript witnesses of Mark 14:62 which attest the customary 'You say that I am'.

The fate of Jesus before the Roman authorities, like that of several self-proclaimed Jewish redeemer figures listed by Flavius Josephus (cf. above, p. 27), demonstrates the risk that anyone rumoured to be a political Christ incurred in the powder keg of Palestine in the first century AD. If Jesus had had political ambitions, if he had as it were run for the office of Messiah and had encouraged his partisans to proclaim it to all and sundry, it is most unlikely that the Romans would have allowed his public career to last even the one year envisaged by the Synoptic Gospels.

## The title 'son of God'

Various aspects of the 'son of God' concept have been investigated in earlier sections, from the biblical and post-biblical meanings of the expression to the use made of it in the Fourth Gospel, Paul and the Acts of the Apostles. Before coming to grips with the Synoptics, we must remember that the Jewish attestations of 'son of God' are all metaphorical. Secondly, we can also safely put aside as irrelevant to the portrayal of Jesus those scriptural and intertestamental texts which represent the general sense of 'son of God', i.e. every son (or daughter) of Israel irrespective of his or her religious and moral standing. We should focus our attention instead on the biblical and post-biblical patterns of the Messiah and of saintly or charismatic Jews. Finally, dealing with Jesus during his lifetime, we need not take into account the specific application of the title 'son of God' to Christ *after* his resurrection, which figures in Paul and the Acts of the Apostles.

We can distinguish two kinds of Synoptic use of the title 'son of God' as applied to Jesus, depending on whether we are dealing with self-identification or with an address or description formulated by a third party. Every passage in which Jesus speaks of God as his Father, whom he used to call *Abba* in his Aramaic prayer (Mark 14:36), may be treated as an indirect self-reference with the meaning of the term remaining wide open. Only two texts qualify as direct self-identification. In the first, not even 'the Son' shares the Father's knowledge of the arrival of the Kingdom of God (Mark 13:32; Matt. 24:36). The second appears in a poem ascribed to Jesus: 'All things have been delivered to me by my Father, and no one knows the son except the Father, and no one knows the Father except the son' (Matt. 11:27; Luke 10:22). The first, probably a genuine saying of Jesus, implies that the 'Son' is not equal, but inferior to the Father. He is less privileged than the Teacher of Righteousness of Qumran who possessed the key to all the eschatological mysteries (1QpHab 7:3–5). The second excerpt sounds more like John than the Synoptics, and is best understood as part of a primitive Christian hymn.

Among the numerous examples in which Jesus is described or directly addressed as 'son of God', we have already touched on two cases where the title is synonymous with the royal Messiah who, like the Jewish king of former times, was seen symbolically as a progeny of God. I have in mind Peter's confession as reported by Matthew, 'You are the Christ, the son of the living God' (Matt. 16:16), and the high priest's question to Jesus, 'Are you the Christ, the son of the Blessed [or: the son of God]?' (Mark 14:61; Matt. 26:63; Luke 22:70). To these can be added the proclamation heard at the moment of Jesus' baptism by John in the river Jordan. This heavenly voice, a 'daughter of the voice' or *bat qol* in the language of the rabbis, was either addressed to Jesus, 'Thou art my beloved son; with thee I am well pleased' (Mark 1:11; Luke 3:22), or to the assembled company, 'This is my beloved son, with whom I am well pleased' (Matt. 3:17). Its likely messianic connotation may be deduced from the Baptist's hint at someone to come who will be greater than he (cf. p. 155). The same *bat qol* is reported as testifying at the scene of the Transfiguration too (Mark 9:7; Matt. 17:5; Luke 9:35). However, Jewish literature also associates such heavenly pronouncements with charismatic holy men without a messianic reputation (see Chapter 7).

Another group of sayings reported by the evangelists centre on the idea of miraculous power. This power may be demonstrated through the casting out of evil spirits and in other extraordinary happenings, or just in the awe inspired by a 'son of God'. The Synoptists write of exorcized individuals proclaiming, 'You are the son of God' (Mark 3:11; Luke 4:41) or the complaints of demons after receiving marching orders from the exorcist, 'What have you to do with me, Jesus, son of the Most High God?' (Mark 5:7; Matt. 8:29; Luke 8:28). In a completely different context, the phrase was used sarcastically by the jeering onlookers who taunted the dying Jesus, 'If you are the son of God, come down from the cross' (Matt. 27:40; cf. 27:43; Mark 15:32; Luke 23:35). On the other hand, at the sight of the extraordinary events which according to the Gospels accompanied the death of Jesus (the earthquake, and the rent of the Temple curtain), Mark and Matthew make the Roman centurion supervising the execution cry out, 'Truly this was a son of God' (Mark 15:39; Matt. 27:54).

## The title 'Lord'

The title 'Lord', as we have seen in John (cf. pp. 34–5), Paul (cf. pp. 82–3) and the Acts (cf. pp. 119–20), is common currency in the New Testament. Yet here is one of the oddities of modern biblical scholarship, namely the view that this title says nothing about the historical Jesus, or even about Palestinian Christianity's understanding of Jesus. It is widely held, under the influence of the renowned German scholars Wilhelm Bousset and Rudolf Bultmann, that the New Testament use of 'Lord' originated with the Gentile church, in imitation of the terminology of mystery religions (the worship of the Lord Osiris or Hermes) and of the imperial cult of Rome where the emperor was addressed as 'Lord' (*Kyrios*) or 'our Lord and God' (*Dominus et Deus noster*). So that the perplexed reader can grasp the full significance of the phrase in the Synoptic Gospels and form his own judgement, I will discuss this crucial title in the light of its Semitic and Greek linguistic background.

Both Hebrew/Aramaic and Greek-speaking Jews of the intertestamental age were familiar with the term 'lord' (*'adon, mar(e)* or *kyrios*) in various senses, but the precise nuance of the word entirely depends on the context in which it appears. An outline of the linguistic phenomenon will be enough to enable the non-philologist to assess the Gospel usage.

In the human context, the title 'lord' in the sense of 'master' or 'Sir' is regularly used in all the Jewish languages (Hebrew/Aramaic and Greek) of the intertestamental period, as well as in later rabbinic literature. In the non-religious field it denotes persons in authority. Beginning with the family, in the Aramaic Genesis Apocryphon from Qumran Methuselah addresses Enoch with 'Oh my father, oh my lord', and Lamech is spoken to by his wife with similar solemnity, 'Oh my brother, oh my lord' (1QapGen 2:9, 24). Likewise, in a Greek funerary inscription from the Jewish cemetery of Bet Shearim, two sons describe their dead parents as 'my lord father' and 'my lady mother'. This is echoed in rabbinic literature when it stipulates that after his death a father should be referred to as 'my father, my lord' or 'my father, my master' (*abba mari*).

Moving to the top position in the secular field, we find the king invoked as 'Lord'. In the Genesis Apocryphon from Qumran Pharaoh of Egypt is so addressed by one of his princes, and the king of Sodom by Abraham. Likewise in rabbinic literature the Patriarch Judah the Prince salutes the Roman emperor as 'Our Lord, the King' (Gen Rabba 75:5).

In the religious field, the Aramaic *mar/mari* in the sense of 'master' regularly refers to a teacher, as do the Hebrew titles *rab* and *rabbi*, as well as *rabbun/rabbuni*. However, since among both the Palestinian and the Mesopotamian Jews teachers wielded administrative power, the Patriarch or 'chief rabbi' in Galilee was called 'Rabban' and the Exilarch, the corresponding dignitary in the Babylonian Jewish community, *Mar*. A similar terminology was in use in the Syriac church with bishops, priests and saints being designated as *Mar*. But *mar*, rather than Rabbi, characterizes the first-century BC charismatic Abba Hilkiah. When the humble Hilkiah refused to admit before rabbinic emissaries that he was responsible for ending a long drought, the rabbis declared, 'We know full well that the rain came on account of *mar*' (bTaanit 23b).

At the summit of the religious ranking, but still in the human sphere, 'lord/*mar*' is addressed to the prophet Elijah by a saintly rabbi (Gen Rabba 94:9) and also to the Messiah who was asked, 'When will the

Lord come?' (bSanhedrin 98a: *athe mar*, a phrase reminiscent of *Maran atha* in the New Testament).

Finally, it is well known that in direct continuity from 200 BC to AD 300 Jews used the title 'Lord' in speaking of, or to, God in Hebrew, Aramaic and Greek. The author of the bilingual (Hebrew and Aramaic) biblical book of Daniel, completed in the second century BC, employs both *'adon* and *mare*. Outside the Bible, the Qumran Genesis Apocryphon among the Dead Sea Scrolls makes frequent use of the same terminology in phrases such as 'Lord of greatness', 'Lord of heaven and earth', 'Lord of the worlds' (the latter is the rendering of the tetragram YHWH), etc. The sectarian Thanksgiving Hymns from Qumran Cave 1 always invoke God as 'my Lord' (*adonay*). In Jewish Greek, be it a free composition like the Wisdom of Solomon or a translation from the Hebrew such as Ben Sira or Ecclesiasticus, *Kyrios* is substituted with monotonous regularity for both YHWH and *'adon*. God was still called *Kyrios* in ossuary inscriptions from the third century AD at Bet Shearim, and 'Lord' continued to be steadily employed in Jewish prayer recorded in the classic sources of rabbinic Judaism.

The constant use of 'lord' in its various meanings represents therefore a deep-seated Jewish linguistic custom which can be traced unchanged over five centuries. In fact, this continuity provides the best refutation of the thesis that the title 'Lord' entered the Gospels as a loan from Hellenism via Gentile Christianity, with no Palestinian Semitic antecedents.

Set against its linguistic backcloth, the Synoptic use of 'lord' stands out distinctly. Negatively, there is not a single instance in Mark, Matthew or Luke in which Jesus as 'Lord' is associated with anything to do with divinity. Only in John, and even there only once, are the two concepts formally linked by Thomas's invocation of Jesus as 'My Lord and my God' (John 20:28). It is therefore beyond doubt that this reverential title, in addition to being applicable to God, possesses a variety of other meanings so that its precise significance cannot be determined without a context any more than, for instance, that of the English 'Sir', the title of a schoolmaster in a school and the form of address of a king in a royal palace.

It is very important to note that 'lord' is never linked in the Synoptics to the messianic function of Jesus. The nearest we come to it is in the interpretation of Psalm 110:1, 'The Lord said to my *lord*, Sit at my right hand', where the Christ is labelled 'the *lord*' and not 'the son' of David (Mark 12:35–7; Matt. 22:41–6; Luke 20:41–4). However, the passage is presented in the Gospels as a (probably spurious) exegetical debate with the Pharisees, having no direct link with Jesus himself.

The largest group of the Synoptic examples using the invocation 'Lord' comprises miracle stories. 'Lord, if you will, you can make me clean', a leper begged Jesus (Matt. 8:2; Luke 5:12); so did the centurion from Capernaum, 'Lord, I am not worthy to have you come under my roof' (Matt. 8:8; Luke 7:6). The moving words of the Syro-Phoenician woman, pleading for her sick daughter, exude limitless trust in the power of the not very forthcoming healer: 'Yes, Lord; yet even the dogs under the table eat the children's crumbs' (Mark 7:28; Matt. 15:27). To these and many other appeals by outsiders we may add similar requests by members of Jesus' entourage. 'Save, Lord, we are perishing' is the cry attributed to the apostles in a boat tossed by the storm (Matt. 8:25; 14:28, 30). Amazement at the realization of their own charismatic power inspires the childlike enthusiasm of the disciples at their first success: 'Lord, even the demons are subject to us in your name' (Luke 10:17; cf. also 5:8; 9:54), and the experience of the miraculous prompts the question, 'Lord, Lord, did we not prophesy in your name, and cast out demons in your name, and do many mighty works in your name?' (Matt. 7:22).

In spite of such an abundance of evidence to the contrary, scholars inclined to deny the authenticity of the use of 'Lord' in Palestinian Jewish circles do not fail to underline the fact that this title never figures in Mark, the oldest Gospel, excepting in the case of the Syro-Phoenician woman who was neither Jewish nor an Aramaic speaker. Their argument is, however, insubstantial and incomplete. It entirely relies on the text printed by the scholarly editors of Mark and pays no attention to that part of the manuscript evidence which shows Mark's familiarity with the mode of address, 'Lord' (see, for example, Mark 1:40; 9:22; 10:51).[2] The same scholars also overlook the role of the narrative

2. Quoting from one edition of the Greek New Testament rather than another may alter the picture. For instance my 1964 Nestle edition of *Novum Testamentum Graece* lists the manuscripts which have 'lord' in the above quoted passages of Mark, but the more recent 1981 *Greek–English New Testament* with the critical apparatus prepared by Kurt and Barbara Aland ignores all the variants which attest 'lord'. So user beware!

style of Mark. Whereas Matthew adopted the biblical manner of story-telling with speeches reproduced in the form of a direct quotation, Mark opted for succinctness and indirect speech. Compare, for instance, 'She came and knelt before him, saying, *Lord*, help me' of Matthew 15:25 with 'She begged him to cast the demon out of her daughter' in Mark 7:26.

After its use in the context of the miraculous, the title 'lord' most frequently appears as an equivalent of 'teacher'. In fact, Luke tends to confuse the two (cf. 8:24; 9:49; 17:13). In Mark, too, the blind Bartimaeus from Jericho seeking the restoration of his eyesight turns to Jesus with the Aramaic word *rabbuni* or 'my Teacher' (Mark 10:51) and not with 'Lord', as in Matthew (20:33) and Luke (18:41). However, this apparently inappropriate title may not be as unsuitable as that if it is borne in mind that *rab* has a much broader meaning than 'teacher', and often designates a chief, i.e. a person in authority, close to 'lord' or 'master'.

## The title 'Prophet'

The various categories of prophet with which Jews of the first century AD were familiar, the teacher, the eschatological prophet and the wonder-worker, have already been outlined and discussed in earlier chapters (see above, pp. 27–8 and p. 118). However, both the Acts of the Apostles and John represent an already developed stage of New Testament reflection on the prophetic idea. For them Jesus was *the* prophet, the ultimate and decisive spokesman of God. The Synoptic Gospels, revealing an earlier portrait, present their readers with *a* prophetic figure more in tune with the ideology of first-century Jews in general.

### PROPHECY IN JUDAISM

'Since the death of the prophets Haggai, Zechariah and Malachi the holy Spirit ceased from Israel' (tSotah 13:2) is a famous rabbinic saying, signifying that Israelite prophecy came to an end in the late sixth century BC, shortly after the rebuilding of the Temple of Jerusalem by the Jews who had returned from Babylonian captivity. From then on divine revelation was conveyed according to the belief of the rabbis by the *bat qol* or heavenly 'daughter of a voice' like the one introduced by the evangelists at the moment of the baptism of Jesus. The cessation of prophecy is referred to also in the First Book of the Maccabees (9:27) and in Flavius Josephus, who wrote: 'From Artaxerxes [fifth-century BC Persian ruler of Palestine] to our own time the complete history has been written, but has not been worthy of equal credit with the earlier records, because of the failure of the exact succession of the prophets' (*Contra Apionem* i. 41). Nevertheless, intertestamental literature, the Dead Sea Scrolls, Josephus in a roundabout way, and the New Testament all seem tacitly to contradict this view and attest that up to the time of the first Jewish war against Rome (AD 66–70), prophetic activity among Palestinian Jews continued and further prophets were still awaited.

For the sake of formal classification, biblical prophets may be divided into two categories. While they were all recognized as communicators between God and the Jewish people, some of them were primarily preachers and poets, and the others primarily doers. The political, religious and eschatological message of the former was recorded in the prophetic books of the Bible; they are of no special concern for us here. On the other hand, the historical compositions of the Old Testament, especially Samuel and Kings, testify to the deeds, often the miraculous deeds, of the wonder-working prophets among whom Elijah and Elisha were the most famous. The Bible credits them with stopping and starting the rain, making polluted water drinkable, curing the sick, and reviving the dead (cf. above, p. 170). It is this miraculous aspect of prophecy that is relevant to the Jesus picture in the Synoptic Gospels as well as to popular Palestinian Judaism, which will be examined in the next chapter.

The continuing speculation surrounding the figure of Elijah, the prophet who having escaped death was believed to have gone to heaven in a chariot of fire, played an important part in the thinking of the evangelists. Building on the prediction of the prophet Malachi that Elijah would return (Mal. 4:5), a tradition evolved beginning with the Book of Enoch (90:31, 37) and the Wisdom of Ben Sira or Ecclesiasticus in which this Elijah was identified as the forerunner of the Messiah who would be sent to prepare the day of the Lord: 'It is written that you are to come at the appointed time with warnings' (Ecclus. 48:10).

But in addition to Elijah, the Jews of the time of Jesus expected another prophet, promised by Moses in Deuteronomy 18:15–18. He, like Moses himself, would be the transmitter of the final message of God. This messenger, *the* Prophet, the ultimate mouthpiece of God or messianic Prophet, mentioned in 1 Maccabees (4:46; 14:41) and in the Cave 1 manuscript of the Qumran Community Rule (1QS 9:11), is identified, as we have seen, with Jesus in the Acts of the Apostles and the Fourth Gospel.

Our survey should end with mention of the hybrid figure combining the prophet and the political Messiah (cf. above, p. 27). Characters identified as such were held responsible for the recurring upheavals and the ensuing death of many gullible Jews in the years leading up to the first Jewish revolt against Rome. The *bêtes noires* of Josephus, who called them 'deceivers and impostors' promising miraculous signs of impending liberation, like the parting of the river Jordan or the collapse of the walls of Jerusalem (*Jewish Antiquities* xx. 167–8). Two of them, Theudas and the one nicknamed 'the Egyptian', mentioned by Josephus (*Ant.* xx. 97, 169–70), also appear in the New Testament.

## Jesus as prophet in the Synoptic Gospels

If it is true that Jesus entertained no political aspirations, we need not linger here with this last group, or with the figure of the final prophet already known from the later Christian adjustment in the Acts and John of the Jewish prophet concept based on the expectation of a new Moses.

In its turn, the Elijah imagery played a central part in the thought of the Synoptists, but the New Testament writers primarily associated Elijah with John the Baptist. This is obvious from the opening of the Gospel of Mark, where the arrival on the public scene of John the Baptizer is introduced by the words of Malachi 3:1: 'Behold I send my messenger' – cf. 'Behold, I will send you Elijah' (Mal. 4:5), the same verse quoted by Jesus in his praise of John (Matt. 11:10). A direct connection existed between Jesus and Elijah, the Elijah who was expected to return, or the Elijah *redivivus*. This view was not generally embraced by the primitive Christian church, but was one of three opinions held by Jesus' contemporaries, the other two being that Jesus was the reincarnation of some other prophet of the Old Testament, or of John the Baptist (Mark 8:28; Matt. 16:14; Luke 9:19). According to Matthew, Herod Antipas himself dreaded that Jesus was the decapitated John the Baptist risen from the dead (Matt. 14:2), and a similar idea was attributed by Mark and Luke to members of the court of the ruler of Galilee (Mark 6:14; Luke 9:9). Fringe opinions though these may have been, they were typical of the mentality of a society which instinctively placed Jesus within the framework of the prophetic tradition.

Indeed, the unanimous testimony of the evangelists leaves one in no doubt that sympathetic Galilean folk regarded Jesus as a prophet. This was not on account of his ability to teach or foretell the future. The popular definition, 'the prophet Jesus from Nazareth of Galilee' (Matt. 21:11), was based on the miracles and wonders ascribed to him. Witnessing the re-awakening of the young man in Nain, the crowd exclaimed: 'A great prophet has arisen among us!' (Luke 7:16). The same observation is expressed in the closer circle of the followers of Jesus; the two disciples on the way to Emmaus described the dead Jesus to the unrecognized risen Christ as 'a prophet mighty in deed and word before God and before the people' (Luke 24:19). Even Simon the Pharisee, though personally unconvinced, knew that Jesus had the reputation of a prophet (Luke 7:39). Furthermore we are told that the deeply hostile chief priests hesitated to arrest Jesus because they feared the reaction of ordinary people for whom the charismatic Jesus was a messenger of God (Matt. 21:46).

At this point we may venture one step further and note that according to the evangelists Jesus perceived himself explicitly as a miracle-working prophet. The famous Nazareth episode is profoundly revealing. 'A prophet is not without honour except in his own country, and among his own kin, and in his own house' (Mark 6:4; Matt. 13:57; Luke 4:24). The context of the story makes it plain that Jesus' disillusioned declaration was sparked off by the dislike of the locals for his charismatic teaching and '*mighty works*' (Mark 6:2; Matt. 13:54). Conversely, since people of his home town had no faith in him, the spiritually paralysed Jesus was incapable of curing and exorcizing among them.

According to Luke's version, the Galilean Jesus saw a link between his charismatic deeds and those of Elijah and Elisha, the two foremost wonder-workers active in the northern kingdom of Israel, when he remarked: 'No prophet is acceptable in his own country. But in truth I tell you, there were many widows in Israel in the days of Elijah . . . and Elijah was sent to none of them but only to Zarephtah, in the land of Sidon, to a woman who was a widow. And there were many lepers in Israel in the time of the prophet Elisha; and none of them was cleansed, but only Naaman, the Syrian' (Luke 4:24–7).

It is impossible to prove the verbal authenticity of these sayings, but as far as their substance is concerned I have no doubt that it was not in the interests of the evangelists or of the primitive church to invent them. They definitely went against the grain. Indeed the tendency revealed in both the Acts of the Apostles and John was to enhance the stature of Jesus from miracle-working prophet to ultimate mouthpiece of God through the correcting prism of the church's faith. Unsurprisingly, Paul preferred to disregard the issue, and one observes throughout the centuries a definite coolness on the part of Christian New Testament exegetes towards that very Jewish concept of the prophet Jesus, perfectly at home in the world of unsophisticated Galilean Jews of his age. Consequently the vignette of Jesus, the Elijah-like charismatic prophet, enjoys all the credentials of truth.

## THE PORTRAIT OF JESUS EMANATING FROM HIS TEACHING

Until now the elements used in reconstituting the Synoptic picture of Jesus have been borrowed either from attestations ascribed to contemporaries or from the anonymous tradition ultimately formulated by the three evangelists. From these we learn about the impression made by Jesus on Palestinian Jews and about how the Synoptists endeavoured to present him to their readers. At such a distance in time and with the kind of evidence at our disposal certainty is clearly unattainable, but the coherence of the sketches gives grounds for moderate optimism. Fortunately we can further check the evidence collected from the Gospel narratives against the testimony of the maxims, proverbs and parables of Jesus, and against the broader canvas of first-century Jewish religious ideas and aspirations, which will be investigated in the next chapter.

It goes without saying that this search for the 'self-portrait' of Jesus, his characterization from his own sayings, cannot incorporate a full-scale study of his teaching in the present volume. The task is exceptionally arduous, and Jesus did not facilitate historical research by his deliberate abstention from leaving any personally written record of his ideas. The only occasion on which he is reported to be engaged in writing is in the story of the woman caught in adultery (John 8:8), a definitely inauthentic passage of the New Testament as it does not appear in the most important Greek manuscripts. Even then he wrote in the dust, a fickle substance to preserve one's thought for posterity, and to crown it all, the narrator of the story failed to disclose the actual content of the scribbled note. Would that Jesus had beaten Paul to it, and had himself summarized the salient traits of his preaching in a letter or two! As things are, he must bear his share of the blame for centuries of misrepresentation. Be this as it may, three particular aspects of his central message will be used in this quest for the *face* or *faces* of Jesus: his attitude to the Jewish religion of his day, to God the Father, and to the idea of the Kingdom of heaven.

## The 'Jewish' Jesus

Most of the headings under which Jesus has been approached in the foregoing pages, especially 'lord', 'prophet' and 'Messiah', imply a teaching function, and this in turn raises the question of the exact position of Jesus towards Judaism as it was understood and practised in his time. Christian tradition, nourished on Paul and John, has always held that as a messenger of God, he stood above, and considered himself apart from, the degenerated Jewish religion of first-century Palestine, whose representatives predictably gave him such a hostile reception. So to justify our basic stand, that Jesus of Nazareth was thoroughly Jewish in his roles of teacher, exorcist and preacher, prophet and son of God, we must investigate his pronouncements on the Law of Moses which lay at the heart of the religion he taught and practised.

The evangelists implicitly portray Jesus as a Jew profoundly attached to the laws and customs of his people, and some of his most obviously authentic sayings confirm this picture. The Gospels attest his presence in Galilean synagogues and in the Temple of Jerusalem. We are told that he had eaten the Passover just before he was arrested. His garment was like that of the Pharisees (Matt. 23:5), with the traditional tassels hanging from its edge (Matt: 9:20; Luke 8:44; Mark 6:56; Matt. 14:36; cf. Num. 15:38–40; Deut. 22:12). Following an anecdote, which is to be taken with a pinch of salt, he arranged for a miracle to find the right amount of money to pay the Temple tax (cf. above, p. 163). His respect for the ritual legislation is revealed in the story of the leper already cured by him whom he ordered to submit himself to the judgement of the priests and offer the prescribed sacrifice in the Temple (Mark 1:44; Matt. 8:4; Luke 5:14; cf. Lev. 14:1–7).

Such conduct is in perfect harmony with Jesus' teaching regarding the permanent validity of the Torah, which has been preserved in two versions. The first is in Matthew: 'Till heaven and earth pass away, not an iota, not a dot, will pass from the Law' (Matt. 5:18), and the second, almost identical, in Luke: 'It is easier for heaven and earth to pass away, than for one dot of the Law to become void' (Luke 16:17). Once more the best guarantee of the authenticity of this statement is its very survival in the New Testament in the face of the deep embarrassment caused by it in the antinomian Gentile church, which provided the Gospels of Matthew and Luke with a permanent home.

Admittedly attempts have been made both in the primitive church and in later Christianity to eviscerate Jesus' affirmation of the permanence of the Torah, and insinuate that the parting of the ways between Law-centred Judaism and the new spiritual Christian religion was initiated by Jesus himself. To demonstrate his superiority towards the religion of the Old Testament, it is claimed that he disregarded two of the most fundamental obligations imposed by the Law, the observance of the sabbath and the dietary regulations of the Bible, and deemed himself greater than Moses whose precepts he felt free to abrogate and replace. None of these allegations can stand up to an objective examination.

In our discussion of Jesus as healer and exorcist we have already encountered the criticism that by curing the sick on the sabbath Jesus broke the Law. The question of healing on the day of rest is explicitly raised in the Gospels themselves (Mark 3:4; Matt. 12:10; Luke 6:9), as well as in the debates of rabbis outside the New Testament. The evangelists make Jesus answer it affirmatively through his action, and this is in conformity with the view of the rabbis for whom the saving of life superseded the sabbath precepts. In any case, the form of healing by word of mouth or touch which Jesus had adopted did not really count as 'work' prohibited on the sabbath. We discover from the evangelists that the only issue which genuinely preoccupied scrupulous people in his Galilean surroundings was the degree of severity of an illness which would justify therapeutic 'work', for example the carrying and administering of medicines. But even in this respect the head of a synagogue quoted by Luke put the blame not on the healer, but on those who sought cure on the sabbath: 'There are six days on which work ought to be done; come on those days and be healed, and not on the sabbath day' (Luke 13:14). Enlightened rabbis of the Mishnah advocated leniency and held that if any doubt existed about the potentially life-threatening character of a sickness, that was enough to overrule the sabbath precepts (mYoma 8:6). In fact, even the apparently more shocking statement of Jesus concerning the sabbath being made for man and not man for the sabbath (Mark 2:27) does not exceed the opinion expressed by a rabbi of the second century AD, 'The sabbath is delivered to you and not you to the sabbath' (Mekhilta on Exod. 31:14).

The food laws (kosher v. non-kosher) constitute the second area of Jesus' supposed conflict with the Torah of Moses, but the claim that he abolished the distinction between clean and unclean is based on a crass misunderstanding of a subtle saying, 'There is nothing outside a man which by going into him can defile him; but the things that come out of a man are what defile him . . . Whatever goes into a man from outside cannot defile him, since it enters not his heart but his stomach, and passes on' (Mark 7:15, 18–19); Matt. 15:11, 17–18). The patent meaning of the words is that defilement is caused not by the foodstuff as such but by the heart's disregard of a divine prohibition, a customary ethical interpretation of a legal precept. Such a moralization of the

Law is traceable, apart from the biblical prophets, to the author of the Letter of Aristeas in the first half of the second century BC, according to whom God is honoured not with gifts and sacrifices, but with purity of soul and holy convictions (234). The same idea underlies the teaching shared by Philo of Alexandria and Jesus that identifies the Ten Commandments as the epitome of the Law (Special Laws I, 1; Mark 10:17–19; Matt. 19:16–19; Luke 18:18–20) or the so-called Golden Rule – 'Whatever you wish that men would do to you, do so to them' – which in varying forms runs from Tobit (4:15) and Philo (*Hypothetica* 7:6) to Hillel, a leading Jewish teacher at the turn of the era (bShabbat 31a), and Jesus himself (Matt. 7:12; Luke 6:31).

To return to the dietary laws, the comment by the editor of the Gospel to Mark 7:19 – 'Thus he [Jesus] declared all foods clean' – is a secondary gloss which had nothing to do with Jesus and was meaningful and beneficial only in the Gentile-Christian church for which this Gospel was ultimately destined. Jewish Christianity's difficulty with prospective Gentile converts in the Acts of the Apostles and Paul's row with Peter in Antioch (cf. above, pp. 65–6, 142) demonstrate that in the first Christian generation no one was aware of Jesus having declared all foods clean!

The third proof, as spurious as the preceding two, of Jesus' claim of superiority over the Law lies in the sayings assembled in the Sermon on the Mount known as the 'antitheses' (Matt. 5:21–48). In these an Old Testament precept, for example 'Thou shalt not kill', is introduced with the words, 'You have heard that it was said to the men of old' and followed by Jesus' proclamation, 'But I say to you' something else, such as 'every one who is angry with his brother shall be liable to judgement' (Matt. 5:21–2). However, when objectively analysed, his declarations strengthen and clarify, rather than contradict the Torah. By forbidding anger Jesus does not permit murder but ensures that its root is pulled up. To mistake the antitheses for a 'shattering of the letter of the Law', as Ernst Käsemann, a German New Testament scholar, put it, reveals an extraordinary blindness to which theologians of a certain type are often prone.

## Jesus, the worshipper of God the Father

If the Torah is presented by the Synoptists as the focal point of the devotion of the 'Jewish' Jesus, careful examination of the Gospels indicates that the wellspring of his religion lay in his perception of God as Father, his Father, the Father of the Jewish people and of the whole of mankind. The God of Jesus is less remote, transcendent and awesome than the God who could show Moses not his face, but only his back (Exod. 33:21–3).[3] Isaiah believed that he himself would perish because of his vision of the heavenly throne (Isa. 6:5). As for Ezekiel, in his trance he was allowed to behold only a God four times removed through the 'likeness' of the glory of the Lord in the form of the 'likeness' of a human shape sitting on the 'likeness' of a throne above the 'likeness' of the firmament (Ezek. 1:26).

By the time of Jesus, the God contemplated by Jews appeared less awe-inspiring. Already the post-exilic Third Isaiah (sixth century BC) repeatedly addressed the deity as 'our Father' (Isa. 63:16; 64:8), and the paternal imagery is regularly employed from the second century BC onwards in Jewish literature, including the Dead Sea Scrolls. Listen to the Qumran psalmist's moving words: 'Until I am old Thou wilt care for me; for my father knew me not and my mother abandoned me to Thee. For Thou art a father to all the sons of Thy truth' (1QH 17 [9]:34–5). Indeed, by the earliest stages of the era of the rabbis the phrase 'the Father who is in heaven' was a standard formula.

The loving and caring heavenly Father is the model for Jesus' religious action. His imitation of God is epitomized in the commands, 'You must be perfect, as your heavenly Father is perfect' (Matt. 5:48), or 'Be merciful, even as your Father is merciful' (Luke 6:36). The imitation of God was direct, without intermediaries, and his disciples were encouraged to follow the same direct path. In framing his principle, Jesus relied on and softened the biblical injunction, 'Be holy, for I the Lord your God am holy' (Lev. 19:2).

Jesus was the imitator of the forgiving and merciful Father. This central topic of his teaching occurs throughout the Synoptics. 'When-

---

3. A jovial rabbi called this 'the vision of the buttocks' (Sifre on Num. 12:8).

ever you stand praying, forgive if you have anything against any one; so that your Father also who is in heaven may forgive you your trespasses' (Mark 11:25; Matt. 6:14). The same message is embedded in the parable of the prodigal son (Luke 15:11–32), in which the compassionate father, symbolizing God, is ready to pardon even before his wayward child had repented and confessed his sorrow.

In addition to the quality of forgiveness, the divine virtue extolled by the Jesus of the Synoptics as supreme and essential to emulate is the Father's solicitude towards the weak, the poor and the helpless, a solicitude inspiring limitless trust. The words of the Sermon on the Mount speak for themselves. 'Do not be anxious about your life . . . Look at the birds of the air: they neither sow nor reap . . . and yet your heavenly Father feeds them . . . Consider the lilies of the field . . . they neither toil nor spin, yet . . . even Solomon in all his glory was not arrayed like one of these . . . Do not be anxious about tomorrow . . . Let the day's own trouble be sufficient for the day' (Matt. 6:25–34; Luke 12:22–31).

With eastern Mediterranean Semitic exaggeration Jesus opted for an extreme example to bring home his admiration for the paternal generosity of God. Wishing to put into relief the difference between returning love for love received, or being generous with the secret hope of a reward, and true, uncalculating benevolence, he chose what goes most against the grain, the love for an enemy. 'Love your enemies . . . so that you may be the sons of your Father who is in heaven' (Matt. 5:44–5; Luke 6:27). God makes the sun shine and the rain fall for the wicked (his enemies) just as for the good. So generosity must know no bounds. The idea is startling and is often thought to be exclusive to Jesus. However, in a less spectacular fashion Flavius Josephus attributes a similar outlook to Moses: 'We . . . must show consideration even to declared enemies' (*Contra Apionem* ii. 211).

Prayer is the most direct source disclosing a person's attitude and feelings towards God. It is important to note that although the Gospels frequently locate Jesus in synagogues, and during his Passover pilgrimage in the Temple of Jerusalem, they never mention that he prayed there, let alone that he participated in sacrificial worship. With the exception of the Lord's Prayer, which is meant for a group, he is always depicted as a practitioner of individual prayer either in solitude or at least at some distance from other people. We see him praying in the desert (Mark 1:35; Luke 5:15), on a mountain (Mark 6:46; Matt. 14:23; Luke 6:12) and in a garden away from his disciples (Mark 14:35; Matt. 26:39; Luke 22:41). His advice on prayer insists on privacy: 'When you pray, go into your room and shut the door and pray to your Father who is in secret; and your Father who sees in secret will reward you' (Matt. 6:6).

Whether the words reported as his in the Gospels are authentic or not, there is no doubt about the conviction of the evangelists who make him address all his supplications to God the Father. On this point at least we can be sure that their report is truthful. Mark quotes only a single prayer of Jesus (Mark 14:36), but in doing so he goes to the heart of the matter in citing a petition addressed to *abba* ('Father' or possibly 'my Father') in Jesus' own Aramaic. This is an invocation in which reverence and intimacy are mingled. That *abba* represents baby language, as some have claimed, is complete nonsense. I strongly recommend James Barr's paper bearing the telling title, 'Abba isn't Daddy!' (*Journal of Theological Studies* 39, 1988, 28–47).

All the other prayer formulae preserved in Matthew and Luke begin in Greek with 'Father' or 'Our Father', and convey ideas of blessing, supplication and thanksgiving. All three are comprised in the most famous of them, the Lord's prayer *par excellence*, a paradigm of a plea to God taught by Jesus to his disciples (Matt. 6:9–13; Luke 11:2–4). It has survived in a longer and a shorter form respectively in Matthew and Luke, but contrary to the common view that the shorter version is nearer the original, I can see arguments in favour of both. Indeed, various elements in Matthew are endowed with an authentic Semitic flavour missing from Luke.[4] As far as the substance is concerned, both seem to reflect the religious cast of mind of Jesus. The Lord's Prayer is

---

4. There are two particular arguments in favour of Matthew's version. Both accounts contain the Semitic metaphor of 'debt' for sin, but whereas Matthew is consistent: 'Forgive us our debts as we also have forgiven our debtors' (Matt. 6:12), Luke, less familiar with things Jewish, spoils the imagery by substituting 'sins' for 'debts': 'Forgive our sins, for we ourselves forgive everyone who is indebted to us' (Luke 11:4). Moreover, since the prayer is framed for a group ('we', 'us'), Matthew's 'our Father who art in heaven' is more appropriate than Luke's 'Father', which is found in all the individual prayers of Jesus in the Synoptics.

admirably concise, corresponding to the command not to be loquacious when addressing God since 'your Father knows what you need before you ask him' (Matt. 6:7). The chief topics concern the sanctification of God's name in harmony with the 'Holy, holy, holy' of the angelic choir; a plea for *today*'s bread, not the food of tomorrow or the day after, and for divine remission of our debts presupposing repentance and mutual forgiveness among the members of the company. These are all typical of Jesus' thinking. In fact the petition, 'Thy Kingdom come' is the best warranty for tracing the Lord's Prayer to Jesus himself, for the primitive Christian community would have expressed its eschatological hope in a prayer for the return of Christ, *Marana tha*, rather than for the advent of the Kingdom.

## Jesus and the Kingdom of God

The development of primitive Christian thinking about the Kingdom of God traceable in the Acts of the Apostles and in Paul and the virtual extinction of the idea in the Fourth Gospel have been dealt with earlier (cf. above, pp. 135, 71, 17). Now we must examine, in the religious outlook of Jesus, the significance of this powerful concept which figures more than a hundred times in the Synoptics. Since it was not Jesus' creation, but permeated the whole Palestinian thinking of the epoch, a brief introduction will set the scene in the wider context of Judaism.

Modelled on the biblical idea of God being the king of Israel, the Kingdom of God, or Kingdom of heaven, conveys a picture of God's sovereignty over the Jewish people in the first instance, but also as Creator over the entire world. In the perspective of the Old Testament the establishment of God's dominion over the whole of mankind was envisaged in the form of a universal conquest of the nations by the royal Messiah followed by their conversion to belief in the one true God (cf. Isa. 45:14; 60:3, etc.). The same notion continued to flourish in the post-exilic age to the end of the period of the Second Temple (538 BC to AD 70). The literature of the intertestamental era, including the Dead Sea Scrolls, further enriched the Kingdom imagery with the apocalyptic features of a cosmic battle between good and evil on the eve of the final manifestation and triumph of the divine King. Needless to say, apocalyptic fervour often transformed itself into political action, as the history of Palestinian Jews shows over the century that preceded the great war against Rome (AD 66–70) which took place a generation after the life of Jesus.

In the subsequent centuries, despite two calamitous defeats, the political concept lingered on, contrasting the Kingdom of heaven with the wicked Roman empire. Nevertheless Jewish religious thinkers increasingly imagined entry into the Kingdom in a non-violent form, through taking on the 'yoke of the Kingdom' by means of a whole-hearted obedience to the Torah. A typical example is furnished by the famous Aramaic prayer called *Kaddish*, the origins of which are thought to belong to the earliest phases of the rabbinic era, if not before. In it, without reference to the destruction of Jerusalem, and presumably antedating it, God is asked to establish his Kingdom in the present time: 'in your life and in your days . . . speedily and in a short while'. As one might have guessed, Jesus' Kingdom perfectly fits between the apocalyptic and the rabbinic pictures and due to its unwarlike character it rather foreshadows the latter than develops the former. The idea of a bellicose march towards the new Jerusalem in the footsteps of a combative Messiah is exclusive to the Book of Revelation in the New Testament (cf. above, p. 57).

Nothing indicates more clearly the importance ascribed by the writers of the Gospels to the idea of the Kingdom of God than the fact that it opens and closes the story of Jesus. The very first of his proclamations, quoted in Mark, relates to the imminent arrival of the Kingdom and the necessity of a total change of behaviour: 'The Kingdom of God is at hand; repent and believe in the gospel' (Mark 1:15; Matt. 4:17). This can be set against the final naive question which the author of the Acts makes the apostles put to Jesus after the forty-day-long instruction he gave them on the Kingdom of God, 'Lord, will you at this time restore the kingdom of Israel?' (Acts 1:6).

The evangelists give us correctly to understand that preoccupation with the Kingdom of God and devotion to doing what he had to do about it constitute the essence of the vocation of Jesus. Not being an abstract thinker, he never set out to determine the exact meaning of the concept; he sought to describe the Kingdom in similitudes rather than to define it, and strove to make known how he and his followers were to act when the moment was ripe for action.

Jews and Christians loved to speculate about the date of the coming of the Kingdom. The Book of Daniel, echoed by intertestamental Judaism, sketched step by step, sign by sign, the approach of the day of the Lord (Dan. 9–12); the so-called eschatological discourse of Jesus, a piece composed by the primitive church, also amasses hint after hint leading to the end – war, persecutions, false Messiahs, the statue called 'abomination of desolation' installed in the sanctuary, the destruction of the Temple (Mark 13:5–20; Matt. 24:4–22; Luke 21:8–24). St Paul drew up a detailed map and timetable for the second coming of Christ (2 Thess. 2:1–9). Yet with the exception of the dissonant eschatological discourse, the Synoptics depict Jesus as someone whose mind was totally alien to such an outlook. He was opposed to giving clues because he did not believe in premonitions: 'The Kingdom of God is not coming with signs to be observed' (Luke 17:20; cf. Mark 8:11–13; Matt. 12:38–9; 16:1–4; Luke 11:16, 29). Even more positively – and flatly contradicting all the warnings he is supposed to have issued in the eschatological discourse – Jesus firmly denied any knowledge of the date of the coming of the Kingdom; it was the exclusive privilege of God: 'But of that day and that hour no one knows, not even the angels of heaven, nor the son, but only the Father' (Mark 13:32; Matt. 24:36).

In many of the relevant parables and in all the preserved sayings the Kingdom is an existing but as a rule concealed reality which nevertheless at times allows its presence to be felt. According to Jesus, the Kingdom is symbolized by the concerted action of the field, the farmer sowing and the seed (Mark 4:26–9), or by the tiny mustard seed which invisibly and astonishingly grows and is transformed into a tall plant (Mark 4:30–32; Matt. 13:31–2; Luke 13:18–19), or by the leaven which mysteriously turns flour into bread (Matt 13:33; Luke 13:20–21). The co-existence of good and evil shows that the scene is in the here and now, antedating the final settlement and the new age. Seeds of corn and weeds, fish fit and unfit to eat remain together in the parables of the sower and of the net (Matt. 13:24–43, 47–50). As for the similitudes of the wedding feast, wise and foolish virgins and worthy and unworthy guests await together the bridal procession or try to enter the banquet hall (Matt 25:1–13; 22:1–14; Luke 14:16–24). In the words of the Jesus of the Synoptics, 'the Kingdom of God is in the midst of you' (Luke 17:20).

However, another aspect of the teaching of Jesus which the evangelists emphatically underscore is that the still hidden Kingdom now and then reveals its presence in charismatic manifestations. Jesus declares that victory over evil in the form of exorcism by the spirit or by the finger of God signals that the Kingdom 'has come upon you' (Matt. 12:28; Luke 11:20). The quest for the Kingdom, Jesus tells his hearers, has attracted ever since the days of John the Baptist large and bustling Jewish crowds elbowing their way forward: 'The good news of the Kingdom is preached, and everyone enters it violently' (Luke 16:16; cf. Matt. 11:12).

The conduct prescribed by Jesus in the age of the latent presence of the Kingdom of God is set out with absolute clarity in the Synoptic Gospels. The gate opens only to those who have the simplicity, trust and intensity of desire of a child: 'Unless you turn and become like children, you will never enter the Kingdom of heaven' (Matt. 18:3; Mark 10:15; Luke 18:17). Continuing along the same lines, he impressed on his disciples that no one could become a citizen of the Kingdom without total devotion to the cause: the merchant seeking to acquire the legal ownership of the most precious pearl ever heard of, or of a treasure trove, must be prepared to give up all that he owned to achieve his aim (Matt. 13:44–6). The ideal devotee is the destitute widow who gave 'everything she had, her whole life' (Mark 12:44; Luke 21:3–4). Finally, the Jesus of the Synoptics asserted that it is preferable to rid oneself of an eye or a limb and to sacrifice sex if that is the price of entry into the Kingdom of God (Mark 9:45–7; Matt. 18:9; 19:12).

This willingness to surrender oneself for the sake of the Kingdom is an empty pretence in Jesus' eyes unless it is turned into immediate action. In harmony with his stress on the primacy of today over tomorrow (cf. above, pp. 199, 201), he obliged his disciples to throw themselves at once into the work for the Kingdom. No delay, no procrastination was tolerated, not even on the pretext of filial piety: 'Leave the dead to bury their own dead, but as for you, go and proclaim the Kingdom of God' (Luke 9:60; Matt. 8:22). In fact, once recruited by Jesus, a labourer for the cause of heaven was no longer allowed to hesitate or wonder. He had to press ahead: 'No one who puts his hand to the plough and looks back is fit for the Kingdom of God' (Luke 9:62).

If we bear in mind the constant emphasis laid on immediacy, single-mindedness and unrestrained giving of the self *vis-à-vis* the Kingdom of God, the inescapable conclusion will be that the eyes of Jesus were resolutely focused on the present, on the duty of the moment, and closed to anything pertaining to the more distant future. Indeed, if we take his words in their most obvious sense, we are compelled to accept that Jesus refused to contemplate or prepare for eventualities that lay far ahead. For if the Kingdom of God was already there and its glorious manifestation was due any moment, it would have been nonsensical to be concerned with matters of this age whose time would soon run out. Such a perspective has no room for the idea of an organized society, a church, destined to last until heaven and earth pass away in a far distant age to come. Those who find such an assessment of the world view of Jesus difficult to swallow need only re-read his parable of the wealthy landowner. This man, expecting a particularly rich harvest, launched himself into a detailed process of forward planning. He would demolish his old barns and construct new ones with greatly increased capacity, only to discover that he, like the present era, had no tomorrow. 'Fool!' he was told, 'This night your soul is required of you' (Luke 12:16–20).

Unshakeable faith and trust in God, the biblical *emunah*, was the hallmark, the ideal of Jesus which he preached and practised. It was the spiritual engine of his whole life's work and we may reasonably believe that it continued to his last day, during his trial before the high priest and Pilate, and even on the way to the cross. But there came the moment of realization that his Father would not intervene, which provoked the cry of anguish, '*Eloi, Eloi, lama sabachtani? . . .* My God, my God, why hast thou forsaken me?' (Mark 15:34).[5]

---

5. The words correspond to the opening line of Psalm 22. New Testament interpreters, disturbed by the tone of despair, like to point out that this psalm ends on a note of triumph and the vindication of the sufferer, and suggest that Jesus quoted the beginning of the psalm but was thinking of its concluding verses. This looks very much like special pleading especially when it is taken into account that the words quoted represent the

A well-known contemporary writer has characterized such an under-standing of the outlook of Jesus as that of 'doom and gloom'. Nothing is further from the truth. Even according to Mark, the dying Jesus emitted another last cry, and nothing prevents us from imagining that it was similar to his supplication in the garden of Gethsemane, 'Remove this cup from me; yet not what I will, but what thou wilt' (Mark 14:36), or even shorter, as the 'Thy will be done' of the Lord's Prayer.

Far from being a 'doom and gloom' merchant, Jesus was an eschato-logical enthusiast. It is a single-minded dedication to what he believed to be his special mission, the leading to a safe haven those entrusted to his charge, that defines the role of Jesus in the last act of the final drama. He is depicted in the Synoptics as the compassionate, caring and loving pilot and shepherd who, imitating the merciful, caring and loving God, guides those most in need, the little ones (Matt. 18:10), the sinners, the whores and the publicans, towards the gate of the Kingdom of the Father.

The Synoptic Gospels intimate that in the judgement of Jesus the saving of a single lost sheep was the cause of more rejoicing in the Kingdom than the safe arrival of ninety-nine just (Luke 15:7; cf. Matt. 18:14), and he envisaged as the ultimate fulfilment of his dream the picture in which penitent tax-collectors and harlots overtook the right-eous in the race towards the Kingdom of God (Matt. 21:31).

Our three-pronged approach – from stories, titles and teachings – to the Jesus of Mark, Matthew and Luke has yielded a coherent picture, the portrait of the Jesus intended by the Synoptics. It mirrors in some way, but is not identical with, the Jesus of history. Alas, owing to the nature of the Gospel material, strict historical accuracy is bound to elude us, but a strenuous effort can be made – and will be attempted presently – to authenticate this image as far as possible by integrating it into the cultural and religious setting of contemporaneous Palestinian Judaism.

To begin with a negative, but fundamentally important observation,

---

Aramaic translation of the biblical verse. In a prayer one would expect the original Hebrew, Eli, Eli lema 'azabtani?, to figure. My surmise is that the Aramaic sentence was a proverbial exclamation of a man in despair.

the Jesus of the Synoptics, like that of the Acts of the Apostles, is not an other-worldly figure, but one that is firmly planted in our universe of man. His apotheosis was not sudden; it was reached step by step. It started with the miraculous birth recorded in Matthew and Luke, and continued through Paul and John by the Fathers, the theologians and the councils of the Hellenized Gentile church. Formal deification, though looming on the horizon from the second century on, was not achieved until the Council of Nicaea in AD 325. But let it be forcefully underlined once more, and finally, that in the minds of first-century Palestinian Jews no human being, not even one celebrated as 'son of God', could conceivably share the nature of the Almighty.

The Jesus of Mark, Matthew and Luke (and of the Acts) comes onstage as an itinerant Galilean preacher, healer and exorcist, admired and followed by many, but also distrusted and opposed by others, especially the central religious Establishment responsible for maintaining law and order in rebellion-threatened Jerusalem. According to the common testimony of the Synoptics, wherever he went Jesus was recognized as the spokesman of God by the simple folk of Galilee. We know that they saw in him a prophet. Indeed, the Gospels give us every reason to believe that Jesus personally envisaged himself as such and that this was also the earliest quasi-definition applied to him at the start of the Christian preaching: 'Jesus of Nazareth, a man attested . . . by God with mighty works and wonders and signs' (Acts 2:22).

However, from an early stage of his public career, but it would seem without any encouragement on his part, the name of Jesus began to be linked to that of the Messiah. For though he appeared as an eschatological leader, he eschewed any association with the traditional political figure of the royal son of David. Indeed nothing in his background, teaching or aspirations would lead one to believe that he sought recognition as the king of the Jews. Only his opponents, and then only at the very last moment and for want of something more solid, had recourse to the flimsy charge of false messianic pretension. I have repeatedly stressed that his friendly contemporaries, instinctively and indirectly rather than rationally, took him for the Messiah, not for political considerations, but in view of his beneficial charismatic actions in which they recognized the portents of the messianic age. This charismatic, non-political perspective is evident in the answer of

Jesus to John the Baptist's question whether he was the awaited Christ. He did not reassure John with words such as, 'Yes, I am the new David and my troops allied to the host of the fighting angels will soon be on the march.' The message quoted in Matthew and Luke is roundabout, slightly mysterious, but nowhere touches on political Messianism: 'Go and tell John what you hear and see: the blind receive their sight and the lame walk, lepers are cleansed and the deaf hear, and the dead are raised up, and the poor have good news preached to them' (Matt. 11:4–5; Luke 7:22).

The Synoptic use of the title 'son of God' reinforces the same proposition. The unwillingness of Jesus to be seen as the Davidic Messiah, liberator of Israel and conqueror of nations, obliges the informed reader to discard the aspect of 'sonship' which is intrinsically linked to the concept of the eschatological King. However, the most prominent facet of the 'son of God' concept was revealed by the historical-spiritual surroundings of Jesus. As a miraculous healer and teacher, displaying the outward signs of the age of the Kingdom already come, Jesus fulfilled in the minds of simple people the principal non-political quality expected of a 'Messiah, son of God'.

Again, the title 'lord' regularly evoked in the minds of the evangelists and of the contemporaries of Jesus, as well as in the earliest thinking of primitive Christianity, the icon of a man endowed with power and authority and triumphant over the forces of darkness, sickness and evil. With all its potential implications in Graeco-Roman society, it is normal that *Kyrios*-Lord progressively and inexorably acquired higher religious associations in the Gentile church and, freed from the control of the cultural tradition of biblical Judaism, itself became a powerful instrument in the creation of a free-ranging speculative Christology.

Finally, when the contribution of Jesus' own doctrine about Jewish religion, God the Father and his nearly present Kingdom is assimilated, and the later Christian distortions imposed on his message are corrected, the picture sketched with the help of the Gospel stories and titles may be further enriched. Jesus is revealed there as a respectful observer of the Torah and a penetrating expositor of its enduring ethical message. He manifests himself as the devout worshipper of the heavenly Father along the path of repentance, trust and imitation of the ways of God.

Needless to say, the image of the loving and solicitous deity does not truly reflect the human experience of a harsh, unjust and cruel world. Jesus too witnessed fledglings fall from the nest, little ones perish and the innocent suffer. Yet it would be a mistake to imagine that he allowed himself to be deluded by what seems to be a sentimentally anthropomorphic image of the Father. But what he was motivated by and what lay at the heart of his intuition was the feeling of certainty that the eternal, transcendent and tremendous Creator was also, and for him above all, a near and approachable God.

Perhaps the most striking aspect of the Gospel portrait of Jesus is its overwhelmingly eschatological colouring. From the very moment of his proclamation of the imminence of the Kingdom of God, he showed himself, and exhorted his followers to be single-minded, absolute and decisive, concentrating on the inward aspects, and putting the accent on the root causes of every religious action. The best summary of the programme pursued by Jesus, presenting also the quintessence of his religious persona, is the resolute determination to do all that is required for the fulfilment of the plea, 'Thy Kingdom come'. And the absence of a literal fulfilment of his belief does not detract in any way from the fundamental truth that no religious attitude is real without an all-pervading sense of urgency which converts ideas into instant action.

I have used all the tools at our disposal to sketch the face of Jesus with the help of the Synoptic Gospels. I have attempted to come as close to the Jesus of history as Mark, Matthew and Luke would permit. But the picture arrived at is only the evangelists' picture, or if you like the Gospel truth about Jesus. In the next chapter I shall embark on the final stage of our search, looking for the Jesus hidden beneath the Gospels – on the quest for the truth about the real Jesus of Nazareth.

## PARTICULAR FEATURES OF JESUS
## IN THE THREE SYNOPTIC GOSPELS

In building up the image of Jesus from the Synoptics, I have relied mostly on evidence attested by more than one Gospel, paying no special attention to tendencies typical of individual evangelists, or for that matter to the significant lack of such tendencies. Not wishing to overcrowd the argument, I will restrict this section to the presentation of the evidence emerging from the so-called 'Infancy' gospels in Matthew and Luke; to a review of the pro-Jewish and anti-Jewish features in Matthew and of some universalistic trends in Luke; and to aspects of the characterization of Jesus in Mark which are either modified or ignored by Matthew and Luke.

### The 'Infancy' gospel in Matthew and Luke

The genealogies of Jesus in Matthew and Luke, although substantially different from one another, serve a common theological purpose, namely the authentication of the descent of Jesus from King David. As a secondary echo, they correspond to, and reflect, the teaching of the primitive church expressed not in the Synoptic Gospels, but in the Acts of the Apostles (cf. p. 128) and in Paul (cf. p. 81).

Matthew makes himself clear from the start, opening his Gospel with 'This is the genealogy of Jesus Christ, *the son of David*'. He traces schematically in three units of fourteen generations the male-line pedigree of the Messiah: from Abraham to David, from David to King Jechoniah, and from Jechoniah to Jesus through Joseph. From Abraham to Zerubbabel (Matt. 1:2–12) the evangelist follows the Old Testament, but the rest of his list is based on an otherwise unknown source which does not tally with the genealogy employed by Luke.

Luke has a more grandiose theological perspective than Matthew. He starts in reverse order with Jesus and Joseph, and reaches back via David to Abraham and to the first man, qualified as 'the son of God' (Luke 3:23–38), thus tacitly endorsing Paul's teaching on the universality of the mission of Jesus, the second Adam.

Both evangelists were aware of the difficulty created by the legal need to chart Jesus' claim to royal succession through the male line, that is, through Joseph, at a stage when the miraculous conception of Jesus, unknown to Mark, had already become part of the teaching of the primitive Gentile church. Luke, writing for non-Jews, adopted an easy solution to the problem by quietly suggesting that Joseph was merely the putative father of Jesus ('being the son – *as was supposed* – of Joseph', Luke 3:23). Matthew's tradition, on the other hand, reveals embarrassment and hesitation, indicated by a number of variants in the text. According to the logic of his account of *A* begot *B* who begot *C*, etc., the register should have ended with 'and Jacob begot Joseph, and *Joseph begot Jesus*' (Matt. 1:16). Instead, Matthew's textual witnesses are unstable. We have 'and Jacob begot Joseph, the husband of Mary, of whom [Mary] was born Jesus'; 'Joseph, to whom was betrothed the virgin Mary, who bore Jesus'; and 'Joseph, to whom was betrothed Mary the virgin, begot Jesus'. The latter formulation, attested among others by an ancient Syriac (i.e. Christian Aramaic) version of Matthew, became part of the creed of the Judaeo-Christian community known as the Ebionites, or the Poor, who professed according to early patristic authorities that Jesus was born naturally from Mary and her husband.

In trying to prove the Davidic legitimacy of Jesus as Messiah through Joseph and simultaneously assuming his miraculous birth of a virgin, the tradition of Matthew had to make a way through rough terrain before reaching, in the fold of the not very well informed Gentile Christian church, the orthodox compromise: a supernatural virginal conception and an imputed, yet legally valid, descent from King David.

According to Matthew, the belief of the Greek-speaking church was further confirmed through an assurance given by an angel to Joseph, Mary's prospective husband. When, in the certain knowledge that he was not responsible for her pregnancy, Joseph was pondering on a quiet dismissal – a public charge laid against his fiancée might have threatened her with the death penalty – he was informed that the conception was miraculous.[6] Mary's pregnancy was the work of the

---

6. In the Qumran Genesis Apocryphon, the father of Noah wondered whether his wife had had an affair with one of the fallen angels. A firm and spirited denial by his wife brought him to his senses (1QapGen. 2:3–10).

holy Spirit (Matt. 1:20), and was intended to fulfil the prophecy of Isaiah 7:14, 'Behold a *virgin* shall conceive and bear a son, and his name shall be called Emmanuel, which means God with us' (Matt. 1:23). The reading 'virgin' is that of the Septuagint version of the *Greek* Bible, and Matthew's gloss, interpreting the symbolic name Emmanuel as a pointer to the superhuman nature of the miraculous child, also implies that a non-Jewish readership was envisaged. Jews would have known that the name Emmanuel ('God is with us') signified not the incarnation of God in human form, but a promise of divine help to the Jewish people.

Readers familiar with the Hebrew Isaiah would have been perplexed by Matthew's argument because the word used by the Old Testament prophet was 'young woman' (in Hebrew *'almah*), and not 'virgin' (in Hebrew *betulah*). A young woman becoming pregnant is not the same as a virginal conception. The misleading rendering of *'almah* as *parthenos* ('virgin', 'maid') was corrected in the later (first or second century AD) Greek translations of Isaiah; all of them substituted 'young girl' (*neanis*) for the Septuagint's 'virgin' (*parthenos*). In plain language, Matthew's genealogy and account of the birth reflect an image of Jesus born of a virgin which was exclusively designed for, and meaningful in, the Hellenistic church.

Luke's account is entirely different and theologically more advanced. The announcement of the miraculous birth of Jesus is preceded by that of the quasi-miraculous birth of John the Baptist, son of the aged Elizabeth, a kinswoman of Mary. An angel told Mary that although she was unmarried, she would conceive of the holy Spirit and bear the 'Son of the Most High' who would sit on 'the throne of David' (Luke 1:31–2), and that such a miraculous conception would be no more unimaginable than the pregnancy of her cousin Elizabeth, for long infertile and well past child-bearing age (Luke 1:36–7).

To see the story of the conception of Jesus in a broader context, it is necessary to set it against other birth legends current in intertestamental Judaism. The authors of the Old Testament believed that sterility in a woman was caused by God closing her womb, but he could also re-open it and so render her fertile. Many of the biblical heroes, including the patriarchs Isaac, Jacob and Joseph, as well as the prophet Samuel, were born to women considered to be barren – and in the case of Sarah, the wife of the ninety-nine-year-old Abraham, after lifelong sterility. In ancient Jewish society and culture these births were considered miraculous.

Next, we must not overlook in our evaluation of the Infancy gospels that the term 'virgin' was capable of various interpretations among Jews. Of course, the absence of sexual experience was one, but the Greek *parthenos* could also mean that the girl was young and/or unmarried. In fact, in the Septuagint translation of the Old Testament *parthenos* was used to render three distinct Hebrew words, 'virgin', 'girl' and 'young woman'. Already rabbis in the Tannaitic era (first to second century AD) subscribed to further nuances, and there is no reason to think that all these were invented by them. Even the word *betulah*, which normally means *virgo intacta*, when used by them could carry the lateral sense of bodily immaturity with the consequential inability to conceive. In rabbinic terminology this type of virginity in a woman ceased with the physical onset of puberty. The Mishnah, the oldest of the rabbinic codes, defines a virgin as a female who 'has never seen blood even though she is married' (mNiddah 1:4). The Tosefta, another early Jewish code of law, claims in the name of Rabbi Eliezer ben Hyrcanus (late first century AD) that such a woman would continue to count as a virgin even after she had conceived and borne children without prior menstruation (tNiddah 1:6)!

To understand these statements, we must remember that in the intertestamental and early rabbinic age, pre-puberty marriage was generally permitted.[7] In fact, rabbis seriously debated whether bloodstains found after the wedding night in the nuptial bed of a minor, i.e. a 'virgin in respect of menstruation', marked her first period or the consummation of the marriage. So the idea of conceiving on the first physical opportunity and thus becoming a 'virgin mother' was not a mere flight of fancy of the over-imaginative rabbinic mind.

---

7. A woman could marry on reaching majority, which by legal fiction was set at twelve years and one day irrespective of whether or not she had reached puberty. The marrying branch of the Essene sect prohibited cohabitation until the young woman had proved by three consecutive periods that she was physically mature (Josephus, *Jewish War* ii. 161). It is likely that 'fornication with one's wife', mentioned in one of the manuscripts of the Damascus Document from Qumran (4Q270), was committed through disobeying this rule.

Yet another aspect of the ancient Jewish representation of virginity is supplied by the famous philosopher, Philo of Alexandria, a contemporary of Jesus. He described the post-menopausal wife of Abraham as a woman who had become a virgin for a second time (*De posteritate Caini* 134). In his usual allegorical mode of thinking, he characterized Isaac, the miraculously born child of Sarah and Abraham, as the 'son of God' (*De mutatione nominum* 131). Quoting the words of Sarah from Genesis 21:6, 'The Lord has made laughter for me' (Isaac means 'He laughs'), Philo commented, 'Open your ears and accept most holy teachings: *laughter* is "joy", and *has made* equals "to beget". So that which is said is similar to this: "The Lord begot Isaac"' (*De allegoria legum* iii. 219). Or opting for an even more striking symbolism, Philo ascribes Sarah's pregnancy to her encounter with God: 'For Moses shows us Sarah conceiving at the time when God visited her in her solitude; but when she brings forth, it is not to the author of her visitation, but to Abraham' (*De cherubim* 45). The only conclusion one needs to draw from all this is that virginity and virgin birth were much more elastic notions in Jewish antiquity than Christian tradition allows.

The rest of the Infancy gospel of Matthew seeks to reinforce the messianic traits of Jesus; it emphasizes that Jesus was born in Bethlehem, the city of David, and by tradition the expected birthplace of the Christ. In fact, it is implied that Joseph and Mary lived there. Matthew knows of no imperial census and of no birth in a stable. The astrologers or 'wise men from the East' visited father, mother and baby 'in the house' (Matt. 2:11).

Superimposed on the story of the virgin birth is the image of Jesus as the new Moses, signalling that he was to be not only the Messiah, but also the ultimate teacher and law-giver. The life of the infant Jesus, like that of the baby Moses and all the new-born Jewish boys in Egypt, was threatened by the new Pharaoh, the wicked King Herod. But Jesus, too, was miraculously saved and found refuge in Egypt. He and his parents were subsequently ordered to migrate to Nazareth on the death of Herod the Great in 4 BC.

Luke's narrative presents an entirely different picture. Joseph, of the lineage of David, and his heavily pregnant fiancée, normally resident in Nazareth, travelled from Galilee to a crowded Bethlehem as a result of the otherwise unknown and improbable decree of world census issued by the emperor Augustus.[8] Jesus was born in a stable and laid in a manger because all the inns were fully booked. Luke knows of no danger threatening the infant from King Herod. On the contrary, the family is shown as quietly devoting itself to carrying out the duties imposed by the Mosaic Law. Jesus was circumcised on the eighth day – this is the Jewish rite that Christians are supposed to celebrate on New Year's day – and a sacrifice was offered in the Temple of Jerusalem forty days after the birth of a boy (cf. Lev. 12:2–6; Exod. 13:2, 12; Luke 2:21–4).

A final amusing snippet of a semi-legendary nature about the precocious wisdom of Jesus is provided in Luke's reference to the twelve-year-old youth's visit to Jerusalem for the pilgrim festival of Passover. It took his parents a day to realize that he was missing, and another three days' search before they spotted him in the Temple, 'sitting among the teachers . . . and asking them questions; and all who heard him were amazed at his understanding and his answers' (Luke 2:41–6). Luke's purpose in telling the story was to foreshadow the supernatural knowledge of Jesus. Leaving aside rabbinic and later examples, a perfect parallel to Luke's account is furnished by Josephus in his autobiography. 'While still a mere boy,' he wrote, 'about fourteen years old, I won universal applause for my love of letters; inasmuch that the chief priests and the leading men of the city used constantly to come to me for precise information on some particular in our ordinances' (*Life* 9). The idea of the wonder-child is not a modern phenomenon but has been part of Jewish family lore throughout the ages.

8. There is no record of any general imperial census in the time of Augustus. There was a tax registration in Judaea in AD 6/7 under Quirinius, governor of Syria, after the deposition of Herod Archelaus and the transformation of his ethnarchy into the Roman province of Judaea. But no Roman census would have been imposed on a client king such as Herod, neither was Quirinius legate of Syria in Herod's lifetime. Finally, even if there had been a census at the time of the birth of Jesus, under Roman rules Joseph would not have been compelled to travel to the ancestral home of his tribe, nor would Mary have been obliged to accompany him. Luke seems to have combined the real census under Quirinius, about a dozen years after the birth of Jesus, with his theological scenario.

## Further peculiarities in Matthew and Luke

Perhaps the easiest way to trace changes in the depiction of Jesus is to concentrate our inquiry on the attitude to Jews and Gentiles assigned to Christ in these two Gospels.

In this respect, Matthew showed himself contradiction incarnate. On the one hand, he was an arch-Jew. His favourite persona was the learned 'scribe', not only expert in ancient wisdom, but also 'trained for the Kingdom of heaven', and distributing from his treasure things both new and old (Matt. 13:52). Among all the evangelists Matthew was the most expert practitioner of the biblical argument, especially the use of fulfilment (or *pesher*) interpretation (cf. pp. 123-9), demonstrating from Old Testament predictions details of the destiny of Jesus. Some of the most familiar 'prophetic proofs' of the messiahship of Jesus come from Matthew. To Isaiah 7:14 ('Behold the virgin shall conceive') should be added Micah 5:2 ('And you, O Bethlehem ... from you shall come a ruler'), identifying the birthplace of the Christ (Matt. 2:6); Hosea 11:1 ('Out of Egypt have I called my son'), used to explain Jesus' journey from Egypt to Galilee (Matt. 2:15); Jeremiah 31:15 ('Rachel weeping for her children'), accounting for Herod's massacre of the innocent children (Matt. 2:18). Isaiah 9:1-2 ('The land of Zebulun ... toward the sea ...') is seen as the prophetic prediction of Jesus' choice of 'Capernaum by the sea' as the centre of his Galilean ministry (Matt. 4:15-16). The fact that some of the scriptural arguments (for instance Isaiah 7:14) work only from the Septuagint, and not from the Hebrew Bible, provides grist to the mill of those who see in Matthew a Greek-speaking Jew.

In presenting polemical diatribes between Jesus the moralist and his opponents – the 'scribes' in Mark (12:38), the 'scribes' and 'lawyers' in Luke (20:46; 11:52) – Matthew regularly shows him in conflict with 'scribes and *Pharisees*' although there is no evidence of an established influence of Pharisees in Galilee in the time of Jesus (cf. pp. 167 and 229). The first evangelist also lays greater stress on Jesus' interest in legal niceties, the size of the phylactery (*tefillin*) and the fringe (*tzitzit*), formulaic details which may invalidate an oath, or the rules relating to the cleansing of pots and pans (23:5, 16-22, 25-6), than we normally encounter in the sayings and parables which are generally acknowledged to be authentic. Both the *pesher* argument and the legalistic debates mirror the controversies with Pharisees in which Jewish Christians in Jerusalem and Pauline Christians in the diaspora were engaged in the second half of the first century AD. They are anachronistically backdated by Matthew to the life of Jesus and have substantially contributed to the blackening of the name of the Pharisees.

Matthew's 'schizophrenia' shows itself in many ways. He is more pro-Jewish than Mark, and much more than the Gentile Luke. He portrayed a Jesus who was concerned only with Jews – 'I was sent only to the lost sheep of the house of Israel' (Matt. 15:24) – and who actually forbade his disciples to take an interest in non-Jews: 'Go nowhere among the Gentiles, and enter no town of the Samaritans, but go rather to the lost sheep of the house of Israel' (10:6). However, in a complete volte-face from the chauvinism expressed in the preceding passages, Matthew laid a heavier emphasis than any other evangelist on the Christian mission to all the nations, and on the church being substituted for Israel. His Jesus, no longer preoccupied with lost Jewish sheep, firmly proclaimed: 'I tell you, many will come from east and west and sit at table with Abraham, Isaac, and Jacob in the Kingdom of heaven, while the sons of the Kingdom will be thrown into the outer darkness' (Matt. 8:11–12). Even the non-Jewish Luke, who reports a similar saying (Luke 13:28–9), abstains from dispossessing 'the sons of the Kingdom' as such.

Another passage exclusive to Matthew, and as poisonous in its after-effects as John's demonization of the Jews (cf. above, p. 19), contains the frightening words of a curse intended to counter Pilate's profession of innocence of Jesus' death: 'His blood be on us and on our children!' (27:25–6). By ascribing this curse to 'all the people', Matthew laid the foundation of the Christian concept of the universal and permanent Jewish guilt for deicide which, unhesitatingly embraced by the church, was responsible for the shedding of much innocent blood over the ages.

In parenthesis: it took more than nineteen centuries for the Roman Catholic church to revoke, in highly diplomatic language at the Second Vatican Council, the universal and enduring charge of deicide levelled against the Jewish people as such. 'Even though the Jewish authorities and those who followed their lead pressed for the death of Christ (cf. John 19:6), neither all Jews indiscriminately at that time, nor all Jews today, can be charged with the crimes committed during his passion' (A. Flannery (ed.), *Vatican Council II*, 741). This was a giant step towards the restoration of historical truth. Yet the statement shows no awareness of the fact that the large majority of Jewish contemporaries of Jesus – those who lived outside Palestine – had never heard of him and consequently could not possibly have 'pressed for his death'. It is also permissible to wonder what the Council meant by declaring that not all Jews today can be charged with crimes committed more than nineteen centuries ago. Did the fathers of the Council think that some could?!

The apparently irreconcilable features in Matthew are best explained as the result of evolving attitudes towards the Jews, starting with the original enthusiasm for their impending entry into the Kingdom of God, continuing with the strenuous but largely inefficient preaching to them of the fulfilment of messianic prophecies inside and outside Palestine, and ending with the conclusion – based on Paul's success among the Gentiles – that it was the will of Jesus that the nations should inherit all the biblical promises made to the Jewish people.

Turning to Luke, his omissions in the portrayal of Jesus are particularly significant. In addressing what was primarily a Gentile public, he deleted or dropped the passages which in Mark and/or Matthew underline the exclusively Jewish orientation of the mission of Jesus and of his immediate disciples. Luke is silent on the story of the Syro-Phoenician woman, getting rid of the declaration that Jesus was sent only to the lost sheep of Israel (Matt. 15:24) and of his reference to non-Jews as 'dogs' and 'swine' (Mark 7:27; Matt. 15:26; cf. also Matt. 7:6). By excising the prohibition to visit Gentiles and Samaritans, he abbreviated the account of the apostles' commission to preach and to heal (cf. Matt. 10:5–8 against Luke 9:2). The affirmation that the message of Jesus and the church was intended for the whole world opens and closes Luke's Gospel. When the forty-day-old Jesus was presented in the Temple he was met there by Simeon, an old man who, in his prayer of thanksgiving, recognized in Jesus the salvation prepared by God not just for the Jews but for 'all the peoples' (Luke 2:30–32).

At the end of the story, in Luke's description of the apparition of Jesus to the apostles, the mandate to preach repentance and forgiveness of sins was extended to 'all the nations' (24:47).

In a similar manner, Luke either completely left out or partly modified those sayings of Jesus which indicate eschatological urgency. One would search in vain in Luke's Gospel for Jesus' first proclamation that the Kingdom of God was at hand (Mark 1:15; Matt. 4:17), or his identical assertion in the instruction he gave the apostles before dispatching them on their initial preaching expedition (Matt. 10:7; Luke 10:11). Even when Luke reproduced eschatological sayings of Jesus, he tried to soften their impact by the removal of key words. In Luke's wording, 'You will see the son of Man seated at the right hand of Power, *and coming with the clouds of heaven*' (Mark 14:62; Matt. 26:64), the final italicized apocalyptic clause is left out (22:69). As a result of these manipulations, Luke altered the overall picture of an eschatologically oriented Jesus and opened the gate for a lasting and universal church.

## Distinctive features in Mark

It is generally agreed that the best path leading to the human and Aramaic-speaking Jewish Jesus is the Gospel of Mark. Because this thesis has momentous implications in the quest for the historical Jesus, I will set out here some passages in Mark which deal with emotions and ignorance or indicate various degrees of imperfection in Jesus, passages which the other Synoptic evangelists expunge or correct.

Before healing a leper, Mark's Jesus is moved *by pity* towards the sick man, or according to a manuscript variant *by anger*, no doubt directed at the demonic source of the disease (Mark 1:41). Neither Matthew nor Luke refers to the state of mind of Jesus. Again, in Mark Jesus looks at his critics *with anger* (3:5). Luke omits 'with anger' (Luke 6:10) and Matthew deletes the whole sentence (cf. Matt. 12:12–13). The comment by Jesus' relatives that *he is out of his mind* recorded in Mark (3:21) proved too much for both Matthew and Luke; they ignore the words altogether. The Pharisees' request for a sign from heaven makes Jesus groan before replying (Mark 8:12). Luke implies that Jesus did not answer (Luke 11:16) and Matthew overlooks the undignified sigh (Matt. 16:2). Luke and Matthew edit out Mark's allusion to Jesus' annoyance with his disciples when they tried to keep children away from him (Mark 10:14; cf. Matt. 19:14; Luke 18:16). Mark's Jesus frequently displays ignorance: he asks for the name of a demon (5:9). The question is copied by Luke (8:30), but left out by Matthew. Mark's report on a less than perfect healing performance by Jesus is upwardly revised by Matthew and Luke: instead of curing 'many' (Mark 1:34; 3:10), he cures them 'all' (Matt. 8:16; Luke 4:40). In Mark, Jesus' inability to perform 'mighty works' in Nazareth apart from healing a 'few' sick people (6:5) becomes in Matthew 'he did not do *many* mighty works there' (13:58); there is no parallel in Luke.

Lastly, a particular feature of Mark to which attention should be drawn is his liking for the quotation of Aramaic words in the sayings of Jesus. Only he reports that Jesus nicknamed the hot-headed apostles James and John *Boanerges*, 'sons of thunder' (Mark 3:17), or used the healing word *Ephphatha*, 'Be opened', when treating a deaf-mute (7:34). He called a sacrificial gift *Corban*, for which the Greek paraphrase 'given to God' is provided (7:11). The blind man of Jericho bears the Aramaic name *Bar*timaeus, correctly explained as 'the son of Timaeus' (10:46), and Bartimaeus calls Jesus *Rabbuni*, which is left untranslated as everyone was expected to know that it signified 'My Master' (10:51). Neither Matthew nor Luke used any of these words.

Mark's (and Matthew's) Simon the Cananean (*qannay*: Mark 3:18; Matt. 10:4) is translated into Greek as 'Zealot' by Luke (6:15). *Talitha cum*, Jesus' command to the daughter of Jairus, is amplified in Greek as 'Little girl, *I say to you*, arise' (Mark 5:41). These words, which are ignored in Matthew (9:25), are abridged in Luke's Greek simply as 'Child arise' (Luke 8:54). As we discussed earlier, Mark quotes a prayer of Jesus in which he addresses God in Aramaic as *Abba*, followed by the Greek 'Father' (14:36). Matthew substitutes 'My Father' (Matt. 26:39) and Luke 'Father' (Luke 22:42), both in Greek. Finally, Mark reproduces fully in Aramaic the cry of Jesus on the cross, *Eloi, Eloi lama sabachtani* ('My God, my God, why hast thou forsaken me', Mark 15:34). He is followed by Matthew, but with the substitution of the Hebrew *Eli, Eli* for the Aramaic *Eloi, Eloi* (Matt. 27:46).

Brief though this survey is, it will serve to show that Mark's Gospel brings us nearer the Jesus of history than any other New Testament writing, and that Mark is the only evangelist who enables us to hear today an occasional and faint echo of what may have been the *ipsissima verba*, Jesus' own words in his own language.

# 7

# Beneath the Gospels:
# The real Jesus

The most prominent features of the Synoptic portrait of Jesus, those of a charismatic healer and exorcist, teacher and champion of the Kingdom of God, are essentially dependent on the historical figure which other authors of the New Testament progressively disguised. The fact that Jesus was admired, or suspected, as a potential Messiah started a complex process of theological speculation which in the course of three centuries culminated in the elevation of the carpenter from Nazareth to the rank of the second person of the triune Godhead, the Holy Trinity. In other words, it is to be feared that not even a highly critical treatment of the New Testament evidence can enable the most adroit historian to re-convert the Christ of the Gospels – even the Jesus of Mark, who is the least concealed – into the real, tangible, flesh-and-blood person who once used to walk on the rocky and dusty paths of first-century rural Galilee.

Is, then, a full recovery of the personality of Jesus of Nazareth beyond anyone's reach? In the footsteps of generations of critical scholars, I have lamented the absence of direct evidence, a genuine Gospel of Jesus by Jesus, or just a synopsis of his ideas prepared by him. Unfortunately the missive, which in any case is devoid of doctrinal content, that Jesus is said to have sent to Abgar, a first-century king of Edessa in Mesopotamia, is patently spurious and apocryphal, and no other document is extant on which we could fasten our hopes. The only chance to transform Jesus into a lifelike character beckons from the realities of the Jewish world of his day. By recreating the milieu of his time, we may be able to catch a glimpse of what he really was. So we must try to retrieve the atmosphere he breathed, together with the ideas and ideals which animated his small world of people living in first-century Palestine, and especially in the backwaters of Galilee: their religious dreams and petty jealousies, and – particularly in Galilee – their love of (relative) independence springing from a freedom from immediate Roman rule and the direct influence of the distant Judaean priestly authority, and from the doctrinal domination of the urban intellectual classes represented by the Pharisees.

## GALILEE IN THE AGE OF JESUS

The Galilee of Jesus differed from Judaea as it differed also from the post-AD 70 Galilee, which underwent major changes during the last decades of the first and in the course of the second century AD. It came more and more under the influence of the Judaean rabbinic authorities. Indeed the rabbis opted for, or were forced to select, the less oppressive conditions prevailing in the north after two Roman victories had finally brought to an end Jewish independence in Judaea as well as in Jerusalem, which after AD 135 was rebuilt and transformed into the pagan city of Aelia Capitolina.

Following the death of Herod the Great, who from 37 to 4 BC ruled over the whole of Palestine, his territory was divided between three of his sons who were lucky enough to survive their father. Three other sons, one of his wives and his mother-in-law had been put to death by this murderous king, who was justifiably given the leading part of the wicked in the Gospel legend of the massacre of the innocents. Herod's eldest son, Archelaus, who inherited Judaea and Samaria, was ten years later deposed and exiled to France, and from AD 6 onwards Judaea and Samaria came under direct Roman administration; Pontius Pilate (AD 26–36) was the best known of the imperial prefects. These governors resided not in Jerusalem but in Caesarea Maritima on the Mediterranean coast. In Judaea the presence of the Roman army and officialdom was visible everywhere, and taxes were collected for the imperial exchequer. However, the northern sectors of the land remained in the hands of the two surviving sons of Herod the Great. Philip (4 BC to AD 33/4) ruled over the north-eastern districts of Batanaea, the Golan and Ituraea, and his brother Antipas was the ethnarch of Galilee from 4 BC to AD 39, that is during the whole lifetime of Jesus. As long as the tributes were paid the Roman overlords did not interfere with his running of the country, which continued to enjoy comparative freedom and autonomy.

Galilee, which in earlier centuries had possessed a substantial non-Jewish population, was largely re-Judaized after the victory of the Maccabees in the second century BC. They even forcibly converted to Judaism some of the neighbouring Gentile peoples. In the days of Jesus the country was completely surrounded by non-Jews. To the west, the Mediterranean coast was Hellenized, and so was Phoenicia (Lebanon) in the north. The east (southern Syria and Transjordan) was held by the confederation of ten Greek city-states, known as the Decapolis. One of these, Scythopolis (the biblical Beth Shean), at the lower extremity of the Lake of Galilee, blocked the road to the south. Beyond it lay the unfriendly province of Samaria, which Galilean Jews were well advised to bypass and to use the valley of the Jordan as a safer route for their pilgrimage to Jerusalem. Inhabiting a Jewish island in the midst of a Gentile sea, the Galileans were renowned for their fighting spirit, courage and chauvinism.

Agriculture was flourishing in the province, especially in the southern half of it or Lower Galilee. An enthusiastic account by Josephus furnishes a vivid background to the parables of Jesus relating to fields, wild flowers, trees and vineyards: 'The land is everywhere so rich in soil and pasturage and produces such variety of trees, that even the most indolent are tempted by these facilities to devote themselves to agriculture. In fact, every inch of the soil has been cultivated by the inhabitants; there is not a parcel of waste land' (*Jewish War* iii. 42–3). Josephus further speaks of 'abundant resources': Galilee produced olive oil in large quantities, some of which could be exported (*War* ii. 592). Agriculture was complemented by fishing in the Lake of Gennesaret, again the home of many a Gospel episode; an ancient boat similar to those used by Peter and his colleagues for earning their living, and by Jesus for travelling and occasionally as a kind of pulpit for preaching, was discovered at the bottom of the lake in 1985. It may have sunk during a storm like the one described in the Gospels.

The area of the lake lying about 200 metres below sea-level was the chief venue of the ministry of Jesus. According to Josephus it was exceptionally rich and beautiful:

There is not a plant which its fertile soil refuses to produce, and its cultivators in fact grow every species; the air is so well-tempered that it suits the most opposite varieties. The walnut, a tree which delights in the most wintry climate, here grows luxuriantly, beside palm-trees, which thrive on heat, and figs and olives, which require a milder atmosphere. One might say that nature had taken pride in thus assembling, by a *tour de force*, the most discordant species in a single spot, and that, by a happy rivalry, each of the seasons wished to claim this region for her own. For not only has the country this surprising merit of producing such diverse fruits, but it also preserves them: for ten months without intermission it supplies those kings of fruits, the grape and the fig; the rest mature on the trees the whole year round. Besides being favoured by its genial air, the country is watered by a highly fertilizing spring, called by the inhabitants Capharnaum. (*War* iii. 516–19)

The little fishing village after which the spring was named was Jesus' own town, the place where he felt 'at home' (Matt. 9:1; Mark 2:1).

Galilee had its towns, but they play no part in the life of Jesus. The chief city, Sepphoris, never appears in the Gospels; nor do other important localities like Gabara, Tarichaeae or Gischala. The Synoptics, unlike John (John 6:1, 23; 21:1), do not mention the new city built by Herod Antipas between AD 17 and 20 in honour of the emperor Tiberius and named Tiberias after him. City life had no appeal for Jesus.

If on the one hand nature might have predisposed the Galileans to enjoy a quiet and peaceful existence, on the other hand its remoteness from the centre and the rugged mountains of Upper Galilee seem to have made of the area an ideal home for revolutionaries. Josephus, at the beginning of the first war against Rome commander-in-chief of the revolutionary forces in both Galilees, praised the bravery of the inhabitants who from childhood were trained for war (*War* iii. 42). The province was the seat of unrest from the mid-first century BC to the great rebellion in AD 66–73/4, and together with the neighbouring Golan produced the most notorious leaders of the fight against Rome. The list begins with Ezekias, the chief brigand or revolutionary, active in northern Galilee, who was captured and summarily executed by the young Herod in 47 BC (*War* i. 204). His example was emulated by his son Judas, who after the death of Herod raided the royal arsenal in the half-Greek, half-Jewish regional capital of Sepphoris, next door to Nazareth, and created chaos in the area, motivated by 'ambition for the royal rank' (*Jewish Antiquities* xvii. 271–2). The general unrest which also extended to Judaea was quelled by Publius Quinctilius Varus, the Roman governor of Syria (7/6–4 BC), who put an end to the uprising by crucifying 2,000 leading rebels. The dreaded cross was not an unusual sight in Roman Palestine.

At the time of the tax registration ordered by Publius Sulpicius Quirinius, another governor of Syria, in AD 6 – the census which the Gospel of Luke wrongly connects with the birth of Jesus – Judas 'the Galilean', no doubt identical with Judas son of Ezekias, launched in the company of a Pharisee called Saddok or Zadok, the rebellious association of the Zealots, who forbade Jews to pay taxes to Caesar and acknowledge any Lord but God (*War* ii. 118; *Ant.* xviii. 4–10). Two of his sons, also revolutionaries and contemporaries of Jesus, were subsequently crucified by Tiberius Julius Alexander, the Romanized nephew of the Jewish philosopher Philo of Alexandria, who was the governor of Judaea between AD 46 and 48 (*Ant.* xx. 102).[1] It is easy to understand, therefore, that the Galilean origin and messianic reputation of Jesus, as well as the fact that one of his apostles was nicknamed 'the Zealot', had sinister connotations in the eyes of those whose principal aim was to secure the goodwill of the Romans towards the Jewish people in Palestine.

As far as the culture of Galilee in the first century is concerned, although commerce with neighbouring regions obviously entailed the importation of Hellenistic industrial products, it should be emphasized that Hellenization as such, apart from the Greek cities, was very superficial in Galilean peasant society and that in the countryside the Greek language had made little inroads. The idea that the Galileans were bilingual, speaking both Greek and Aramaic, is not based on any

---

1. Menahem, another of Judas's sons, was one of the rebel captains in Jerusalem at the outbreak of the first war in AD 66 (*War* ii. 433). Finally Eleazar the son of Jairus, a further descendant of Judas the Galilean (probably his grandson), led the last stand against the Romans in Masada in AD 73/74 (ibid., vii. 253). Josephus' characterization of the Galileans as champions of Jewish independence is echoed in the Mishnah, where a 'Galilean heretic' criticizes the Pharisees for including the name of the emperor in dating a divorce document (mYadayim 4:8).

factual evidence. It should be borne in mind that according to the famous church historian Eusebius, even in the third century AD the rural Gentile-Christian population of the environs of the south Galilean Greek city of Scythopolis required a translator to render into Aramaic a sermon preached in Greek in the church. Over the first few centuries of the Christian era, Greek loan words, especially relating to administration and material culture, were progressively creeping into the Aramaic vernacular of Galilee, but this is a far cry from the theory of bilingualism. As for Jesus himself being a Greek speaker, this is a wild flight of fancy.

Some further aspects of Galilean culture and its relation to that of Judaea can be tentatively reconstructed with the help of the relevant evidence in rabbinic literature. The Mishnah and the rest of the writings of the rabbis postdate the period of Jesus, and their testimony cannot automatically be applied to the situation prevailing in the first century AD; yet historical circumstances point in the direction of the relative reliability of stereotypes regularly repeated. After the fall of Jerusalem in AD 70, and even more so after the defeat of the rebellion of Simeon bar Kosiba or Kokhba in AD 135, the cultural elite of Judaea emigrated to Galilee and soon gained control of the province. Thereafter any distinction between Judaean and Galilean became blurred if not meaningless unless it referred to the pre-AD 70 situation. But fortunately a good many of the anecdotes exemplifying the cultural differences between the two regions presuppose the existence of the Temple of Jerusalem, and consequently presume a first-century AD background. They relate to the language spoken in the north and to the Galileans' lack of familiarity with the sophisticated understanding and practice of the Torah. Both have their impact on the real Jesus and his surroundings.

The dialect of Aramaic used in Galilee seems to have been a permanent topic of sarcasm in Jerusalem circles. As I once light-heartedly remarked, adapting the terminology of Nancy Mitford, the Galileans did not speak U-Aramaic, i.e. the language of the Jerusalem upper classes.[2] The most striking jibe castigates the notoriously slipshod

2. The translator of my comment into French, completely at sea with the phrase U-Aramaic, produced a magnificent howler which, retranslated into English, runs, 'an Aramaic characterized by the pronunciation of the vowel U'. Fortunately the error was noted before it reached the printer.

enunciation of words beginning with a guttural (or deep-throat) consonant. It ridicules a Galilean in Jerusalem trying to buy something in the market. The merchants, unable to make out what he wanted when asking for something which sounded like *amar*, taunted him, 'You stupid Galilean, do you need something to ride on [*hamâr*, a donkey], or something to drink [*hamar*, wine], or something to make a dress with ['*amar*, wool], or something for a Temple sacrifice [*immar*, lamb]' (bErubin 53b). In the light of this story, the Gospel account of Peter's denial of Jesus appears in a new perspective. When he insisted that he did not know 'that man', some Jerusalem bystanders in the courtyard of the high priest retorted, 'Certainly you are one of them, for your accent betrays you' (Matt. 26:73; Mark 14:70; Luke 22:59).

In matters of Torah observance, in particular the observance of regulations relating to offerings in the Temple, Galileans were presumed to be ignoramuses, and for this reason special rules applied to their vows. Thus the Mishnah stipulates that if a vow concerning heave-offerings, i.e. the portion of the harvest set aside for the priests, or other offerings beneficial to the priests, is not clearly defined, it still binds a Judaean who is presumed to be familiar with Temple matters, but is void for a Galilean who knows nothing about them (mNedarim 2:4). In Judaea, work had to cease at midday on the eve of Passover, but Galileans, unsure of such details, abstained from work the whole day (mPesahim 4:5).

Elsewhere noted Galilean rabbinic figures are depicted as ignoring or neglecting the code of conduct binding on the sages. Two rabbis of the first century AD, Hanina ben Dosa (about whom more presently), and Yose the Galilean, are rebuked for venturing out in the street by night or speaking to an unaccompanied woman (bPesahim 112b; bErubin 53b). Though Jesus himself escaped being charged with neglect of this kind, he is certainly not described as paying much attention to conventional religious etiquette. Interestingly, the Fourth Gospel several times expresses the Judaean disparagement of Galilee familiar from rabbinic literature. 'Is the Christ to come from Galilee?' we read. Nicodemus, who spoke up for Jesus, found himself sarcastically rebuked: 'Are you from Galilee too? Search and you will see that no prophet is to rise from Galilee' (John 7:41, 52). A rural holy man from the Galilean lakeside could do little against such superiority and bigotry.

Lack of legal sophistication in Galilee is attributable to the absence of rabbinic schools in the province in the first half of the first century AD. This does not mean that there were no 'scribes' or 'lawyers' in the district to draw up contracts, marriage deeds or divorce documents. Josephus sarcastically referred to them as village clerks or *komogrammateis* (*Ant.* xvi. 203; *War* i. 479). Apart from the Talmudic story relating to Yohanan ben Zakkai, there is no evidence that in the age of Jesus Pharisee luminaries settled in Galilee. Yohanan ben Zakkai, we are told, wasted eighteen years in the Galilean town of Araba (or Gabara) during which he made hardly any impact on the local people. With the usual oriental hyperbole he is said to have accused them of hatred of the Torah (yShabbat 15d). We learn from the Gospel of Mark that some of the Pharisees/scribes whom Jesus encountered in Galilee did not function locally, but were visitors from Jerusalem (Mark 7:1; 3:22). Likewise, the only Pharisees in Galilee mentioned by Josephus while he was the revolutionary commander of the province in AD 66 were members of a delegation dispatched from Jerusalem by Simon son of Gamaliel, the Pharisee leader, with a view to engineering Josephus' removal from office (*Life* 189–98). So it is highly unlikely that Jesus came across Galilean Pharisees of note during his activity in the province. Hanina ben Dosa (see below) – if he was really a Pharisee – was too young to count, and Yose the Galilean, who flourished at the end of the first century AD, lived several generations after Jesus. The sufficiency of the surname, 'the Galilean', to identify Yose, one of the commonest Jewish names, implies that there cannot have been many Pharisee rabbis operating in Galilee in the years following the destruction of Jerusalem. Even if one were to concede that there might have been a sporadic Pharisee presence there, it would have affected the cities more than Jesus' rural surroundings, for according to Josephus the Pharisees operated in urban environments and their main impact was felt among the townsfolk (*Ant.* xviii. 15). So the historical circumstances confirm our earlier conclusion that the downfall of Jesus was not religiously, but politically motivated. Jesus was free from high-level Pharisee influence, and his occasional mini-conflicts with small-minded local scribes were of negligible importance.

As for the few chaotic days of his only public appearance in Jerusalem just before the feast of Passover, neither the shortness of the time nor the circumstances allowed for a serious conflict with the Pharisee masters to develop.

## POPULAR RELIGION
## IN THE AGE OF JESUS

Throughout the existence of Israelite sanctuaries in early biblical times – starting in the tenth century BC with temples in various cities and ending with a single one in Jerusalem after the reform of King Josiah in the late seventh century BC – the Jewish religion was practised on two levels. Its official form was in the hands of the priests who in addition to conducting the sacrificial worship acted as judges and teachers. But parallel to it, and often away from the centres, a popular version of Judaism existed. It was not presided over by an established caste of leaders but by persons believed to be directly chosen by heaven. The 'man of God' (*ish ha-elohim* in the Bible) was the medium through which the ordinary Israelite could come into contact with God. As J. B. Segal, the author of an illuminating essay on the subject, remarked, the 'men of God' were seen as endowed with what in Arabic is called the *barakah*, a mystic divine gift, enabling them to speak and act on behalf of the deity. Prophets and seers belonged to this category, but the field of action of the 'men of God' extended far beyond verbal communication. They were revered, especially the prophets Elijah and Elisha, as workers of miracles. 'When he was angry [the man of God] could summon fire from heaven' (2 Kings 1:9–10). He could make iron float on the water (2 Kings 6:6). In times of famine he brought about the return of food in plenty. The poor wife of a member of the prophets' guild was saved from her creditors by the flowing oil (2 Kings 4:1–7). A small quantity of grain would suffice to feed, and feed generously, a hundred men (2 Kings 4:42–4). The 'man of God' made poisonous food fit to eat (2 Kings 4:38–41). So, too, Elisha not only healed the great Naaman from leprosy, but restored from death a small child (2 Kings 5:8–14; 4:32–7). And it was when Elijah had resuscitated her son that the widow of Zarephat knew that he was a 'man of God'

(J. B. Segal, 'Popular Religion in Ancient Israel', *Journal of Jewish Studies* 27 (1976), 8–9). Segal includes Jesus in the same category. 'It should be remarked that, like Elijah and Elisha, the "man of God" *par excellence*, Jesus came from northern Palestine . . . We have miracles – of the food that is not exhausted, and especially the healing of the sick . . . Jesus, like the "men of God", was not deterred by fear of ritual uncleanness from contact with the dead and the sick . . . Like the "men of God" of the Old Testament, Jesus stood outside the established order' (ibid., 20–21). As we know, in the case of Jesus the healing of the sick and the casting out of evil spirits dominated the scene. To grasp this in its true reality, we must take a closer look at three connected notions in intertestamental Judaism: sickness, the devil and sin.

All those Jewish mothers who proudly refer to 'my son, the doctor' would be greatly surprised if told that the profession of the physician is hardly mentioned in biblical Israel. Of course, medicine existed in the ancient Near East. It was a lucrative but also dangerous calling. According to the Babylonian code of law of Hammurabi (eighteenth century BC), a surgeon who operated on a noble man 'with his bronze scalpel' and saved his life, earned ten shekels of silver. However, if the operation failed and as a consequence the patient died, he was not sued for incompetence or malpractice, but instead had his operating hand cut off.

The Law of Moses only once, and implicitly, refers to Jewish doctors. The case is that of a man causing bodily harm to another. If he is found guilty, the judge will order him to compensate his victim for 'the loss of his time' and pay in full the unnamed physician for the treatment of the victim (Exod. 21:19). Voluntary recourse to a doctor, as opposed to employing him by judicial order, was met with disapproval, probably because medicine was held to be tainted with magic. The Judaean king Asa was blamed in his illness for seeking help from physicians who were incapable of restoring him to health. He should have turned to God instead, we are told by the biblical historian (2 Chron. 16:12).

In the minds of the authors of the Old Testament, God alone was the master of sickness and health: 'See now that I, even I, am he, and there is no god beside me; I kill and I make alive; I wound and I heal' (Deut. 32:39), or more positively, 'I am the Lord, your healer'

(Exod. 15:26). In fact, in most of the cases the verb 'to heal' has God for subject in the Bible. The few exceptions concern not professional physicians, but representatives of God. Among these, priests were entrusted with the task of diagnosing leprosy and recovery from it. If it is legitimate to seek guidance from the Damascus Document from Qumran, we find that the priests possessed quite a detailed knowledge of the symptoms, making it possible to determine whether the disease was progressing and the patient had to be quarantined, or receding and the patient heading for complete cure (4Q266, 272). Apart from the priests, the only other approved healers were prophets, i.e. God's delegates. Chief among them, as we have seen, were Elijah and Elisha, but Isaiah is also credited with the prescription of a fig cake which cured the boils of King Hezekiah (2 Kings 20:7–8; Isa. 38:21–2).

For the final compromise we have to wait for Jesus ben Sira, author of the Book of Ecclesiasticus in the Apocrypha, at the beginning of the second century BC. In the view of this sage the medical art, far from being contaminated with magic and sorcery, was a divine gift. God created the doctor and endowed him with skill, and also created the healing substances to be used by the physician. The sick person was advised to pray, repent and mend his ways. Jesus ben Sira, being himself a priest, exhorted him also to offer a sacrifice. After such preliminaries, the patient was allowed to summon the doctor. Sometimes, ben Sira commented, recovery lay in the physician's hands as long as he prayed for divine help to save life (Ecclus. 38:1–14).

The physician thus rehabilitated by Jesus ben Sira was available only to those who could afford him, the kings (Ecclus. 38:2) and the wealthy devout; in his world there was no health service for poor lepers and blind beggars. For help they had to fall back on the men of God. Moreover, it is also unclear whether diseases attributed to demonic possession came within the sphere of competence of the physician. For in the popular belief of Jews living in the age of Jesus, devils were acknowledged as the cause of all spiritual and bodily evil. This idea is richly documented in intertestamental writings as well as in rabbinic literature. Already in the Greek Book of Tobit in the Apocrypha, Aramaic and Hebrew fragments of which survive at Qumran, we learn how the healing angel Raphael saved the life of the young Tobit from the evil demon Asmodeus. This devil, in love with Sarah, young Tobit's bride, and determined to keep her for himself, had managed to kill seven of her previous bridegrooms on their wedding nights before any of them could sleep with Sarah. On angelic advice, Tobit brought live ashes of incense into the bridal chamber and burned on them the heart and liver of a fish, producing such a foul odour that Asmodeus, who like demons in general was sensitive to smell, fled from Media, where the wedding took place, to the remotest parts of Egypt. There Raphael bound him with chains (Tobit 3:7–8; 6:13–17; 8:1–3).

The First Book of Enoch also depicts the same Raphael as God's agent in binding hand and foot the chief of the demons, Azazel, and healing the earth from all corruption and sin (1 Enoch 10:1–6). Meanwhile men were instructed by the angels how to combat the evil which humans had learned from the demons. Jewish tradition refers to two principal revealers of anti-demonic secrets, the patriarch Noah and the Jewish King Solomon. According to the Book of Jubilees (second century BC), an angel was commissioned by God to teach Noah the art of healing, and Noah in turn was to pass on this arcane science to his descendants. 'And we explained to Noah all the remedies against their diseases, together with their seductions and how to heal them with herbs. And Noah wrote down everything in a book, as we instructed him about every kind of remedy: thus were the evil spirits kept from doing harm to Noah's sons. And he gave everything he had written to Shem, his eldest son' (Jub. 10:10–14).

Josephus is our next most important source on esoteric medicine. His chief authority was the biblical sage, King Solomon, whom he described both as a philosopher for his Graeco-Roman readers, and as the hero of the art of healing mysteries for his Jewish audience. In addition to writing 'a thousand and five books of odes and songs, and three thousand books of parables and similitudes' (1 Kings 4:32; Ant. viii. 44), he subjected every aspect of nature to thorough philosophical investigation and testified to a complete mastery of its properties. Moreover, 'God granted him knowledge of the art used against demons for the benefit and healing of men. He also composed incantations by which illnesses are relieved, and left behind forms of exorcisms with which those possessed by demons drive them out, never to return' (Ant. viii. 45). The last clause recalls the command of Jesus to an evil spirit to get out of a man and never to re-enter (cf. above, pp. 161–62).

We also learn from Josephus of the therapeutical expertise of the Essenes.[3] 'They display an extraordinary interest in the writings of the ancients, singling out in particular those which make for the welfare of soul and body; and with the help of these, and with a view to the treatment of diseases, they make investigations into medicinal roots and the properties of stones' (*War* ii. 136). It is worth noting that in the Instruction on the Two Spirits in the Community Rule of the Qumran Essenes, healing heads the rewards of the children of light (1QS 4:6), and that their wisdom literature includes poems of exorcism (4Q510–11).

Enoch, Jubilees, Josephus and Qumran substantiate the close link in the minds of Jews of the intertestamental age between healing and exorcism which we have observed in the stories concerning Jesus. Actual descriptions of casting out demons display both similarities and notable differences. Perhaps the most detailed of these is provided by Josephus' account of an exorcism performed by a Jew called Eleazar and witnessed by Vespasian, commander-in-chief of the Roman army in Palestine and future emperor, together with his sons, tribunes and soldiers. Eleazar according to Josephus, 'put to the nose of the possessed man a ring which had under its seal one of the roots prescribed by Solomon' – probably the *baaras* root growing in the region of Macha-erus in Transjordan, which was held to be capable of expelling demons (*War* vii. 185) – 'and then, as the man smelled it, drew out the demon through his nostrils, and, when the man at once fell down, adjured the demon never to come back into him, speaking Solomon's name and reciting the incantations which he had composed' (*Ant.* viii. 46–7).

Knowledge of particular features of the demon was considered a distinct advantage for the exorcist. We are told that two rabbis of the second century AD, Simeon ben Yohai and Eleazar ben Yose, liberated the daughter of the emperor from a demon by addressing it by name: 'Ben Temalion, get out! Ben Temalion, get out!' (bMeilah 17b). No

---

3. The etymology of the name 'Essenes' has been the subject of much controversy. In my opinion the most satisfactory derivation is from the Aramaic word *assayya*, or healers. The Egyptian group akin to the Essenes also bears the name *therapeutai*, which means both 'worshippers' and 'healers' of the spirit and the body (Philo, *De vita contemplativa* 2).

doubt Jesus is supposed to have sought the same advantage when he inquired of the devil possessing the Gergesene demoniac, 'What is your name?' To which the demon replied, 'My name is Legion, for we are many' (Mark 5:9; Luke 8:30). Jesus attributed the failure of his disciples to cast out an evil spirit to their ignorance of the nature of the enemy: 'This kind cannot be driven out by anything but prayer' (Mark 9:29).

A successful exorcism by Jesus was usually marked by the calming of the previously distraught, often convulsing patient. The professional exorcist, however, was keen to supply a more spectacular proof of his competence. We learn from Josephus that the same Eleazar who had performed in the presence of Vespasian prepared a dramatic demonstration of the departure of the devil. 'He placed a cup or foot-basin full of water a little way off and commanded the demon, as it went out of the man, to overturn it and make known to the spectators that he had left the man' (*Ant.* viii. 48). The evangelists allude to an even more sensational proof of efficient exorcism in the transfer of the demons into a herd of swine in Gergesa (cf. above, p. 165).

Finally, before turning to the portrayal of the holy man outside the New Testament, we have to confront the reaction of non-believers to the phenomenon of exorcism. Were they witnessing the tricks of a magician? In the Gospels, opponents of Jesus assigned his exorcizing power either to his being possessed by Beelzebul or to acting by means of the power of the prince of demons (Mark 3:22; Matt. 12:24; Luke 11:15). In fact, as we shall see presently, detractors of Jesus in the post-New Testament period, both pagan and Jewish, uniformly branded him as a sorcerer. In a roundabout way, the famous Rabban Yohanan ben Zakkai (late first century AD) compared the levitical ritual of purification to exorcism, and believed the efficacy of both derived not from the ceremonial acts themselves but from God. Yohanan sought to demonstrate to a Gentile intellectual, with the help of the practice of exorcism, the non-magical nature of the rite of the red heifer, i.e. the cleansing power of water mixed with the ashes of a sacrificed female calf (Num. 19:1–10):

A Gentile said to Rabban Yohanan ben Zakkai: 'Some things you Jews do are like sorcery! A heifer is killed and burned. It is converted to ashes which are collected. After that if one of you is defiled by touching a corpse, he is sprinkled twice or thrice and told, You are clean.' Rabban Yohanan ben Zakkai answered: 'Has the spirit of madness ever entered you?' The Gentile replied, 'No.' 'Have you seen a man into whom the spirit of madness has entered?' 'Yes,' he answered. Yohanan asked, 'What does one do to him?' The Gentile said, 'They bring roots and make them smoke under him and splash water on him and the spirit flees.' So Rabban Yohanan ben Zakkai asked, 'Do your ears hear what your mouth is saying? The spirit of madness is the same as the spirit of uncleanness' [i.e. if one can be disposed of without sorcery, so can the other]. (Pesikta de-Rab Kahana 40ab)

The pupils of Yohanan found this argument worthless, and remarked after the departure of the Gentile that he had been 'knocked down with a straw'. They also thought that there was no rational basis on which the potency of the rite of the red heifer could be vindicated. Indeed it looked like magic. But Yohanan ben Zakkai explained that it worked on account of the faith of the worshipper who was convinced that he was doing the will of God: 'No dead body defiles and no water cleanses, but this is a precept of the King of kings' (ibid.). The underlying logic recalls Jesus' statement about defilement being caused from within and not from without (cf. above, p. 196).

## MODELS OF CHARISMATIC
## HOLY MEN IN THE AGE OF JESUS

We have already reviewed the role of the holy man as enacted by prophets, in particular Elijah and Elisha. In a peculiar way David may be added to them as one whose musical skills provided relief to King Saul: 'And whenever the evil spirit from God was upon Saul, David took the lyre and played it with his hand; so Saul was refreshed, and was well, and the evil spirit departed from him' (1 Sam. 16:23). Intertestamental literature introduced further healers or exorcists among the biblical heroes. The list begins with Abraham, who, as a holy man, was called on in the Qumran Genesis Apocryphon to repair the damage inflicted by his lack of honesty on the king of Egypt. Pharaoh thought that Sarah was free to be his wife – 'She is my sister,' the Patriarch deceitfully told him – but he was prevented by a plague caused by an evil spirit from harming Sarah's virtue. In fact both the king and all the male members of his court were sick (and impotent) for two years without any professional medicine men being able to assist them. 'He [Pharaoh] sent for all the sages of Egypt, for all the magicians, together with all the healers of Egypt, that they might heal him and all his household of this scourge. But not one healer or magician or sage could stay to cure him, for the spirit scourged them all and they fled' (1QapGen. 20:18–21). In the end, when the innocent Pharaoh discovered the reason for his troubles, he summoned Abraham himself and requested him to do the honest thing, which he did. 'So I prayed for him . . . and laid my hands on his head; and the scourge departed from him and the evil spirit was expelled from him and he lived' (ibid., 20:28–9). Healing by the laying on of hands was part of the healing and exorcistic practice of Jesus (cf. above, pp. 159–60) and of the apostles too (cf. Acts 28:8).

After Abraham comes Moses. The Hellenistic Jewish historian Artapanus of the second century BC depicted him as the restorer of Pharaoh's health after he had collapsed lifeless (Eusebius, *Praeparatio evangelica* ix. 29, 24–5). As for David, a list of his poetic output found at Qumran refers to four songs composed by him to make music on behalf of people stricken by evil spirits (11Q5, 27). Finally an exorcist (probably the prophet Daniel, about whom we shall hear more later) is portrayed in the so-called Prayer of Nabonidus (4Q242) in the Dead Sea Scrolls as healing the last Babylonian king by pardoning his sins and thereby removing the ulcer with which he had been afflicted for seven years. In brief, charismatic healing and exorcism were regular features of the religious landscape of intertestamental Judaism.

All these biblical and post-biblical antecedents are highly illuminating in the attempt to understand the real Jesus. They would, however, remain somewhat theoretical without the support of more or less contemporary figures with whom Jesus can be compared. The two leading characters, one of them from the first century BC and the other from the first century AD, are known from rabbinic literature, but the story of the earlier is also recorded in Josephus. Studying them will enable us to see the traits common to charismatics and the distinguishing marks which give Jesus his characteristic individuality. First we shall review the stories relating to Honi the Circle-Drawer and his two grandsons, and to Hanina ben Dosa, and then follow this up with a survey of the assessment of these holy men contained in Josephus and in rabbinic literature.

Of the two, Honi was chronologically the first to appear on the scene. Despite the magical overtones of the title 'the Circle-Drawer' which he bears in the Mishnah and the Talmud, he was venerated as a holy Hasid so close to God that his prayer exhibited miraculous efficacy. Therefore people in need came to solicit his help, especially in periods of drought when it was feared that all the crops might fail and a disastrous famine threatened.

Let me clarify one point before going into details. By using the descriptions of the two men given in the Mishnah and the Talmud, I am, need I say, perfectly aware of the time factor: most of the written sources postdate them by several centuries. Therefore I will not argue on the basis of details, but from typology which is verifiable in all the periods from the age of the prophets down to that of the rabbis. Some New Testament scholars, disturbed by the comparison between Jesus and the charismatic Hasidim, cavil about calling them miracle-workers. They simply petitioned God, and their prayer was instantaneously answered. The objection displays a typically Western theological thought process. The Jewish texts again and again explicitly attribute the 'miracle' to the Hasid. When Honi's grandson Hanan was invoked, 'Abba, abba, give us rain', the children surely did not mean, Please pray and may God listen to you and grant us rain. For them the rain was brought by the Hasid, just as in the case of the prophet Elijah (1 Kings 17:1).

Returning to Honi, the principal anecdote preserved about him in the Mishnah depicts him as a spoilt child secure in the knowledge that he can obtain whatever he asks from his heavenly Father.

Once Honi the Circle-Drawer was asked: Pray that it may rain. He answered, 'Go and bring in the Passover ovens [made of dried clay] that they may not become soft.' He prayed but it did not rain. What did he do? He drew a circle and stood in it and said to God, 'Lord of the world, Thy children have turned to me because I am like a son of the house before Thee. I swear by Thy great name that I will not move from here until Thou hast mercy on Thy children.' Drops of rain fell. 'I have not asked for this,' he said, 'but for rain to fill the cisterns, the pits and rock-cavities.' There came a cloud-burst. 'I have not prayed for this but for a rain of goodwill, blessing and grace.' Then it rained steadily until the Israelites were compelled to flee from Jerusalem to the Temple Mount. So they went to him and said, 'As you prayed for the rain to come, now pray that it may cease.' (mTaanit 3:8)

Irony apart, we have here a story that recalls the prophet Elijah starting and stopping rain on Mount Carmel. The Mishnah tells us nothing about Honi as a person, when he lived or where he came from, although we can deduce that the event related above took place around Passover and that the venue was Jerusalem where in the days of the Temple every pious Jew was duty-bound to be at the approach of the festival. Fortunately the historian Josephus comes to our rescue; alluding in passing to the rain-making episode, he firmly sets the hero in a historical context. Josephus is neither disparaging nor starry-eyed, but respectfully tells his story. The event occurred in the midst of political turmoil in Jerusalem where the high priest Aristobulus II was besieged in the Temple by an army led by his brother Hyrcanus II, and his ally, the Nabataean king Aretas III, at Passover, probably in April 65 BC. This is Josephus' report.

Now there was a certain Onias [the Hellenized form of Honi] who, being a righteous man and beloved by God, had once in a rainless period prayed to God to end the drought, and God had heard his prayer and sent rain. This man hid himself when he saw that the civil war continued to rage, but he was taken to the camp of the Jews and was asked to place a curse on Aristobulus and his fellow rebels, just as he had by his prayers put an end to the rainless period. But when in spite of his refusals and excuses he was forced to speak by the mob, he stood up in their midst and said, 'O God, king of the universe, since these men standing beside me are Thy people, and those who are besieged are Thy priests, I beseech Thee not to hearken to them against these men, nor bring to pass what these men ask Thee to do to those others.' And when he had prayed in this manner the villains among the Jews who stood round him stoned him to death. (*Ant.* xiv. 22–4)

If the pieces of information supplied by the Mishnah and Josephus are combined, we have a man renowned for a rain miracle or for the infallible efficacy of his prayer, of whom the party of Hyrcanus tried to make use in their efforts to defeat Aristobulus. Onias, however, was unwilling to play their game, and when forced to speak to God he refused to take sides and paid with his life for his courageous act.

Josephus has nothing further to say about Onias, but in rabbinic literature he is presented as if he were the founder of a dynasty of wonder-workers. As I have noted, nothing is said directly about the geographical origin of the family, but an episode associated with the grandson Abba Hilkiah is linked elsewhere to 'a Hasid from Kefar Imi', a village which figures in a Galilean context in the Palestinian Talmud (yTaanit 64b). Two of Honi's grandsons also had a reputation as charismatic rain-makers with the difference that they were exceedingly modest, unworldly and humble, unlike their petulant grandfather. Abba Hilkiah, mentioned above, is described as an impecunious hired labourer, who in his humility attempted to deny that he had anything to do with the instant rain; it came from God, or was possibly due to his wife's prayer. But the rabbinic envoys could not be fooled: 'We know full well that this rain is come through you,' they said (bTaanit 23ab).

The second grandson, Hanan the Hidden, was so designated because of his self-effacing personality. In times of drought rabbis encouraged children to pull the fringes of his garments in the street and beg him, 'Abba, Abba, give us rain!' He turned to God with the words, 'Lord of the universe, do this for the sake of those who cannot distinguish the Father [Abba] who gives rain from the abba [he was no doubt known as Abba Hanan] who does not' (bTaanit 23b). Both Hanan and his cousin Hilkiah, and in an odd way even grandfather Honi, are portrayed as typifying the Hasidim, or particularly pious men.

Before turning to Hanina ben Dosa, the most remarkable example of this category of Jewish men of God, let me sketch with the help of the rabbinic sources the portrait of these ancient Devout. In addition to the proverbial humility and unworldliness, poverty was one of their hallmarks. They lived frugally and had scarcely enough to eat. Hilkiah was unable to invite visitors to share his supper because he had no more than the day's bread in his house (bTaanit 23b), and Hanina's weekly food ration was one *kab* (the equivalent in volume of two pints or 1.2 litres) of carob beans, the poor man's diet (ibid., 24b), and it was rumoured that he was unable to afford bread even for the Sabbath (ibid., 24b–25a). The Hasidim lived in a state of total detachment from earthly possessions and were ready to share with others the little they had. They professed as their philosophy, 'What is mine is yours, and what is yours is yours' (mAbot 5:10). They rated piety higher than mere ritual (cf. above, p. 238; bBerakhot 33a) and one of them, the Galilean Hasid of the second century AD, Rabbi Pinhas ben Yair, extolled sexual abstinence among the Hasidic virtues (mSotah 9:15). But above all the Hasid was famous for his prayer, which was believed to be all-powerful, capable of performing miracles and revealing his closeness to God, the heavenly Father: 'The ancient Hasidim used to pause for an hour before reciting the Prayer [the Eighteen Benedictions] that they might direct their hearts towards their Father in heaven. Should the king salute him, he may not return his greeting; should a snake be wound around his leg, he may not interrupt his prayer' (mBerakhot 5:1). Many of these traits reflect the Synoptic portrait of Jesus, in particular the absence of anxiety for daily needs, the divesting oneself of riches, even the lack of a home where he could lay his head and the conviction that faith can perform miracles: 'If you have faith as [tiny as] a grain of mustard seed, you will say to this mountain, "Move from here to there" [or "Be taken up and cast into the sea"], and it will move; and nothing will be impossible to you' (Matt. 21:21; Mark 11:23).

Hanina ben Dosa was a first-century Galilean, probably a younger contemporary of Jesus, from the town of Araba or Gabara, about a dozen miles north of Nazareth. Rabbinic sources represent him as a pre-AD 70 personality associated with Yohanan ben Zakkai (cf. above, pp. 228–9), who is located in the same place before the first Jewish war (AD 66–70). The earliest layers of the rabbinic tradition depict him not only as a holy man who, like Honi and his grandchildren, could miraculously bring rain and stop it again, but as a person of outstanding devotion who was a famous healer and a master over the demonic powers. He was, in short, rabbinic Judaism's most prominent wonder-worker whose death marked the end of the era of the 'men of deeds' (mSotah 9:15), but he is also remembered as the author of a small number of moral teachings. To understand the title 'man of deeds' it should be remembered that the miracles of Jesus were also designated as 'deeds' (Luke 24:19; Matt. 11:20; Acts 2:22).

Hanina's fame was primarily based on his charismatic healings, which at the request of the family of the sick person he was able to perform even from a distance. His prayer was seen not simply as an intercession to God, but as directly efficient. In fact he was aware in advance of the efficacy of his words: 'If my prayer is fluent in my mouth,' he is quoted as saying, 'I know that he [the sick man] is favoured' (mBerakhot 5:1).

His two most renowned healings are associated, genuinely or typologically, with the leading Pharisee masters of the first century AD: Gamaliel, probably the one mentioned in the Acts of the Apostles (5:34) and claimed by St Paul as his Jewish teacher, and Yohanan ben Zakkai, allegedly Hanina's own master and the leader of the Jews after the fall of Jerusalem. He was much sought after in high places. In the Yohanan story all the actors are located in the town of Araba, but in the case of Gamaliel, the head of the Pharisee confraternity is in Jerusalem and the humble charismatic resides in remote Galilee. Both accounts derive from early traditions from the first or second century AD, incorporated into the Talmud. The second of these healings, already cited (cf. p. 13, n. 2), is reminiscent of Jesus healing the servant of the centurion from Capernaum.

In connection with the cure of Yohanan's son, one must observe the stress laid on the miraculous power of the prayer directed to heaven from a strange crouching devotional position which recalls the prophet Elijah on Mount Carmel, who bowed down to earth and put his face between his knees (1 Kings 18:42). Here, as in the case of Jesus' miracles, Elijah appears as the prototype. The spontaneous recognition of the superiority of the young charismatic by the leading Pharisee is also noteworthy.

It happened when R. Hanina ben Dosa went to Rabban Yohanan ben Zakkai to study Torah, the son of Rabban Yohanan ben Zakkai fell ill. He said to him, 'Hanina, my son, pray for him that he may live.' He put his head between his knees, and prayed, and he lived. Rabban Yohanan ben Zakkai said, 'Even if ben Zakkai had squeezed his head between his knees all day long, no attention would have been paid to him.' (bBerakhot 34b)

In regard to the Gamaliel story it should be pointed out that before the arrival of his envoys and the disclosure by them of the object of their visit, Hanina had already perceived the purpose of their mission. He assured them of the child's recovery before they had had a chance to open their mouths.

It happened that when Rabban Gamaliel's son fell ill, he sent two pupils to R. Hanina ben Dosa that he might pray for him. When he saw them, he went to the upper room and prayed. When he came down, he said to them, 'Go, for the fever has left him' . . . They sat down, wrote and noted the hour. When they came to Rabban Gamaliel, he said to them, 'By Heaven, you have neither detracted from it, nor added to it, but this is how it happened. It was at that hour that the fever left him and he asked us for water to drink.' (bBerakhot 34b; yBerakhot 9d)

Apropos the Elijah connection, like the Old Testament prophet Hanina and Honi were credited with both bringing rain when it was needed and stopping it in due course. The rabbinic narrative, tainted with irony, presupposes a period of drought during which official prayers for rain were recited by the high priest in the Temple.

R. Hanina ben Dosa was once travelling along the road when it began to rain. He said, 'Lord of the universe, the whole world [waiting for rain] is comforted while Hanina is in distress.' The rain stopped. When he reached his home, he said, 'Lord of the universe, the whole world is in distress while Hanina is in comfort.' The rain started again. (bTaanit 24b)

The comment appended by a later rabbi, Rav Joseph, is meant to underscore the pre-eminence of the charismatic over the high priest: 'What is the use of the high priest's prayer [for rain] against that of R. Hanina ben Dosa?' (ibid.)

Three more little stories will complete this sketch intended to furnish the charismatic activity of Jesus with a context from outside the New Testament. The first and probably the most significant of these is the account of Hanina and the 'snake', or to be precise, the story refers to a poisonous reptile, a cross (according to popular zoology) between a snake and a lizard. It has been handed down in various forms. They are all linked to the account, referred to above, of Hanina's supreme concentration during prayer which he would not interrupt even though a snake had wound itself around his leg.

It is said concerning R. Hanina ben Dosa that when he stood and prayed, a snake bit him, but he did not interrupt his prayer. His disciples departed [ran away] and found the snake dead at the entrance of its hole. They said, 'Woe to the man bitten by a snake, but woe to the snake which has bitten ben Dosa.' (tBerakhot 3:20)

The same story is more dramatically told in the Talmud, where it conveys both the belief in Hanina's benevolent protective action and the allegorical interpretation of the physical harm caused by a snake, and the spiritual ill-effects of sin. Indeed, it would seem that the story in Genesis 3:15 of the serpent striking man's heel underlies the talmudic saga.

Our masters taught: It happened that there was a snake in a locality which injured people. They went and reported it to R. Hanina ben Dosa. He said to them, 'Show me its hole.' He placed his heel on the entrance of the hole, and the snake came out, bit him and died. He put it on his shoulder and carried it to the school. He said to them, 'See, my children, it is not the snake that kills, but sin.' In that hour they framed the saying, 'Woe to the man who meets a snake, but woe to the snake that meets R. Hanina ben Dosa.' (bBerakhot 33a)

In connection with this tale, it is worth noting that in line with the general Hasidic custom to concentrate more on religion and morality than on ritual, Hanina had no scruples in touching the dead snake and thus becoming unclean for the rest of the day (cf. Lev. 11:29–31; bHullin 127a). Rabbinic writings include further examples of a Hasidic lack of enthusiasm about purity regulations. One Hasid spoke lightly of a matter relating to uncleanness; another was apparently ignorant of a biblical law in the same domain (yTerumot 45c; Abot de-R. Nathan B, 27). A well-known expert on the Talmud writes that the legal teaching (*halakhah*) of the Hasidim 'was highly individual and sometimes . . . opposed to that generally prevailing', and that in particular it did not display any trace of austerity in the field of ritual purity.[4]

Of the other two stories, the first relates to the supernatural transformation of vinegar into oil – similar to the changing of water into wine by Jesus. Hanina's daughter in error filled the sabbath lamp with

4. Cf. S. Safrai, 'Teaching of Pietists in Mishnaic Literature', *Journal of Jewish Studies* 16 (1965), 19–20, 33.

vinegar and noticed it too late to correct the mistake. Her father told her to light it and the lamp went on burning all day long (bTaanit 25a). The second story deals with the miraculous production of bread, and incidentally illustrates Hanina's poverty and the common belief that around him miracles were commonplace.

His wife used to light the oven every Friday and throw twigs into it because she was ashamed that it would be known that she had nothing to bake. She had a neighbour woman who said, 'I know very well that she has nothing. Let me see therefore what all this is about.' She went and found the oven full of bread and the basin full of dough. She said, 'You there, bring a shovel for your bread is getting burned.' It is taught that she [Hanina's wife] went for a shovel because she was so used to miracles. (bTaanit 24b–25a)

Finally, whereas no actual exorcism is attributed to Hanina the healer in rabbinic writings, nevertheless he is hailed there as a master over the forces of evil. The following story has the form of a folk legend, but seen in the light of parallel accounts it makes of Hanina an admirable benefactor of his people and of mankind. The anecdote is linked to a rule governing Pharisaic-rabbinic proper conduct according to which no respectable Jew was to be seen alone in the street at night, first and foremost to prevent any suspicion of an immoral purpose, but also, deeper down, because of the danger of bumping into demons in the dark. Hanina in his innocence paid no attention to the *petit bourgeois* regulations of conventional rabbis.

'Let no man go out alone at night.' Not on Wednesday night, nor on sabbath night, for Agrat daughter of Mahlat [queen of the demons] and eighteen myriads of destroying angels are on the prowl and each of them is empowered to strike. In former times she was seen every night. Once, however, she met R. Hanina ben Dosa and said to him, 'Had there not been a commendation from heaven [by means of a heavenly voice], "Take heed of R. Hanina ben Dosa and of his teaching!", I would have struck you.' He said to her, 'If I am so highly esteemed in heaven, I decree that you shall never again pass through an inhabited place!' She begged him, 'Please allow me in there for a limited time.' He then left her the sabbath nights and the Wednesday nights. (bPesahim 112b)

Despite his generosity towards the demonic queen, Hanina is shown to be in total control over the forces of hell, and the saviour of humankind from their threat. Compared with him, two of the greatest rabbis straddling the first and second centuries AD, Meir and Akiba, although ultimately escaping harm after an encounter with Satan (no doubt on a Wednesday or sabbath night when he was free to come to town and tempt), showed their human weakness and emerged from the story cut down to size. In both cases, Satan appeared in the guise of an attractive woman and when the rabbis had nearly succumbed to her lures, Satan informed them that their escape was due only to the praise which their teaching had received from heaven (bKiddushin 81a).

Hanina was better known in rabbinic tradition for his marvels of benevolence than for his teaching, of which in fact precious little has survived. Apart from the proverb, 'It is not the snake that kills, but sin', only three other sayings are attached to his name. They all emphasize the correct order of spiritual priorities: fear of sin and good deeds should come before wisdom, and no man can please God unless his neighbours are pleased with his behaviour towards them (mAbot 3:9–10). Hanina has left no lasting mark on rabbinic tradition in the doctrinal, legal, or exegetical fields. Indeed, on the sole and almost certainly fictitious occasion when he plays the role of a teacher – bringing the dead snake to school – he is pictured rather as a primary-school master instructing children.

## RABBINIC PRAISES AND QUIBBLES

This vignette of Hanina ben Dosa suitably concludes the overall presentation of the figure of the charismatic holy man in the intertestamental age. However, a brief survey of the rabbinic attitude towards Honi and Hanina, and Josephus' view of Onias, will help the reader to grasp the full significance of the comparison with the Synoptic portrait of Jesus.

The opinion of the rabbis represents a broad spectrum from high acclaim to sarcasm and carping, but it always falls short of outright condemnation. Apropos of Honi, the Mishnah passage describing his rain miracle continues with an evaluation of the Hasid by the leading Pharisee of his time, Simeon ben Shetah. In his view, Honi's behaviour towards God was impudent and broke the accepted rules of piety; consequently he deserved a severe formal condemnation. Nevertheless, unenthusiastically recognizing Honi's exceptional closeness to his heavenly Father, Simeon restrained himself from pronouncing the ban on him.

Simeon ben Shetah sent a message to him [Honi]: 'If you had not been Honi, I would have excommunicated you. But what can I do with you? You pester God, yet he performs your will, like a son who pesters his father and obtains from him what he wants.' (mTaanit 3:8)

In time this positive evaluation gained strength, and in some manuscripts of the great rabbinic commentary on the Book of Genesis (Genesis Rabba 13:7) Honi is turned into the ultimate model, equalled only by the prophet Elijah, of the holy man bringing people to the service of God. The author had in mind the life-giving effect of the rain in a period of drought: 'There was no one comparable to Elijah and Honi the Circle-Drawer, to cause people to worship God.'

Josephus, as might be expected from a historian, offers a more sober but wholly appreciative picture of Onias. The circle-drawing episode is ignored, the rain-making performance is alluded to without the paraphernalia of miracle, and the holy man or 'son of God' of the rabbinic texts becomes 'a righteous man and beloved by God (*dikaios kai theophiles*)' (cf. above, pp. 239–40). In contrast to the rabbinic sources, Josephus typically would not venture into a general theological ranking of Onias, a matter to be remembered when we come to his portrait of Jesus.

Praise of Hanina is fulsome and frequent, but here again we come across some slyly derogatory criticisms. Again and again he is presented as a supreme model. We have already seen him characterized as the greatest 'man of deeds' (cf. p. 241). To this may be added the claim in Mekhilta, an early rabbinic commentary on Exodus, that through his honesty and poverty he fulfilled the biblical ideal of 'the man of truth who hates evil gain' (Mekh. on Exod. 18:21). These are already high accolades. Nevertheless, in the centuries that followed, rabbinic eulogy of Hanina, like that of Honi, continued to increase. R. Dimi, a fourth-century Babylonian teacher expert in old Palestinian traditions, described him as the latter-day Elijah on whose account his generation

was saved – from death by famine (bHagigah 14a). The great Babylonian master, Rav (early third century AD) had already gone further.
According to him, Hanina was proclaimed by the heavenly voice the
son of God on whose account the whole world was sustained (bTaanit
24b). Some versions of the saying specify that the heavenly voice
praising Hanina issued from the sacred Mount Horeb, the venue of
the revelation of the Ten Commandments and the rest of the Law of
Moses (cf. bBerakhot 17b; bHullin 86a). The same Rav made himself
responsible for the supreme praise of Hanina as the perfect righteous
man. And since according to a proverb God created the world for the
perfectly wicked and the perfectly righteous, he was able to add:

> The world was created only for Ahab the son of Omri [the wicked king of
> the time of the prophet Elijah], and for R. Hanina ben Dosa [the new Elijah].
> This world was created for Ahab son of Omri; the world to come [the Kingdom
> of God] for R. Hanina ben Dosa. (bBerakhot 61b)

These are only drops of praise dispersed in the ocean of rabbinic
literature. Nonetheless, when collected they reveal a fascinating picture
of a Galilean charismatic of the first century AD crowned with a shining
halo. Yet alongside the acclaim, we encounter comments inspired by
the petty jealousy of small-minded rabbis, rabbis' wives or apprentice
rabbis who were annoyed by the unconventional behaviour of the man
of God.

The messengers dispatched from Jerusalem by Gamaliel, when told
by Hanina that the sick child had been cured, instead of expressing
delight and gratitude sneeringly retorted, 'Are you a prophet?' (bBerakhot 34b). Similarly, on hearing Yohanan ben Zakkai's words of self-
abasement, confessing his own inability to save his son even by
squeezing his head between his knees 'all day long', his angry wife
exploded, 'Is then Hanina greater than you?' Resuming his momen-
tarily lost dignity, Yohanan ben Zakkai reasserted the proper hierarchical order: 'No; he is like a servant but I am a prince before the King'
(ibid.).

In another account, the miraculous protection by Hanina of the life
of the daughter of Nehunyah the ditch-digger (the official in charge of
water supplies for Temple pilgrims) was explained by some as due
instead to the merit of the sacrifice of Abraham (bBaba Kamma 50a).

Again, the legendary story of Hanina's goats which brought home bears on their horns provoked a twofold disparaging comment. 'If Hanina was so poor, how could he own goats?' And worse still, if he owned goats, he transgressed a rabbinic statute: 'Have the sages not said that no small cattle should be raised in the land of Israel?' (bTaanit 25a). These are trifling quibbles which do not diminish the genuine veneration in which Hanina, Honi and the other ancient Hasidim were held by Jews of the intertestamental and rabbinic age. What light, then, do these texts throw on the Jesus of the New Testament when he is seen within the reality of the Palestinian Jewish world of late antiquity?

## THE SHADOWY FACE
## OF THE REAL JESUS

Our panoramic survey of Galilee, its history, society, culture and popular religion has already made our case and has allowed, however vaguely and sketchily, the face of the real Jesus to emerge. His image, drawn by the primitive church in the Acts of the Apostles, and the portrait of the living Jesus contained in the earliest layers of the Synoptic Gospels, largely overlap. They point to a prophet-like holy man, mighty in deed and word, a charismatic healer and exorcist, and to a teacher whose eyes were fixed on the present task envisaged from a practical-existential rather than an abstract and philosophical viewpoint.

Jewish, and perhaps in particular Galilean, popular religiosity tended to develop along the path followed by Honi, Hilkiah, Hanan, Jesus and Hanina. Compassionate, caring and loving, they were all celebrated as deliverers of the Jews from famine, sickness and the dominion of the forces of darkness, and some of them at least as teachers of religion and morality. Indirectly they could even be seen as benefactors of the whole of mankind, since the salutary effects of rain and control over demons reached beyond the boundaries of Jewry. The Jesus of the New Testament fits into this picture, which in turn confers on his image validity and credibility: for there is no denying that a figure not dissimilar to the Honis and Haninas of Palestinian Judaism lurks beneath the Gospels. So in one sense anything additional to what has already been said would only labour the case. On the other hand, a comparison in some detail will help to render the relationship between them more precise and set out the finer points of how they resemble each other – and also how they differ.

Beyond the basic similarity between these charismatic individuals, some features displayed in sources outside the New Testament enable us to bring the Gospel portrait of Jesus into sharper focus. Thus Jesus' harsh utterances and almost uncouth outbursts against non-Jews, which would be hardly appropriate to one whom later Christianity liked to identify as the teacher of the religion of pure love, become understandable when ascribed to the chauvinism of a hot-blooded Galilean. In a way he resembled his impulsive Galilean disciples, James and John, who were keen to bring down fire from heaven on the Samaritan village which refused to receive them (Luke 9:54). Those who shut their eyes to Jesus' character will find it hard to account for Jesus calling the gravely sick daughter of the Syro-Phoenician woman a 'dog'. This was no more a term of endearment in the language of the time and place than Jesus' other designation of non-Jews as 'swine' (cf. pp. 156, 218).

It may also be presumed that like Peter, whose northern identity was betrayed by his speech, Jesus also spoke the Galilean dialect of Aramaic. His command addressed to the 'dead' daughter of Jairus is reproduced as *Talitha kum* ('Little girl', or literally, 'Little lamb, get up') in the oldest codices of Mark 5:41. But *kum* represents Galilean slovenly speech in joining the masculine form of the imperative to a feminine subject, as against the grammatically correct *kumi* which we find in some of the more recent and polished manuscripts of the Gospel.

Again, the petty complaints of Galilean village scribes and small-minded synagogue presidents about the unconventional conduct of Jesus, such as healing on the sabbath and permitting his disciples to eat with unwashed hands, or when hungry to pluck heads of grain on the day of rest, are paralleled by the grievances voiced by the rabbis against the Hasidim. As for advancing the view that healing a sick man and proclaiming his sins forgiven, which the scribes who witnessed the healing of the paralytic in Capernaum held to be blasphemy (Mark 2:5–6), we now know that it was not exclusive to Jesus. According to the Dead Sea Scrolls he was anticipated on this point by the Jewish exorcist who cured King Nabonidus by pardoning his sins (4Q242). Jesus' clash with the Temple authorities which led to his execution belongs, however, to a quite different category and will be examined later.

The insistent, and indeed importuning prayer of the Hasid, practised by Honi and disapproved of by Simeon ben Shetah, is echoed in Jesus' words, 'Ask and it will be given you; seek and you will find; knock and it will be opened to you' (Matt. 7:7; Luke 11:9). It also underlies the Gospel parable of the host, taken unawares by an unexpected guest, who had to go on badgering one of his friends in the middle of the night until he got out of his bed and lent him three loaves of bread (Luke 11:5–8). Jesus would have agreed with the later rabbinic dictum, '*Chutzpah* [impertinence] works even vis-à-vis heaven' (bSanhedrin 105a).

We have seen that the way of life adopted by Jesus as an itinerant preacher is paralleled by the Hasidic style of existence as far as poverty was concerned. The men of God were more concerned with providing for others than with their own well-being. By contrast, Jesus' celibacy – which is implied but nowhere positively stated – has no formal Hasidic counterpart, unless an odd saying of a saintly rabbi of the early second century AD, Pinhas ben Yair, is so understood. The chain of virtues and their consequences drawn up by him lists watchfulness, purity, [sexual] abstinence, holiness, humility, fear of sin, devoutness, holy spirit, resurrection of the dead, and finally Elijah (mSotah 9:15). Whatever the meaning of this curious list, it cannot account for the unmarried state of Jesus, which requires a different explanation.

Needless to say, as healer and exorcist Jesus is perfectly at home in Hasidic company. His *modus operandi* may have differed from that of Hanina – Jesus usually cured by touch, Hanina by miraculously efficient prayer – but their method of healing from a distance coincided. A further common feature is their link with the prophet Elijah, patently the model of the miracle-working charismatic. Elijah has been associated with John the Baptist, Jesus, Honi, Hanina, and concludes Pinhas ben Yair's list of virtues and their rewards. A further common theme is supplied by the snake story in the Hanina saga. The Hasid's immunity due to his total trust in God provides a real context for Jesus' certainty that a man of faith could safely step on, or pick up, serpents without being harmed (Luke 10:19; Mark 16:17). Furthermore – and surprisingly – Jesus and Hanina exhibit a similar responsiveness to pleas voiced by submissive demons. Jesus allowed the Gergesene devils to take possession of the local herd of (unclean) pigs (Mark 5:12–13), while Hanina gave permission to demons to visit towns and villages two nights a week, no doubt to keep the inhabitants on their toes.

Beyond helping to perceive Jesus as a man of flesh and blood firmly set in the Jewish world of his age, comparison between him and the ancient Hasidim affords an insight into the process of his rise on the theological ladder. I restrict a list of examples to the three most significant.

If the Hasid addresses his prayers to his Father in heaven (cf. above, p. 240), it is normal to expect that reciprocally God refers to him as his son. Honi alluded to himself as a son of the divine household, and Simeon ben Shetah unenthusiastically had to admit that not only was Honi the heavenly Father's spoiled child, but a biblical saying appropriately shortened, 'Let your Father . . . be glad' (Prov. 23:23) found its realization in him (mTaanit 3:8). Elsewhere the Sanhedrin is said to have proclaimed Honi the man in whom was fulfilled Job 22:28, 'Whatever you command will come to pass and light will shine on your path.'

In regard to Hanina, no *pesher*-type Bible interpretation is linked to his name which might be compared to New Testament fulfilment exegesis. Instead, we are faced with the testimony of the heavenly voice, similar to that heard at the baptism and the Transfiguration of Jesus (cf. above, p. 184), heard not once, but every day: 'The whole world is sustained on account of Hanina, my son, but Hanina, my son, is satisfied with one *kab* of carob beans from one sabbath to the next' (bTaanit 24b; cf. pp. 239–40).

Finally, the highest eulogy of Hanina, almost comparable to the Johannine association of Jesus with the event of the creation, but without the slightest hint at deification: he is declared to be the purpose and goal of the creation of the world to come (bBerakhot 61b; cf. p. 248).

So far I have dealt with similarities between the Gospel picture of the prophet from Nazareth and the portrayal of the charismatic Hasidim. The aim was to enable the real Jesus to become in the true sense incarnate, a genuine, measurable, palpable, Jewish, Galilean *ish ha-Elohim*, a man of God of the first century AD. But signalling similarities brings us only half-way towards an authentic comparison. In the past I have more than once been accused by Christian theologians of detracting from the stature of Jesus by reducing him to that of a pale Galilean charismatic, nothing more. This charge was rebutted long ago in my description of Jesus as 'second to none in profundity of insight and grandeur of character' and as 'an unsurpassed master of the art of laying bare the inmost core of spiritual truth and of bringing every issue back to the essence of religion, the existential relationship of man and man, and man and God' (*Jesus the Jew*, 224).

Nevertheless, to grasp the real Jesus in his individuality within his historical milieu the resemblances to his Hasidic contemporaries must be balanced against the factors and features which distinguish them. They are momentous and many, but I will consider only the most essential of them.

To begin with, the difference in character needs to be stressed. Even allowing for the lack of historical precision in the portrayals, no one with eyes to see can overlook the manifest disparity between Jesus and the other Hasidim. To use modern jargon, if Jesus is the star, they are mere supporting actors. Honi is the only exception. In spite of his peculiar behaviour, when it came to the crunch he showed himself capable of displaying great courage and, like Jesus, sacrificed his life for his convictions. All the others were gentle, kind, well-intentioned and profoundly saintly, but not particularly significant characters. Hilkiah, the day-labourer, is depicted as a taciturn man of prayer, and his cousin, Hanan, was a rather original fellow, closer to children than to rabbis. Even Hanina ben Dosa, perhaps the greatest of those Hasidim, is depicted as a holy man, sweet, benign, always ready to help and exhibiting the deepest possible devotion to God, but with no great personality and without any popular following.

Jesus stood head and shoulders above them. Indeed, let it be under-lined at the outset that he was not the meek and mild figure of popular Christian imagination. As we have seen, he could be determined, impatient and angry. He inherited the strength, the iron character and fearlessness of his predecessors, the prophets. Like Amos facing up to the priest of Bethel (Amos 7:10–17) and Jeremiah prophesying doom in the face of King Jehoiakim (Jer. 36), Jesus was not afraid to stand up to the powerful. He showed love to children whom he proposed as models for those who sought to enter the Kingdom of God. He welcomed women and felt pity for the sick and the miserable. He surpassed the prophets. They embraced the weak, the poor, the widow, the fatherless; Jesus went further and bravely extended a hand of friendship to the social outcasts, the unclean prostitutes and the despised publicans who were kept at arm's length by his hidebound, pious contemporaries. He is depicted as capable of demonstrating extreme emotions. He could be moved by pity and by anger; he let his fury fly and strike opponents and critics. Slowness in comprehension, let alone lack of understanding, especially on the part of his chosen disciples, often made him indignant. He is on one occasion depicted as being quite unreasonable. When hungry, he apparently cursed a fig tree for being without fruit, although it was not the season for figs (Mark 11:12–14). Or maybe as a Galilean, used to the availability of figs ten months out of twelve, he forgot that Jerusalem at 800 metres above sea-level had a harsher climate than the lakeside! Jesus was a man of steel and warmth at the same time, and a total devotee of God whose perfection and mercy he set out to imitate.

However, there is one aspect of life in which Jesus seems to have been completely different from the men of God of his age. The Hasidim were all married, with children and grandchildren; with Jesus, at least during the public phase of his life, everything points towards a celibate existence (cf. above, p. 152). As is well known, lasting celibacy as distinct from temporary sexual abstinence was not part of the Jewish way of life, indeed it was positively frowned on by the rabbis. They held that permanent renunciation of marriage contravened the first commandment given by God to Adam and Eve, 'Be fruitful and multiply' (Gen. 1:28). Admittedly, abstinence from sex for a period was an integral part of Jewish religion in biblical and intertestamental times; for example, soldiers on campaign, and priests and laymen prior to participating in Temple worship, were forbidden sexual intercourse. Women during their periods and after childbirth were taboo to their husbands. But celibacy coupled with the unmarried state is known only among the Essenes as described by Philo, Josephus and Pliny the Elder, and – or so it would seem – among those Qumran sectaries whose life was regulated by the Community Rule. The Essenes' preference for unmarried life is ascribed by Philo and Josephus to misogyny stemming from the 'wantonness' of women, but the Dead Sea literature would suggest that the motivation was essentially ritual and not social. During the period preceding the restoration of the Temple service according to their rules, the members of the ascetic Qumran community considered themselves as a spiritual Temple and were required to remain in a continuous state of ritual purity to be fit to worship God all the time.

Jesus was certainly not a misogynist; neither did he run his life primarily along ceremonial lines. So if he chose the unmarried state while preaching the Kingdom of God – John the Baptist seems to have done the same – it must have been for some other reason. The only suitable pattern arises from the explanation offered by Philo, Jesus' elder contemporary, of the steps taken by Moses to prepare himself for the office of God's spokesman during the wilderness years. He sought to control all the calls of mortal nature – the Alexandrian sage tells us – above all, food, drink and sex. The latter 'he had disdained for many a day, almost from the time when, possessed by the spirit, he entered on his work as a prophet, since he thought it fitting to hold himself always in readiness to receive the oracular messages' (*Life of Moses* II, 68–9). The same idea appears in a more jolly presentation in rabbinic literature. There we learn that the sister of Moses, Miriam, noticing the unkempt appearance and shabby dress of her sister-in-law, sought an explanation and was promptly told by a depressed Zipporah, 'Your brother no longer cares about the thing' (Sifre on Numbers 12:1). The same document also reports the melancholy groan of the wife of Moses at the sight of two Israelite elders prophesying in the camp of the Jews: 'O the unfortunate wives of these men!' In the light of these testimonies one could already appreciate why Jesus *qua* prophet adopted a celibate lifestyle, but for a fuller comprehension we have to bear in mind the eschatological spirit which animated his teaching and life which the other Hasidim did not share.

It will suffice to look once again at the teaching of Jesus surveyed in the previous chapter (see pp. 193–206) to grasp his otherness as a teacher, compared with Honi, Hanina and their colleagues. Apart from Hanina with his legacy of four sayings, none of the others has left any message which Jewish tradition has found worthy of retention. What is more, not even the prototypes of the charismatic Hasid, Elijah and Elisha, famous for their deeds, have bequeathed ideas and doctrines to later generations to inspire them and oblige them to think. From this point of view Jesus was a solitary giant among the ancient Hasidim. The gospel preached by him is fire, power and poetry, one of the high peaks in the religious creativity of the people of Israel. According to Martin Buber, the great twentieth-century Jewish thinker, one day Jesus will be granted a prominent place among the teachers of the Jewish faith (*Two Types of Faith*, 13). And as Joseph Klausner, the first modern Jewish Jesus scholar, so splendidly put it in this often quoted statement published in Hebrew in 1922, 'In his [Jesus'] ethical code there is sublimity, distinctiveness and originality in form unparalleled in any other Hebrew ethical code; neither is there any parallel to the remarkable art of his parables. The shrewdness and sharpness of his proverbs and his forceful epigrams serve, in an exceptional degree, to make ethical ideas a popular possession' (*Jesus of Nazareth*, 414).

Throughout this book numerous individual points of contact between the New Testament and the Dead Sea Scrolls have been noted, and this is perhaps a suitable moment to summarize the similarities and differences between Jesus and the Qumran community. Both Jesus and the Essene teachers used the religious ideas and imagery of their times and shared the conviction that the end of the present era was at hand. Both Jesus and the Qumran Teacher of Righteousness sought to hand over to their followers the last divine message. Both the primitive church and the Dead Sea community believed that the scriptural prophecies announcing the events of the last times were being fulfilled before their eyes and in the persons and events associated with them. Both Jesus and the Qumran sectaries emphasized the necessity of inward religion combined with the straightforward observance of the Law.

The principal difference between them consisted in their overall outlook and distinctive emphasis on the Torah. The priestly Essenes, while insisting on inward conversion, laid particular stress on the rigorous performance of the minutiae of the biblical commandments, such as the purity, dietary and cultic regulations. Though asserting the permanent validity of the Torah, Jesus, the Galilean popular preacher, in the footsteps of the prophets gave definite priority to the innermost aspects of Mosaic piety. Whereas the religious system of Qumran was exclusive, keeping out outsiders, Jesus was keen to convey his spiritual insights to all and sundry who honestly approached him inspired by faith. The publicans and sinners, the friends and table-fellows of Jesus, would have received curt treatment from the leaders of the Dead Sea communities.

So quite apart from the improbability of contact between Jesus and the Essenes in Galilee where the presence of this sect is nowhere attested, the profound diversity of their respective religious perspectives renders unlikely that in his public career Jesus had anything to do with the Qumran movement. The only possible link between the Essenes and Christianity at its earliest stage must be connected with John the Baptist. This ascetic prophet, who called the Jews to repentance in the wilderness close to the Jordan, may have been associated with the Qumran Essenes. However, the fact that the Baptist, like Jesus after him, appealed to the entire Jewish people, to Pharisees, Sadducees, tax-collectors and soldiers, and not just to a select minority, would suggest that if he ever belonged to the Essenes, by the time of his appearance in the Gospels he was no longer a member of the secretive Dead Sea sect.

To add the final distinguishing touch to the portrait of the real Jesus, emphasis should be placed on the eschatological vision and stimulus of his message which, together with the tragic finale on the cross, invest it with a unique urgency and actuality. Proclaiming not just the nearness, but the virtual and more than once the actual presence of the Kingdom of God, he showed himself an incomparable charismatic and religious teacher. His magnetic appeal became more powerful after his death than it could ever have been during his transient ministry in the late twenties of the first century in the Galilee of Herod Antipas and the Jerusalem of Joseph Caiaphas, the high priest, and Pontius Pilate, the imperial legate of Judaea.

The face of this Jesus, truly human, wholly theocentric, passionately faith-inspired and under the imperative impulse of the here and now, impressed itself so deeply on the minds of his disciples that not even the shattering blow of the cross could arrest its continued real presence. It compelled them to carry on in his name with their mission as healers, exorcists and preachers of the Kingdom of God. It was only a generation or two later, with the increasing delay of the Parousia, that the image of the Jesus familiar from experience began to fade, covered over first by the theological and mystical dreamings of Paul and John, and afterwards by the dogmatic speculations of church-centred Gentile Christianity.

## WHY WAS JESUS CRUCIFIED?

This attempt at discovering the face of the real Jesus hiding beneath the Gospels may be strengthened with the help of the best contemporaneous non-Christian witness, the Jewish historian Yoseph ben Mittatyahu, alias Flavius Josephus (AD 37–c. 100). From outside the New Testament he can shed light on the historical figure of the prophet from Nazareth, and supply the key as to why this politically innocent man of God suffered 'the most cruel and abominable form of execution' (Cicero, *crudelissimum taeterrimumque supplicium*) reserved by the Roman empire for its enemies.

Josephus is the only first-century writer outside the Gospels who provides some biographical information about Jesus. The name of Jesus occurs twice in the *Jewish Antiquities*. On the second occasion the historian relates the execution in AD 62 of 'a man named James' whom Josephus identifies as 'the brother of Jesus called the Christ' (*Ant.* xx. 200). The brevity of the description presumes that this Jesus was a known character, that is to say, mentioned earlier in the work. Indeed there is a paragraph devoted to him (xviii. 63–4), the so-called 'Jesus notice' which Christian tradition has celebrated as Josephus' testimony to Christ, or *Testimonium Flavianum*. In certain circles, Josephus was venerated as the fifth evangelist. Hypercritical scholars consider the entire passage to be spurious, i.e. a Christian gloss inserted into the *Antiquities* to furnish a first-century Jewish proof of the existence of Jesus who was the Messiah. Admittedly, as it stands, the text is unlikely to have originated from the pen of Flavius Josephus. The flat assertions, 'He was the Christ' and that his resurrection on the third day fulfilled the predictions of the prophets are alien to Josephus and must have derived from a later Christian editor of the *Antiquities*. However, declaring the whole notice a forgery would amount to throwing out the baby with the bath water. Indeed, in recent years most of the experts, including myself, have adopted a middle course, accepting that part of the account is authentic.[5] Here we touch the veritable substance of the matter. The passage concerning Jesus, mentioning his crucifixion by the Roman governor on the accusation of the highest Jewish authorities, is inserted among the outrages committed by Pontius Pilate during his prefecture in Judaea. We must focus our attention on the two expressions by which Josephus characterizes Jesus 'a wise man' (*sophos 'anêr*) and a 'performer of astonishing deeds' (*paradoxôn ergôn poiêtês*). Both phrases are complimentary in the terminology of Josephus: talking about Old Testament personalities, he applies 'wise man' to King Solomon and the prophet Daniel, and 'performer of astonishing deeds' to the miracle-working prophet Elisha. It is true that according to Josephus 'paradoxical deeds' could also be achieved by magic rather than by prophecy, but when he intended to disapprove of someone like the pseudo-Messiah Theudas, mentioned both by him and in the Acts of the Apostles, he made quite clear that although the man pretended to be a prophet, in truth he was a sorcerer or *goêtês*.[6] So it would seem that, by describing Jesus with the help of those two basically positive phrases, 'wise man' and 'performer of astonishing deeds', Josephus succeeded in formulating a detached judgement about him. His sketch, though cool, fundamentally coincides with the portrait, painted in warmer colours, of the Jesus we have discovered concealed underneath the Synoptic Gospels.

This brings us to the second point on which Josephus will be of assistance, the puzzle of the execution of Jesus. I have often been confronted by perplexed listeners and readers with the question: If, as you allege, Jesus was a pious Jew guilty of nothing that would carry the death sentence on religious grounds, and if he was not an anti-Roman agitator or a pretender to the throne of the royal Messiah,

5. Cf. L. H. Feldman, in *Josephus* IX, Loeb Classical Library (Cambridge, Mass., 1965), 49, and my study, 'The Jesus Notice of Josephus re-examined', *Journal of Jewish Studies* 38 (1987), 1–10.
6. Celsus, the second-century pagan critic of Jesus, is quoted by the Alexandrian church father Origen as claiming that Jesus performed his *paradoxa* by magic (*Contra Celsum* 1.6, 17–18). The same accusation is levelled against him by later Jewish detractors too (bSanhedrin 43b).

why was he crucified? The answer to this legitimate question is that in the unsettled political and religious circumstances of inter-testamental Palestine someone could easily lose his life without actually committing any culpable act against the Jewish Law or the Roman state. Josephus furnishes three examples in addition to the *Testimonium Flavianum*. In fact, because of its lack of precision the *Testimonium* is the least revealing from this point of view. Josephus seems to have implied that the death sentence pronounced by Pilate was a miscarriage of justice since according to the next paragraph of the *Antiquities* it was followed by another *deinon*, i.e. outrage, calamity, injustice (xviii. 65), but he does not reveal why the sentencing to death of Jesus was an outrage. Nor can we use the story of the condemnation and execution of 'James the brother of Jesus who was called the Christ' by the high priest Ananus, because once more Josephus does not specify the charge against him beyond a vague transgression of the Law. In any case he qualified the whole procedure as illegal (*Ant.* xx. 200–201).

The first of the three parallels is that of Honi, the only other Hasid mentioned in the *Antiquities* (cf. pp. 239–40). This man of God was stoned to death for refusing to employ his praying power on behalf of one Jewish party against another in the context of civil strife. Here Josephus unhesitatingly lays the blame for the murder of the just Onias on Jewish villains.

Quite different, and fully relevant to the case of Jesus, is Josephus' account of the execution of John the Baptist (*Ant.* xviii. 117–19). The historian describes John, whom he does not connect with Jesus, as 'a good man' who 'had exhorted the Jews to lead righteous lives, to practise justice towards their fellows and piety towards God, and so doing join in baptism'. His death sentence by Herod Antipas is seen by Josephus as a crime, and he tells us that some Jews recognized in the subsequent defeat of Antipas' army by the Nabataean King Aretas IV a just divine vengeance for the murder of the Baptist. According to the New Testament, John was thrown into prison for declaring the marriage of the ruler of Galilee with Herodias, his sister-in-law, illegal. Seeking revenge, the furious Herodias tricked her husband into making publicly an open promise to Salome, Herodias' daughter, after he had watched Salome dance. On her mother's advice, Salome asked for

John's head on a salver and the 'exceedingly sorry' Herod felt obliged to comply (Mark 6:17–28).

Josephus offers a less picturesque and dramatic explanation. John's downfall was due to the powerful appeal of his preaching:

When others joined the crowds about him, because they were aroused to the highest degree by his sermons, Herod became alarmed. Eloquence that had so great an effect on mankind might lead to some form of revolt, for it looked as if they would be guided by John in everything that they did. Herod decided therefore that it would be preferable to strike first and get rid of him before his work led to an uprising.

In short, John's removal to the distant and quasi inaccessible stronghold of Machaerus and his execution in secret was a drastic preventive measure against a *potentially* dangerous public figure, who dealt with religion today, but who tomorrow could become the leader of a revolution. In a similar way, Jesus, a persuasive preacher, sealed his fate by the affray he caused in the commercial quarter of the Temple court by overturning the tables of the merchants and money-changers. In Zealot-ridden Jerusalem in the tumult of the Passover pilgrimage this was an act which the high priestly guardians of law and order would have been ill-advised to tolerate. So, figuratively washing their hands, they handed him over to the cruel representative of a political system which, when faced with the threat of insurrection, often demonstrated outstanding brutality and savagery.

Another episode transmitted by Josephus further confirms that toying with potential danger was virtually lethal in first-century Jerusalem, especially when the city was filled with crowds of pilgrims during the great festivals. The story involves another Jesus, Jesus son of Ananias, at the autumn feast of the Tabernacles in AD 62 under the procuratorship of Albinus (*War* vi. 300–310). This Jesus, a 'rude peasant' according to Josephus, behaved like a prophet. Imitating Jeremiah (cf. Jer. 26), day and night he went on announcing woe to Jerusalem and to the Temple. Sensing danger, the Jewish authorities arrested him and, like his namesake, he too was administered a severe beating; but this was to no avail as he carried on with his woes. Apprehensive that after all he might be divinely inspired, yet wishing not to be held answerable for a possible popular upheaval, the Jewish magistrates decided to shift responsibility – as they did in the case of Jesus of Nazareth – and delivered him up to the Roman governor. The second Jesus, like the Jesus of the Gospels, was given a fresh scourging by the Romans, but like the first he remained silent and refused to answer the governor's questions. However, in the end Albinus released Jesus son of Ananias, whose behaviour in his judgement verged on insanity.

Hence the reply to the question, Why was Jesus executed? is this. Had he not been responsible for a fracas in the Temple of Jerusalem at Passover time when Jewish tradition expected the Messiah to reveal himself, very likely Jesus would have escaped with his life. Doing the wrong thing in the wrong place and in the wrong season resulted in the tragic death of Jesus on the Roman cross.

# 8

# The real Jesus at the dawn
# of the third millennium

By the end of the first century Christianity had lost sight of the real Jesus and of the original meaning of his message. Paul, John and their churches replaced him by the otherworldly Christ of faith, and his insistence on personal effort, concentration and trust in God by a reliance on the saving merits of an eternal, divine Redeemer. The swiftness of the obliteration was due to a premature change in cultural perspective. Within decades of his death, the message of the real Jesus was transferred from its Semitic (Aramaic/Hebrew) linguistic context, its Galilean/Palestinian geographical setting, and its Jewish religious framework, to alien surroundings. In other words, the emigration of the Jesus movement from its Jewish home territory to the primarily Greek-speaking pagan Mediterranean world of classical cultural background occurred at too early a stage. The aims, ideas and style of life of Christianity had no time properly to crystallize and develop. The clay was soft and malleable; it could still be easily moulded into any shape the potter cared to choose. As a result the new church, by then mostly Gentile, soon lost its awareness of being Jewish; indeed, it became progressively anti-Jewish.

Another fundamental twist exerted an adverse effect on the appeal of the Christian message to Palestinian and to diaspora Jews. Jesus, the religious man with an irresistible charismatic charm, was metamorphosed into Jesus the Christ, the transcendent object of the Christian religion. The distant fiery prophet from Nazareth proclaiming the nearness of the Kingdom of God did not mean much to the average new recruit from Alexandria, Antioch, Ephesus, Corinth or Rome. Their gaze was directed towards a universal saviour and even towards the eternal yet incarnate Word of God who was God. And so from the second century the growing Christian church, instructed by eminent minds trained in Greek philosophy, such as Irenaeus of Lyons, Clement, Origen and Athanasius of Alexandria, substituted for the existential religious manifesto of the real Jesus advocating repentance, instant readiness and submission to God a programme steeped in metaphysical speculation on the incarnate Christ's person and nature, and his relation to the eternal Son of God, and on the mutual tie between the divine persons of the Holy Trinity. The Scriptures, including the Old Testament, were searched for apparently suitable quotations and interpreted allegorically to prove the conclusions reached by philosophical reasoning. This procedure was made all the easier for these great Hellenistic thinkers since their Bible of both Testaments was in the Greek language with which they were familiar and which they could easily manipulate. And they could do so freely since by that time there was no longer any Jewish voice in Christendom to sound the alarm.

Of course I would not dream of denying the theoretical legitimacy of the primitive Christian mission to the Gentile world. If Christianity had not taken root in the provinces of the Roman empire, it would have remained a tiny Jewish sect with no greater external appeal than ordinary Jewish proselytization in late antiquity. It can also be argued that even if the historical Jesus had no intention of approaching the Gentiles, his essential message contained an implicit universalistic element. So once the primitive church decided that non-Jews could be admitted into the fold without first compelling them fully to embrace the Jewish way of life, it was logical to attempt a 'translation' in the broadest sense of the Christian message for the benefit of the Gentile world. This issue, labelled *inculturation*, is nowadays the subject of a lively debate on the European continent.

Such cross-fertilization is almost a necessary part of any cultural evolution, but it is valid and acceptable only if it does not lead to substantive distortion. If the process of adaptation of, say, the teaching of Jesus is in the hands of representatives of the home culture (Judaism) who competently adapt it with the help of elements borrowed from the foreign culture (Hellenism), the result becomes more easily accessible to Greeks. Adequate handling of cultural exchange may be illustrated from biblical and post-biblical Judaism. Thus the authors of the Old Testament successfully used the imagery of the polytheistic cosmogony of the Babylonians in presenting a colourful picture of the biblical creation story without affecting Jewish monotheism. Likewise rabbinic interpreters cleverly resorted to Plato's concept of the *androgyne*, the mixture of a man and a woman, in explaining the statement that the first human being was created 'male and female' by God (Gen. 1:27), without turning Judaism into wholesale Platonism. In the case of Christianity, however, from the late first century onwards the *inculturation* process was handled by Gentiles only superficially acquainted with the Jewish religion of Jesus. As might be expected, within a relatively short time no Jew was able to find acceptable the new *incultured* doctrinal legacy of Jesus. In fact, I think he himself would have failed to acknowledge it as his own.

Christianity laboured under a serious handicap in understanding and commenting on the Old Testament. The Greek-speaking eastern half of the church was at one remove from the text read by Jesus, but the Western church, where the Greek text had to be translated into Latin, was already at two removes both from the Gospel and the Hebrew Scriptures. When its greatest luminary, St Augustine (354–430), who knew neither Greek nor Hebrew, let alone Aramaic, needed information about the Hebrew original of some unclear passage in the Old Testament, he had to contact from Hippo in Roman North Africa (present-day Algeria) St Jerome, the only Christian Hebraist of the age, who at that time lived in Bethlehem at the other end of the Mediterranean world.

To this linguistic and cultural separation of Christianity from the world of Jesus must be added another dark factor, the growing anti-Judaism of the church. Let me give a brief illustration. The same Jerome, the Hebrew expert of Christendom, described the sound made by Jewish worshippers in the synagogue as the grunting of a pig and the braying of donkeys (*grunnitus suis et clamor asinorum*). In a similar vein, St John Chrysostom, Augustine's other contemporary, compared the synagogue of the Christ-killing Jews to a brothel, a wild beasts' den, the devil's citadel, a precipice and abyss of perdition, fit for people who 'live only for their belly . . . behave no better than pigs and goats in their gross lasciviousness and excessive gluttony'.[1] Chrysostom, the golden-mouthed bishop of Constantinople, anticipated many an anti-Judaic outburst of later Christians such as Luther, a notorious antisemite, and in some ways prefigured the oratory of the twentieth-century Nazis and the wicked and vulgar caricatures of their weekly magazine, *Der Stürmer*.[2]

Although the age-old religious antisemitism continued largely unabated in the Christian world until after the Second World War, a change of tremendous importance took place in the sixteenth century. The Protestant reformation, seeking to bring back the church to her roots and pristine first-century purity, resurrected the Bible and proclaimed the Greek New Testament and the Hebrew and Aramaic Old Testament to be the ultimate repository of the word of God. This brought the Protestant Bible scholars and the Bible-reading believers to some extent closer to Scripture and indirectly closer to Jesus.

This first reformation generated among its followers a profound shake-up in Christian thinking, putting the Bible in the centre of faith and religious inspiration, high above the tradition of the church. Inspired by the ideals of the Renaissance, some Protestant students of the New Testament from the seventeenth century onwards turned their attention to non-biblical Jewish literature too. They used the Talmud and cognate writings in search of background information for their Gospel studies. Thus John Lightfoot (1603–75), the very learned Cambridge divine, advocated in his *Horae Hebraicae et Talmudicae* ('Hebrew and Talmudic Hours', 1658) the study of rabbinic literature.

1. Cf. Marcel Simon, *Verus Israel: A study of the relations between Christians and Jews in the Roman Empire (AD 135–425)* (Oxford, 1986), 217–23. The style of the popular Jewish anti-Christian polemic was equally unedifying, growing from incidental sayings in the Talmud to the grossly disparaging caricatures of the early medieval *Toledot Yeshu* ('Life of Jesus') literature. The gist of the calumnious accounts is that Jesus was the illegitimate son of a spinning-woman or a hairdresser. In some versions the name of his father was Panthera, a Roman soldier. He went to Egypt to learn magic in order to corrupt the Jews, but was condemned to death by them. By an extraordinary twist, a revised version of this saga was used by Hitler to prove that Jesus was not Jewish, as his father was a Gallic legionary. Cf. *Hitler's Table-Talk. Hitler's conversations recorded by Martin Bormann* (Oxford University Press, 1988), 76, 721.

2. The editor of this Nazi journal, Julius Streicher, pleaded during his trial by the Allies that if he was guilty of antisemitism, so was Martin Luther, whose anti-Jewish slogans his magazine was repeating.

However, while he declared these writings to be the useful servants of Christians in their pious and scholarly endeavour, they were also said by him to stink (*faetant*) and act as poison for the Jews.

The strange bedfellowship of anti-Judaic attitude and expertise in Jewish studies in Christian scholarly circles continued until the middle of the twentieth century. For instance, Gerhard Kittel, the editor of the *Theological Dictionary of the New Testament*, was also a regular contributor to one of the official Nazi publications on the Jewish question. In fact, only the realization of the horror of the Holocaust put this line of 'scholarship' beyond the pale. By then the critical treatment of the problem of Jesus and of the New Testament, begun in the late eighteenth century, had made substantial progress and the discovery of an increasing number of forgotten or unknown ancient Jewish documents, culminating in the Dead Sea Scrolls, also came to enrich the field of comparative research. Thus opened a new era in the quest for the original meaning of Christianity. From the 1970s onwards, after fifty years of stagnation, a plethora of books on the historical Jesus began to sprout from every corner of the religious and non-religious scholarly world.[3] By then, Catholic Christianity, having also reasserted its belief in the fundamental importance of the study of Scripture and recognized the significance of the Jewish perspective in the investigation

3. Here is a significant selection: David Flusser, *Jesus* (New York, 1969); Geza Vermes, *Jesus the Jew* (London, 1973); Hyam Maccoby, *Revolution in Judaea: Jesus and the Jewish Resistance* (London, 1973); Morton Smith, *Jesus the Magician* (London, 1978); Charles Perrot, *Jésus et l'histoire* (Paris, 1979); Martin Hengel, *The Charismatic Leader and his Followers* (London, 1981); A. E. Harvey, *Jesus and the Constraints of History* (London, 1982); Geza Vermes, *Jesus and the World of Judaism* (London, 1983); Donald A. Hagner, *The Jewish Reclamation of Jesus* (Grand Rapids, 1984); E. P. Sanders, *Jesus and Judaism* (London, 1985); Marcus Borg, *Jesus, a New Vision* (San Francisco, 1987); Paula Fredriksen, *From Jesus to Christ* (New Haven/London, 1988); James H. Charlesworth, *Jesus within Judaism* (London, 1989); John Dominic Crossan, *The Historical Jesus* (San Francisco, 1991); Maurice Casey, *From Jewish Prophet to Gentile God* (Cambridge, 1991); John P. Meier, *A Marginal Jew*, I–II (New York, 1991, 1994); A. N. Wilson, *Jesus* (London, 1992); A. Roy Eckardt, *Reclaiming the Jesus of History* (Minneapolis, 1992); N. T. Wright, *Who was Jesus?* (London, 1992); Geza Vermes, *The Religion of Jesus the Jew* (London, 1993); E. P. Sanders, *The Historical Figure of Jesus* (London, 1993); Stevan L. Davies, *Jesus the Healer* (London, 1995); Joachim Gnilka, *Jesus of Nazareth* (Peabody, Mass., 1998); John Dominic Crossan, *The Birth of Christianity* (New York, 1998); Paula Fredriksen, *Jesus of Nazareth, King of the Jews* (New York, 1999).

of the life and preaching of Jesus, undertook to play a notable part in a joint scholarly effort together with a small vanguard of Jewish New Testament scholars. Over the last half-century, hand in hand with academics, ordinary Jews and Christians have also been more and more deeply engaged in a friendly and fruitful dialogue.

The perspective has indeed changed to an almost unrecognizable extent since 1945. The Jewishness of Jesus is now axiomatic whereas in 1973 the title of my book *Jesus the Jew* was still capable of sending shock waves across many a sector of the traditional Christian world. The legitimacy of the 'Jewish approach' to the study of the historical Jesus is universally acknowledged, even by those New Testament scholars who can only pay lip service to it.

The vague contours of the real Jesus, the charismatic Hasid, which I have tried hard to make more distinct in this book, meet with growing recognition, and not just in academic circles or exclusively among Christians. So with the arrival of the year 2000 the scene seems to be set for the next stage of the search for and understanding of the genuine Jesus. And who knows, perhaps this fresh understanding will express itself in a reorientation of minds and a renewal of the religious spirit inspired by the real Jesus among the heirs of the Judaeo-Christian civilization and beyond in the third millennium.

# Epilogue:
# A Dream

I have reached the point where my role as historian comes to an end. Preaching is not my job. If I have set out truths which some readers find meaningful and applicable to their lives, it is up to them to choose how to implement them. What follows here is in a sense the consequence of the insights gained throughout the many pages of our inquiry, yet it should not affect its results as it belongs to a totally distinct genre. Let us say that after many years of labour, one afternoon I fell asleep and I, too, had a dream.

In this dream the real Jesus staged a return shortly after the onset of the third millennium. He appeared as a middle-sized, middle-aged, dark-haired Jewish man, with strong arms, and the deep sun-tan of a Galilean from Ginossar or Kfar Nahum. His visage radiated an admixture of wisdom, sympathy and steely determination. He had a resounding voice and his piercing eyes were shining. After two thousand years he came to explain himself and successively addressed Jews, Christians, religious drop-outs from synagogue and church, and men and women belonging to other faiths or to none.

'*Shalom*,' he saluted the Jews.

'*Forget the lies about me. I'm one of yours. Look, my religion is that of Moses and the prophets. I only lay extra emphasis on seeking the Lord our God who is one in and through all that we do to our fellow men in every single humble and love-filled deed of all our todays.*'

He seemed surprised when he saw the many assembled Christians, though the size of the crowd was not quite as big as the one which recently greeted the Pope in Cracow.

'*I am amazed to see so many of you calling yourselves my followers despite some of the unkind words I let out about non-Jews. I'm all the same delighted and grateful. Without you my name would not be remembered all over the place. But I feel I must exhort you to rely more on yourselves, on your own insights – you may call it the voice of the holy spirit – on your strength and goodness. You've been told to expect everything from me. I say, you must save yourselves. Don't forget that the Kingdom of God is always at hand. Get on with it at once. You can do it, on your own, as you are children of our heavenly Father who alone is God, blessed for ever. You may carry on with your rites, customs and prayers, but be careful not to take the symbol for reality. You used to blame my Jewish brethren for turning the spirit into the letter. Aren't you doing the same? By the way, you can learn more about the real me from Luke, Matthew and Mark than from all the rest of what you call the New Testament. I now wish I'd taken the trouble to write myself! In any case, you too need to be truly humble and show love and respect to all, especially to those with whom you disagree.'*

He then turned to the company of those who no longer practised their religion, but who were seekers filled with remorse.

*'I know you well and love you. You remind me of the publicans who were longing for a kind word from me. How I enjoyed the party one of them gave in my honour in Jericho, or was it in Galilee? I recognize you, too, ostracized sinners. Others like you, male and female, scorned by the genteel pious, used to come to me, listen to my words, and they changed their lives. Recognize your weakness and do the right thing. Repent and be confident. You are close to the Kingdom of God. Now as in my lifetime the father welcomes with greater joy the returning prodigal son than the son who has been conventionally (and boringly) good all the time.'*

At this moment I was suddenly woken by the telephone bell. Someone calling himself Jim was trying to interest me in new doors and windows for our kitchen, offered at a specially favourable price. Because of him I lost the end of my dream.

# Chronological Table

Entries in italics relate to New Testament subjects

BC

| | |
|---|---|
| 197 | Seleucid rule in Judaea |
| 175–164 | Antiochus IV Epiphanes |
| 167 | Abolition of Judaism |
| 166 | Maccabaean uprising |
| 152–143 | Jonathan Maccabaeus, high priest |
| 143–135 | Simon Maccabaeus, high priest and ethnarch |
| 135–37 | Hasmonaean rule |
| 130(?) | Start of the Essene settlement at Qumran |
| 65 | Honi (Onias) stoned |
| 63 | Pompey in Jerusalem; Roman province of Judaea |
| 37–4 | Herod the Great |
| 27–AD 14 | Augustus, emperor |
| 20–AD 50(?) | Philo of Alexandria |
| 6/5(?) | *Birth of Jesus* |
| 4–AD 6 | Archelaus, ethnarch of Judaea and Samaria |
| 4–AD 39 | Antipas, tetrarch of Galilee |

AD

| | |
|---|---|
| 6–41 | Judaea governed by Roman prefects |
| 14–37 | Tiberius, emperor |
| 18–36(?) | Joseph Caiaphas, high priest |
| 26–36 | Pontius Pilate |

| 29(?) | *Ministry and execution of John the Baptist* |
| 29–30(?) | *Ministry and crucifixion of Jesus* |
| 37 | Birth of Flavius Josephus |
| 37–41 | Gaius Caligula, emperor |
| 41–44 | Agrippa I, king |
| 41–54 | Claudius, emperor |
| 44–66 | Roman procurators |
| 50–60(?) | *Letters of Paul* |
| 54–68 | Nero, emperor |
| 62 | *Death of James, the brother of Jesus*; Jesus son of Ananias |
| 66–70 | First war against Rome. Destruction of Jerusalem |
| 68(?) | End of the Essene occupation of Qumran |
| 68–69 | Galba, Otho and Vitellius, emperors |
| 69–79 | Vespasian, emperor |
| 70–75(?) | *Gospel of Mark* |
| 73/74 | Fall of Masada |
| 75/79(?) | Josephus' *Jewish War* |
| 79–81 | Titus, emperor |
| 80–100(?) | *Gospels of Matthew and Luke, Acts of the Apostles* |
| 81–96 | Domitian, emperor |
| 93/94(?) | Josephus' *Jewish Antiquities* and *Life* |
| 96–98 | Nerva, emperor |
| 96–100(?) | Josephus' *Contra Apionem* |
| 98–117 | Trajan, emperor |
| 100(?) | *Letters of James, 1 Peter, 1–3 John, Jude; Revelation* |
| 100–110(?) | *Fourth Gospel*; death of Josephus |
| 117–138 | Hadrian, emperor |
| 125(?) | *2 Peter* |
| 132–135 | Second war against Rome |

# Select Bibliography

Aland, Kurt, *et al.* (eds.), *Greek–English New Testament* (1981)

Borg, Marcus J., *Jesus in Contemporary Scholarship* (1994)

Buber, Martin, *Two Types of Faith* (English trans. 1951)

Bultmann, Rudolf, *Jesus and the Word* (English trans. 1934)

— *Theology of the New Testament*, I–II (English trans. 1952–5)

Charlesworth, J. H., *The Old Testament Pseudepigrapha*, I–II (1983–5)

Crossan, John Dominic, *The Historical Jesus* (1991)

Daube, David, *The New Testament and Rabbinic Judaism* (1956)

Fitzmyer, Joseph A., *Scripture and Christology: A Statement of the Biblical Commission* (1986)

Flusser, David, *Jesus* (English trans. 1970)

Freyne, Seán, *Galilee from Alexander the Great to Hadrian* (1980)

Fredriksen, Paula, *From Jesus to Christ* (1988)

— *Jesus of Nazareth, King of the Jews* (1999)

Freedman, David Noel (ed.), *Anchor Dictionary of the Bible*, I–VI (1992)

Goodman, Martin, *State and Society in Roman Galilee* (1983)

Harvey, A. E., *Jesus and the Constraints of History* (1982)

Hengel, Martin, *The Charismatic Leader and his Followers* (English trans. 1981)

Horsley, Richard, *Jesus and the Spiral of Violence* (1987)

Jeremias, Joachim, *Jerusalem in the Time of Jesus* (1969)

Klausner, Joseph, *Jesus of Nazareth* (English trans. 1925)

Koester, Helmut, *Introduction to the New Testament*, I–II (1982)

Kümmel, W. G., *Introduction to the New Testament* (1965)

Meeks, Wayne A., *The First Urban Christians* (1983)

Meier, John P., *A Marginal Jew*, I–II (1991, 1994)

Neusner, Jacob, *Jews and Christians* (1991)

Rajak, Tessa, *Josephus: The Historian and his Society* (1983)

Sanders, E. P., *Jesus and Judaism* (1985)

— *The Historical Figure of Jesus* (1993)

Smith, Morton, *Jesus the Magician* (1978)

Stemberger, Günter, *Introduction to the Talmud and Midrash* (English trans. 1996)

Vermes, Geza, *Jesus the Jew* (1973, 1994)

— *Jesus and the World of Judaism* (1983)

— *The Religion of Jesus the Jew* (1993)

— *The Complete Dead Sea Scrolls in English* (1998)

Wilson, A. N., *Jesus* (1992)

Winter, Paul, *On the Trial of Jesus* (1974)

Wright, N. T., *Who was Jesus?* (1992)

# Index

# READ MORE IN PENGUIN

In every corner of the world, on every subject under the sun, Penguin represents quality and variety – the very best in publishing today.

For complete information about books available from Penguin – including Puffins, Penguin Classics and Arkana – and how to order them, write to us at the appropriate address below. Please note that for copyright reasons the selection of books varies from country to country.

**In the United Kingdom**: Please write to *Dept. EP, Penguin Books Ltd, Bath Road, Harmondsworth, West Drayton, Middlesex UB7 ODA*

**In the United States**: Please write to *Consumer Sales, Penguin Putnam Inc., P.O. Box 12289 Dept. B, Newark, New Jersey 07101-5289*. VISA and MasterCard holders call 1-800-788-6262 to order Penguin titles

**In Canada**: Please write to *Penguin Books Canada Ltd, 10 Alcorn Avenue, Suite 300, Toronto, Ontario M4V 3B2*

**In Australia**: Please write to *Penguin Books Australia Ltd, P.O. Box 257, Ringwood, Victoria 3134*

**In New Zealand**: Please write to *Penguin Books (NZ) Ltd, Private Bag 102902, North Shore Mail Centre, Auckland 10*

**In India**: Please write to *Penguin Books India Pvt Ltd, 11 Community Centre, Panchsheel Park, New Delhi 110017*

**In the Netherlands**: Please write to *Penguin Books Netherlands bv, Postbus 3507, NL-1001 AH Amsterdam*

**In Germany**: Please write to *Penguin Books Deutschland GmbH, Metzlerstrasse 26, 60594 Frankfurt am Main*

**In Spain**: Please write to *Penguin Books S. A., Bravo Murillo 19, 1° B, 28015 Madrid*

**In Italy**: Please write to *Penguin Italia s.r.l., Via Benedetto Croce 2, 20094 Corsico, Milano*

**In France**: Please write to *Penguin France, Le Carré Wilson, 62 rue Benjamin Baillaud, 31500 Toulouse*

**In Japan**: Please write to *Penguin Books Japan Ltd, Kaneko Building, 2-3-25 Koraku, Bunkyo-Ku, Tokyo 112*

**In South Africa**: Please write to *Penguin Books South Africa (Pty) Ltd, Private Bag X14, Parkview, 2122 Johannesburg*

# BY THE SAME AUTHOR

**The Complete Dead Sea Scrolls in English**

'No translation of the Scrolls is either more readable or more authoritative than that of Vermes' John J. Collins, *The Times Higher Education Supplement*

The discovery of the Dead Sea Scrolls in the Judaean desert between 1947 and 1956 transformed our understanding of the Hebrew Bible, early Judaism and the origins of Christianity.

These extraordinary manuscripts appear to have been hidden in the caves at Qumran by members of the Essene community, a Jewish sect in existence before and during the time of Jesus. Some fifty years after the Scrolls' first discovery and following the long-awaited release of all the scroll texts to scholars in 1991, this completely revised and much expanded edition of *The Dead Sea Scrolls in English* crowns a lifetime of research by the great Qumran scholar Geza Vermes.

'Vermes has rendered many difficult texts beautifully, so that their literary value and character come through even in translation. The reader will find many beautiful fragments in this volume' Lawrence H. Schiffman, *Los Angeles Times*

'An excellent up-to-date report on the Dead Sea Scrolls ... will enable the general public to read the non-biblical scrolls and to judge for themselves their importance' Joseph A. Fitzmyer, *The New York Times Book Review*